TBBT

COLLECTED PAPERS ON SOUTH ASIA

POLITICAL IDENTITY IN SOUTH ASIA

CENTRE OF SOUTH ASIAN STUDIES
SCHOOL OF ORIENTAL AND AFRICAN STUDIES
UNIVERSITY OF LONDON

COLLECTED PAPERS ON SOUTH ASIA

1. RULE, PROTEST, IDENTITY: Aspects of Modern South Asia
Edited by Peter Robb and David Taylor

2. POLITICAL IDENTITY IN SOUTH ASIA
Edited by David Taylor and Malcolm Yapp

COLLECTED PAPERS ON SOUTH ASIA NO. 2

POLITICAL IDENTITY IN SOUTH ASIA

Edited by
DAVID TAYLOR and MALCOLM YAPP

CURZON PRESS
HUMANITIES PRESS

First published 1979

Curzon Press Ltd: London and Dublin
and
Humanities Press Inc: Atlantic Highlands, NJ: USA

© Centre of South Asian Studies, SOAS 1978

ISBN
UK 0 7007 0111 7
US 0 391 01005 0

ISSN
0141 0156

Printed in Great Britain by
Biddles Ltd, Guildford, Surrey

CONTENTS

Contributors   **vii**

Preface   **ix**

1   Language, Religion and Political Identity:
A General Framework
Malcolm Yapp   1

2   Elite Groups, Symbol Manipulation and
Ethnic Identity Among the Muslims of
South Asia
Paul R. Brass   35

3   Islam and Muslim Separatism
Francis Robinson   78

4   Language, Religion and Political Identity
- The Case of the Majlis-e-Ittehadul-
Muslimeen in Andhra Pradesh
G. Ram Reddy   113

5   Region and Nation: The Telengana
Movement's Dual Identity
Dagmar Bernstorff   138

6   Conflicting Roles of Language and
Regionalism in an Indian State: A Case
Study of Andhra Pradesh
R.V.R. Chandrasekhara Rao   151

7   Language, Religion and Political Identity
in Karnataka
James Manor   170

8   Ethnic Groups in the Politics of Sri Lanka
Urmila Phadnis   191

9   Language, Religion and Political Economy:
The Case of Bangladesh
T.V. Sathyamurthy   214

10   The Changing Position of Tribal
Populations in India
Christoph von Fürer-Haimendorf   243

11   Political Identity in South Asia
David Taylor   255

CONTRIBUTORS

Dagmar Bernstorff, Research Associate and Lecturer in Political Science, South Asia Institute, Heidelberg University, has written *Indiens Rolle in der Weltpolitik* (1965) and has edited books on elections in India and on the Emergency.

Paul Brass, Professor of Political Science, University of Washington, has written *Language, Religion and Politics in North India* (1974), *Factional Politics in an Indian State* (1965), and has co-edited *Radical Politics in South Asia* (1973).

R.V.R. Chandrasekhara Rao, Professor of Politics, Andhra University, is the author of *From Innocence to Strength* (1973) and editor of *Indian Unity - A Symposium* (1969).

Christoph von Fürer-Haimendorf is Professor Emeritus of Asian Anthropology at the School of Oriental and African Studies. He has written *Morals and Merit* (1967), *Himalayan Traders* (1975) and *Return to the Naked Nagas* (1976) and other works on South Asian anthropology.

James Manor, Lecturer in Politics, University of Leicester, has written *Political Change in an Indian State: Mysore 1910-1955* (1977).

Urmila Phadnis, Associate Professor, School of International Studies, Jawaharlal Nehru University, New Delhi, is the author of *Towards the Integration of Indian States, 1919-1947* (1968), *Religion and Politics in Sri Lanka* (1976), and co-editor of *Women of the World: Illusion and Reality* (1978).

G. Ram Reddy is Vice-Chancellor of Osmania University, Hyderabad, and co-author of *The Voter and Panchayati Raj* (1972).

Francis Robinson is Lecturer in History, Royal Holloway College, University of London, and author of *Separatism among the Indian Muslims* (1974).

T.V. Sathyamurthy, Senior Lecturer in Politics, University of York, is author of *Politics of International Cooperation* (1964) and of a forthcoming study of the political development of Uganda.

David Taylor, Lecturer in Politics, School of Oriental

and African Studies, is co-editor of *Rule, Protest, Identity : Aspects of Modern South Asia* (1978).

Malcolm Yapp is Senior Lecturer in History, School of Oriental and African Studies, and has co-edited *War, Technology and Society in the Middle East* (1974).

PREFACE

The papers collected in this volume have their origins
in a conference held in May 1978 at the School of
Oriental and African Studies. Several of the papers,
notably those by Brass and Robinson, have been
extensively revised and are in effect new papers which
present their authors' ideas in a more fully developed
form. One of the main inspirations for the conference
was Paul Brass's earlier work on the political implications of language and religion in northern India (as
might be deduced from the titles of several of the
papers). His writings have had the salutary effect of
asking students of South Asia to consider carefully
the criteria they used to identify ethnic groups and
the political significance of such groups; the conference was designed both to extend the geographical
scope of the inquiry within South Asia and to discuss
the theoretical problems involved in relating political
identity and action to specific cultural variables.

Political identity in its broadest sense is coeval
with political organization; in another sense it is
part of any conscious political action. Our interest
here is more limited. We are concerned with the
development, during the recent past, of claims that
certain patterns of identity should form the criteria
for the creation of nation states, or of distinct
political arenas within such states, or for the
organization of political bargaining units. We want
to know which patterns of identity have been most
prominent in achieving such a political role and why
men chose them. In general contributors are agreed
about the importance to be attached to claims founded
on language and religion, although there are some
interesting differences of opinion both about the
relative importance of each of them and about the role
of other emblems of political identity. But the
principal differences between contributors concern the
second question, that is, the reasons why these
cultural insignia are chosen as the vehicles of
political ambition.

In their answers to this question the contributors
may be arrayed along a spectrum of which the two poles
are, to use Brass's terminology, the primordialist
and the instrumentalist. The primordialist would hold
that political identities are *given*, that is, they

ix

proceed inexorably from the principal cultural
identity of the past. The instrumentalist, on the
other hand, would hold that political identities are
chosen; that is, out of an infinite range of possible
cultural identities that one is selected as the
political identity which it is believed offers the
greatest hope of political success.

None of our contributors holds either of these two
extreme positions. On the one hand it is conceded that
the identities of the past are materially altered by
the process of modernization, for example the phenomena
of industrialization and urbanization, the growth of
communications and the spread of literacy, the changes
in the nature of state power, and the intellectual
impact of modern science. On the other hand it is
admitted that a free choice of identity is not
possible; there are objective constraints imposed by a
variety of circumstances including men's attachment to
their traditional identities.

The discussions at the conference (and they are
here reflected in the revised papers) focused especially on where, along the spectrum defined above, might
be found the mainspring for the formation of South
Asian political identities. Have political groups
found room for manoeuvre by employing different
aspects of political identity or have their leaders
been so hedged about with the debris of the past that
their choice has been limited to one possibility alone
and they have been driven on by forces too great to be
controlled, though easy to be exploited? The answers
inevitably have varied in their emphasis from region
to region and community to community as well as from
time to time, but the papers may help to widen our
understanding of the processes by which political
identities are formed and teach us something more
about the internal structure of language and religion
both as cultural and as political phenomena.

Largely because of the dramatic denouement in 1947,
the demand for a separate Muslim state in the Indian
subcontinent has always attracted a great deal of
attention, and Brass and Robinson's papers are both
concerned to discuss the way in which Muslim
political identity has developed. They agree on the
one hand on the importance of the material interests
of high-status Muslims especially in the United
Provinces, and on the other on the peculiar problems
created for Muslims by the incompatibility of the

concept of the modern nation-state with traditional
ideas of the relationship between authority, law and
the community. But each attributes primary importance
to what the other regards as a subsidiary factor. Ram
Reddy is concerned with the condition of Muslims in
independent India, and in particular with the Muslims
of Hyderabad. The Majlis-e-Ittehadul-Muslimeen,
although it defines itself in universal terms, is in
fact concerned with the fortunes of a group which at
independence had suddenly found itself marginal to the
political process. Nevertheless, after originally
giving support to left-wing parties many Muslims in
Hyderabad found they preferred to support an overtly
Muslim party which at times reached the limits of
toleration within the Indian political system.

The papers by Bernstorff and Chandrasekhara Rao
deal with the breakdown of the linguistic principle in
Andhra Pradesh, ironically enough the first Indian
state to be created in accordance with that principle.
Both give weight to the struggle for jobs among the
educated, but neither puts forward an extreme
instrumentalist analysis. Bernstorff highlights the
range of ingredients that go into the making of an
identity, while Chandrasekhara Rao is particularly
interested in the importance of institutional arrangements imposed from outside.

Phadnis and Sathyamurthy are concerned with the
development of political identities in states where
the dominant political elite has tried to impose an
identity on the whole population. Sathyamurthy
endorses Brass's conclusion that there is no single
Muslim community in the Indian subcontinent and shows
how the capture of power by Muslims from West Pakistan
led ultimately to East Bengalis putting forward demands
based on a linguistic rather than a religious identity.
Phadnis's analysis of the Sri Lanka experience
reiterates two major points: first, the role of the
political system as a whole in stimulating mobilization
along ethnic lines, and second, the many strands that
make up the identity of an old-established community.
Both Phadnis and Sathyamurthy are concerned with the
way in which dominant groups may deliberately exclude
other groups, or offer them membership of the national
community on terms which are economically damaging and
culturally humiliating.

Manor and Fürer-Haimendorf return our attention to
the local level. In Karnataka, Manor holds, language

and religion are not issues at the state level, and
what matters at the local level are conflicts from
traditional *jati* rivalries or from economic interests.
Language and religion play little part, cosmetic or
otherwise, at this level of politics. Two contradictory factors are at work in the case of India's
tribal population. On the one hand they are offered a
position among the lowest strata of Hindu society; on
the other official policy is to promote their economic
welfare and to maintain their cultural identity.
Fürer-Haimendorf shows how the Nagas, aided by
favourable political and geographical circumstances,
have been able to develop as a community. The Gonds
of Adilabad have suffered economically, and although
their cultural identity remains an important factor
they have not been able to convert it into an effective political force.

About the remaining two papers the editors may be
excused if they say little. They were originally
written to suggest possible lines of inquiry for the
seminar discussions which led up to the conference,
and in their revised forms offer general guidance to
this inquiry into theories of political identity and
their application in South Asia.

As with the first volume in this series we have not
attempted to achieve complete uniformity or consistency in transliteration or editorial conventions.
We have in general followed the most commonly used
forms of proper names and words from South Asian
languages, but in borderline cases we have preferred
the spelling which is closer to the technically
correct transliteration.

Our task has been made easier and more pleasant by
the contributions of all those who attended the
conference or the preceding series of seminars. We
acknowledge with gratitude financial assistance from
the School of Oriental and African Studies towards the
expenses of the conference and seminars. We would like
to record our thanks to Hugh Gray, the convenor of the
conference, B.N. Pandey, the then Chairman of the
Centre of South Asian Studies, and Elizabeth Robb for
preparing the camera-ready copy under unusually trying
conditions.

December 1978   D.D.T. and M.E.Y.

LANGUAGE, RELIGION AND POLITICAL IDENTITY: A GENERAL FRAMEWORK

Malcolm Yapp

The exuberant use of the word 'nationalism' to describe a great variety of political and other phenomena has deprived that term of the precision which scholars require of the language they employ and in the title of this essay, as in the title of this volume, the as yet uncontaminated phrase 'political identity' has been enlisted in its place, in the hope of avoiding the confusion which frequently accompanies the more popular word. Nevertheless it is intended that the new term should embrace much of what was comprehended in the old; a man's political identity derives from the political unit to which his primary allegiance is given. It is hoped, however, to avoid the common implication of nationalism that it leads to the formation of an independent state. Political identities may be realized in this way but they may be and are accommodated in many other fashions.

Our concern is with the extent to which political units based upon language and religion have commanded the loyalties of the people of South Asia; the formulation by no means excludes other objects of political allegiance - indeed it demands that they should be brought into the reckoning - but for reasons which will become apparent the focus of our study is political communities based upon language and religion. The object of this introductory paper is to survey what has already been written upon the subject of the relationship between language and religion on the one hand and political identity on the other and to draw out those questions which may be of especial interest to those concerned with South Asia. The paper is constructed in the form of an examination of four main groups of theories concerning nationalism; I have termed these the natural, the unnatural, the reactive and the modernizing theories.

In considering these theories I have chosen to make a broad and hazardous distinction between operational and analytical theories. By operational theories I mean to designate those which have supplied a programme of action intended to produce a given end, namely the creation or recognition of a national community and its embodiment in certain political forms. By analytical theories I wish to denote those which seek merely to explain the course of past events. Of course the distinction is highly artificial; all theories partake of both natures and no one can control the uses to which they are put. Nevertheless the distinction seems worth making, if for no other reason than that it may explain why totally different theories can exist side by side and suggest to us that we should inquire not only into the evidence but into the motives of those who advocate these various theories. We should be concerned not only with the function of nationalism but with the function of theories of nationalism.

Those theories which hold nationalism to be natural first emerged in Europe during the latter part of the eighteenth century. Although they have often been associated with the beginnings of a Romantic reaction against the eighteenth-century emphasis upon reason as the proper arbiter of human institutions, these theories may also be seen as a logical development of that concept of natural harmony which found its inspiration in Newtonian mechanics and which formed so prominent an ingredient in the early Enlightenment. For the early nationalists held that God, or Nature, had designed certain political communities, recognizable by distinct primordial attributes, through which the various groups of human beings could find fulfilment. The attributes varied: the German nationalists emphasized language; Mazzini, captivated by the physical appearance of Italy, urged the importance of geography; and the Greek nationalists called especially to their aid the historical memory of the glories of ancient Greece. Frequently, different attributes reinforced those cleavages which were held to separate the national community from others; geography, history, religion and language each played a part in creating and fostering a feeling of Irish political identity. The feature which distinguishes all these theories, however, and the one which has led me to describe them as 'natural', is the conviction on the part of their proponents that they were not asserting a novel claim but affirming an ancient truth. For them political identity was a gift of God, a gift of which they had been temporarily deprived by evil men and pernicious institutions. Nationalism therefore needed no explanation because it was natural;

all that needed to be explained, or exposed, was the dynastic perversion of God's purpose which had disfigured the map of Europe. All that was necessary was to remove the obstacles placed by humans in the path of God's will and, once the transitional problems created by centuries of misrule had been solved, the new nation states would flourish in pre-ordained harmony. Peaceful harmony was no doubt both the ideal and the expectation of the early nationalists but their argument was not upset by collisions between national states. These could be regarded as an aspect of that competition between species which neo-Darwinists contemplated as a feature of a greater, more inscrutable harmony. Such a greater harmony was supplied by what may be called the tributary theory of nationalism, according to which small nationalisms build into larger identities and eventually flow into the great cosmopolitan sea. In South Asia we may find this view displayed in the arguments of Gandhi, Bandaranaike and Jawaharlal Nehru, for whom it was the only means by which he could reconcile his emotional attachment to India with his intellectual disposition towards internationalism.

Naive as the natural theories may seem to be when expounded in this manner they have been the dominant operational theories for the past two hundred years. It is unnecessary to proceed beyond the British Isles to encounter at least three versions currently flourishing and it is hardly necessary to point out that such theories have been the mainstay of active nationalist politicians in South Asia. 'The people are one,' cried the proponents of Greater Andhra, in words which would have been instantly familiar to any early Italian nationalist, 'but rulers have divided us'.[1] And just as John Stuart Mill argued that Austrian rule in Italy depended upon the deliberate magnification of divisions so as to obscure the essential unity of Italians so Indian nationalists have argued that the unity of India, once fostered by Britain, was destroyed by the policy of divide and rule.

For the early spokesmen of Indian nationalism Indian unity was natural - a gift of God or of Nature, or, as Gokhale would have put it in his familiar imitation of Edmund Burke, of a benevolent Providence. It was demonstrated by several attributes - geography, history, race, religion and language were each enlisted in varying proportions. For Savarkar India was defined by geography, by the homogeneity of its people and by the

3

circumstance that the motherland was also a holy land.
Essentially his India was a Hindu India and this
characterization was not merely the preserve of that
succession of Indian nationalists which proceeded
through Aurobindo Ghose, Tilak and Malaviya to the
Hindu Mahasabha, but was equally an assumption, spoken
in the case of Annie Besant, unspoken by others, of all
those who contended that Indian identity was defined by
its long history of five thousand years. For Ranade
and Gokhale Indianness was an ancient historic consciousness which had been obscured by centuries of misrule but which was re-awakened by British rule in the
nineteenth century and which was now to be broadcast
through education and by preaching the gospel of love
of country. For these men and for their successors
national unity was a truth before which artificial
divisions must melt away.

The conviction of this natural harmony was never
lost. Although it was administrative rather than
national harmony which the authors had in mind I cannot
resist quoting the plaintive Panglossianism of the
official statement on the language question dated 14
July 1958, which date was of course, by a happy coin-
cidence, Bastille Day.

> The Government regret that the question of language
> has sometimes been considered from a communal point
> of view or looked upon as one of rivalry between
> languages. All the principal languages of India are
> the rich heritage of our country and each of them
> has drawn abundantly from the others. The growth of
> one of them helps others to grow also. The question,
> therefore, should be considered from the point of
> view of developing all our national languages and
> bringing about as large a measure of understanding
> and co-operation between them as possible.[2]

One does not know whether to be gladdened or sad-
dened by man's optimistic faith in natural harmony
which the bitter experiences of two centuries have not
quenched.

It is no part of my task to criticize these theories
in detail and here it need only be observed that the
natural theories fail in at least two respects. First,
they do not explain (except possibly by reference to
the relative strength of oppressive men and institutions) why nationalism should have emerged at the end
of the eighteenth century and not previously. Second,

4

they do not explain the phenomenon of 'nationism'.
If nationalism can be defined as the desire of a
nation to have a state of its own, nationism may be
defined as the desire of a state to have a nation of
its own. While nationalism may have been the problem
of Europe, it is nationism which has been especially
the problem of Africa and to a lesser extent of many
parts of Asia. States which were the outcome of accident seemingly feel impelled to demonstrate to their
inhabitants that their political togetherness is, in
some deeper reality, no accident at all but the consequence of a transcendental imperative. Such states busy
themselves in creating the alleged attributes of a
nation in perfect reliance upon the old adage that
clothes make the man. The natural theory cannot
accommodate these teleological nations for that theory
demands that the attributes create the nation, not the
reverse.

The second group of theories has no problems with
nationism for they assert that nationalism is unnatural,
an artificial contrivance foisted on to naive peoples
by evil or deluded men. This view has two points of
origin. Of these the first lies within that same movement of Enlightenment which begat the natural theories,
but stems from that branch which exhibited the universal, individual and liberal outlook of the eighteenth-century philosophers. For John Stuart Mill
nationalism might be a necessary basis of political
organization at a certain period of human history but
civilization was better than nationalism. As liberals
became increasingly disillusioned by their experience
of the intolerant features of nationalism so this view
gained strength. The second point of origin resides
among those conservative thinkers whose ingrained mistrust of attempts to achieve some striking amelioration
of the human condition by changing political institutions was also reinforced by the spectacle of violence
which Europe and later Asia and Africa afforded them.
Communities which had lived side by side in reasonable
amity for centuries now turned and rent one another
seemingly in the name of a mere idea.

These liberal and conservative reactions are exquis-
itely fused in the elegant, mordant writings of
Professor Elie Kedourie, the most brilliant exponent of
the theory that nationalism is unnatural. 'Nationalism', he wrote in his little book, *Nationalism*, (London
1960) 'is a doctrine invented in Europe at the beginning

of the nineteenth century' and his introduction to the
collection of writings which he edited under the title
Nationalism in Asia and Africa (London 1971) opens with
the remark: 'Nationalism in Asia and Africa, it is
generally agreed, is a reaction against European
dominion.'[3] It is not, he asserts, a reaction against
European political or economic exploitation but essentially an emotional reaction by Asian and African
intellectuals against their rejection by Europeans.
These Asian and African intellectuals solace themselves
by adopting the exclusively European idea of nationalism rather as one might employ a drug to assuage the
pangs of withdrawal; liberty is Librium. In the
unnatural theory nationalism needs no explanation outside the realms of individual psychology; it is the
product of the dark gods of unreason and defies rational
explanation. With such felicity does Kedourie expound
his view that he almost persuades us that it must be
so. Unlike the natural theorists he does provide an
answer to the question why nationalism should have
appeared only during the last two hundred years; it was,
he claims, the only political theory which would fit
the intellectual structure of the Enlightenment. And
yet this very formulation must cause historians to
pause and to ask whether ideas do have such motive
power in history. And even those prepared to concede
such autonomy for ideas may wonder at the implied
contradiction in Kedourie's argument, for if nationalism
is an artificial idea conceived by intellectuals, so
surely are democracy, the rule of law and those very
systems of morality and ethics which inspire Kedourie's
distaste for nationalism. Second, while the adoption
of nationalist ideas by individuals may be explained
by reference to individual psychology there is no
satisfactory explanation of why these ideas found such
wide acceptance among so many people in such different
places nor why they should have flourished so luxuri-
antly. The conspiratorial theory, according to which
a few evil or deluded men impose their views upon
passive, ignorant masses, gives moral satisfaction but
is repudiated by common historical experience; the
most successful leaders are those who have put themselves in a position to be pushed.

To be aware of the moral dimension of the unnatural
theories is essential to their proper comprehension
because they are an affirmation of the moral responsibility of the individual for his own actions. Other

6

theories of nationalism contain, in greater or lesser degree, some element of determinism; nations are the work of God or the product of the action of vast economic, social or political forces. Most of the theories include some attempt to predict the course of future events. To many writers, notably Karl Popper in *The Poverty of Historicism*, London 1957 (1945) and Isaiah Berlin (*Historical Inevitability*, Oxford 1954), determinist theories appear to exempt individuals from the requirement to answer for their deeds: they cannot control the ends and it is implied that they would be foolish to resist them; and certainly individuals would be ridiculous if they sought to pass judgements upon such cosmic dramas. But if prediction can be shown to be impossible and nationalism demonstrated to be no more than intellectual perversion and selfish lust for power then it may readily be combated by reason and by stalwart resistance and the individual has a moral duty to oppose its manifestations.

To comment briefly here on so large and fascinating a controversy as that which surrounds the determinist view would be presumptuous; all that is required is to note that, seen in this light, the unnatural theories of nationalism appear primarily in the light of operational theories. And as an operational programme Kedourie's views may be wholly admirable; but as analytical tools they seem too simple. Yet, as we shall see, the notion that national communities are identified and manipulated by small groups of interested men - an idea which forms an integral part of Kedourie's formulation - is one which plays a significant part in theories which are derived from quite different assumptions.

Before leaving the concept of interested manipulators we may note one further curious connexion which links the exponents of the unnatural theories with their bitter enemies, the Marxists. The Marxist accepts the concept of cultural identity but is puzzled by its politicization. His theory requires that class identity, not ethnic identity, should be projected into the political field. Confronted by the evidence that ethnic nationalism has exerted a force more powerful during the last two hundred years than has the class struggle he explains this phenomenon (in so far as he admits its existence) as being a product of the capitalist system, nationalism being a form of political organization congenial to the bourgeoisie and imposed upon the credulous workers by a deception. And thus returns the *deus ex Machiavello* to salvage the theory.

The third group of theories may be called the reactive theories. In one form the reactive theories simply assert that nationalism is engendered by friction between two cultures living in close proximity. In this form they have frequently been employed to explain the development of a sense of shared identity among communities in South Asia, notably that of Hindus and Muslims, but also in relation to almost every other community one can mention. In another form they assume the appearance of the contention that nationalism is a response to foreign political and economic exploitation. Thus it is claimed that Germans reacted against French dominance, Italians against that of Austria, Americans against that of Britain and the third world generally against the influence of European or Yankee imperialism. In this latter form the reactive theories have several facets ranging from the tightly organized Marxist view which, as remarked above, sees nationalism as a suitable vehicle for the aspirations of the rising bourgeoisie and thereby connects nationalism and liberalism in the manner of Europeans of the early nineteenth century, to looser, wider formulations all of which have in common a concept of nationalism as being in some measure a response to colonialism.

Cast in the imperialist form the reactive theories do have the merit of offering an apparent explanation of why nationalism should be a phenomenon of the nineteenth and twentieth centuries, although this explanation carries less conviction as the natures of nationalism and colonialism and the relationship between them are examined more closely. The reactive theories do not elucidate the problem presented by the peculiar forms which nationalism has taken; they attribute a degree of penetration to European imperialism which modern research suggests was lacking; and they fail to demonstrate why imperialism should have produced so distinctive a reaction - why given quantums of political and economic exploitation should have produced the particular results which are observed. Further, if the postulated connexion between capitalism and imperialism is discarded, the reactive theories do not explain the timing of the emergence of nationalism, so resurrecting the problem, endemic in the close

proximity theory, of why the habitual historical experience of alien rule did not produce nationalist
reactions in earlier centuries. Although the reactive
theories have enjoyed some popularity as analytical
models, in India at least from the time of R.C. Dutt,
they seem too imprecise to serve our purposes. Their
true significance has been their employment as powerful operational myths throughout Asia, Africa and
Latin America. Their moral aspect as legitimizers of
nationalist movements is obvious.

The fourth group of theories are the modernization
theories and are derived from the work of social and
political scientists. These theories all depend upon
a contrast drawn between traditional and modern
societies. Much criticism has been directed against
the use of such paired concepts as tradition and
modernity and it has been questioned whether any of
them have much value, with the possible exceptions of
Laurel and Hardy and fish and chips. Such criticisms
have come especially from Anglo-Saxon writers and may
reflect a common distrust of the dialectic and a
belief that if one is to assume that a synthesis will
emerge it would be better to begin with it, suitably
restyled as a compromise. In this instance, however,
the short circuit is inapplicable, for tradition and
modernity are not thesis and antithesis but ideal
concepts, described by reference to particular attributes and chronologically sequential. A traditional
society is characterized by high ratios of dwellers in
the countryside to those living in towns and of workers
in agriculture to those in industry; by small numbers
of radio listeners, newspaper readers, letter writers,
literates, tax payers, travellers, voters, wage earners
and conscripts; and by a low proportion of the gross
national product derived from industry and a low ratio
of government revenue to gross national product. In
every respect the modern society is characterized by
the reverse of these features. The intermediate stage
is not a synthesis but a transition from traditional
to modern and the transitional stage, not the ideal
types, is the core of the modernizing argument.
Broadly speaking the modernizing theorists assert that
nationalism is a phenomenon of the transition from
tradition to modernity and fulfils a particular function in societies undergoing this change. In traditional societies people lived in a variety of groups,
mainly ascriptive, not mutually exclusive, not arranged

in any particular hierarchy, and above all having no necessary connexion with any political organization; in traditional societies no one supposed that the boundaries of the cultural group should be coterminous with those of the state. In the course of the transition to modernity certain groups, notably those based upon religion and language, become politicized and claim that the boundaries of their group should correspond to those of the political unit in which they live; commonly, that is, they demand a nation state.

At this point it may be useful to try to clear up an unnecessary confusion. Generally speaking social scientists are uninterested in the ideal forms of tradition and modernity and merely postulate their existence in order to focus attention on the only feature which concerns them, namely the change from the first condition to the second. Since they encounter cultural identification primarily at the point at which it becomes politicized they demand that their term for cultural identification (ethnicity) should include some measure of political identification. Other writers, less concerned with the problems of transition, who require some term to describe the phenomenon of cultural identification in traditional societies, have used ethnicity without such political connotations. The dispute between the two groups seems to amount to no more than an argument about which should employ a qualifying epithet, whether we should have cultural or political ethnicity or both. Lovers of the English language may be more repelled by cultural ethnicity.

The questions with which we must here be concerned relate to the factors which have brought about the change from a purely cultural identification to one which relates culture to political action and organization and the reasons why some groups and not others should have lodged such claims. To help in answering these questions we may look at three of the principal modernizing theories, those of Ernest Gellner, Karl Deutsch and Anthony Smith.

Professor Gellner (*Thought and Change*, London 1964) answers the first question in two ways. In the first he distinguishes between *structure* and *culture*. Traditional societies are highly structured: each member has a known position in his society usually acquired by birth. Accordingly, a man's culture (that is his language, religion, race, etc.) matters little, because he knows where he belongs without reference to his

culture. Modern societies, however, are short on
structure; a man's position depends upon achievement
and he is continually reassessed and reassigned. In
order to communicate with others he is obliged to fall
back upon culture, in which form political loyalties
come to be expressed. Thus the cultural group becomes
politicized. The stress upon communication, so apparent in the first part of Gellner's explanation, is
still more explicit in the second, in which he
emphasizes the role of education. To produce a complete modern human being, that is one who is properly
educated, the national state, argues Gellner, is the
smallest necessary unit. Education means education in
a particular language and inevitably the language must
be the language of the political unit. In traditional
states power was decentralized and many languages
employed; in a modern state the single government
language is all-important - its diffusion erodes the
former structure and replaces it with the culture of
the dominant group. Other groups are forced to assimilate themselves to the dominant culture or to try to
break away and form a separate political unit in which
they may preserve their own culture. Whether one
accepts the argument and its sombre implications or not
the relevance of this model to South Asia and to the
language controversy in India in particular is evident.
    Karl Deutsch (*Nationalism and Social Communication*,
Cambridge Mass., 1966; *Nationalism and its Alternatives*,
New York 1964) also emphasizes the importance of
communication but hinges his explanation upon culture
alone. Cultures produce, select and channel information, but what is important is not so much the possession of a single language or religion but the existence
of sufficient facilities to enable men to communicate
well enough for their purposes. Thus, although they
speak different languages, the Swiss understand one
another better than they understand the inhabitants of
surrounding states who speak the same language. To a
German Swiss and a French Swiss *Freiheit* and *liberté*
mean the same but they have quite different meanings for
a German German and a French Frenchman. The point
suggests an interesting line of research which could be
pursued with reference to South·Asia. Nations are
formed, argues Deutsch, when a leading social group,
in possession of good lines of communication with a
larger group, identifies itself with the nation, so
bringing into the political arena vertical lines of

communication which both provide the possibilities of
mobility within the nation and discourage competition
from outside. This last clause brings to our attention
the important question of employment and its powerful,
if often hidden significance in defining the national
group. Until the fall of the Ottoman Empire most
Syrian Muslim Arabs continued to identify themselves as
Muslims and remained content to live within the Muslim
empire. Before 1914, however, a small group had
emerged which came to be recognized as the harbinger of
Arab nationalism, a movement which was clearly an
assertion of linguistic identity. At one time this
movement was regarded as a reaction against the so-
called Turkifying policy of the Young Turks but more
recent research has demonstrated that the movement
can be understood only as an attempt to reserve government jobs for Arabic-speakers, thereby improving their
chances of employment. Observation suggests that the
same motive may underpin some manifestations of Welsh
nationalism. Applications of this line of inquiry to
South Asia are too numerous to mention for they embrace
the growth of Indian nationalism, the formation of
linguistic states and the agitations of minority
groups, as well as the language problems of Pakistan
and Sri Lanka.

Deutsch also offers a partial explanation to the
second question, that is why some groups successfully
converted themselves into national states and some did
not. Deutsch introduces two concepts: those of
community and *society*. Community is that group of
people who can communicate easily with one another.
Society comprises all those people who are mobilized
from the traditional society into the modern industrial
society, thereby entering into close economic, political
and social contacts with others. Most commonly, of
course, this mobilization takes the form of urbanization: the movement of people from traditional agricultural occupations into the cities. If the growth of
community keeps pace with that of society the nation is
smoothly enlarged; if however the rate of expansion of
the numbers of those mobilized exceeds that of those
who are able to communicate with one another a crisis
will occur and the state will fall apart or undergo
some other major change. Deutsch illustrates this
process by reference to Finland, where a former Swedish
colony in which Swedish was the town language was
transformed into a Finnish national state because the

influx of Finns into the towns exceeded the possibilities of assimilation. In similar fashion Czecho-
slovakia shed its character as a German colony and
emerged as a Czech national state. On the other hand
Spanish culture has retained its predominant position
in the towns and government of Peru by successfully
assimilating Quercha speakers who came in from the
rural areas. The theory has recently been applied to
the USSR in a manner which, because of the similarities
which exist between the language situation in the USSR
and that in India must be of interest to students of
South Asia. Of the minor nationalities of the USSR the
Ukrainians are the most numerous and if they were to
become indistinguishable from Russians then the two
nationalities would together form a block equal to
three-quarters of the population of the USSR. If,
on the other hand, the Ukrainians asserted their
separate identity the position of the Russians would be
much weakened and that of the minor nationalities
greatly strengthened, an event which would make more
likely the break up of the USSR. The future, it is
argued, depends upon whether Ukrainians now entering
the cities in great numbers are assimilated to the
predominantly Russian urban culture or whether they
retain and exploit their links with the countryside and
eventually replace the Russian town culture with a
Ukrainian culture.

As has been suggested India offers the most intrigu-
ing possibilities for the study of the relationship
between language and political identification during a
period of modernization. The problems can be studied
at the all-India level in the competition between Hindi
and English, at the provincial level in the conflict
between Hindi and the provincial languages, and at the
local level in the competition between the provincial
language and minority languages. The early language
controversy was dominated by the Hindi-English debate
and by the sustained discussion concerning the type of
Hindi which should be adopted. Almost unobtrusively,
however, the provincial languages were establishing a
position of regional dominance under the umbrella
provided by the system of linguistic states. As new
groups were mobilized from the countryside they were
assimilated to the provincial language, whether it was
Hindi or another. In the process tensions were set up
between the provincial languages on the one hand and
the minority languages within the states on the other.

The latter appealed to the central government for help
and the centre found itself in the curious position of
being the supporter both of Hindi and of the minority
languages. Linguistic communities were politicized and
although that development has not yet taken, with very
few exceptions, the form of a demand for separation,
the argument of Deutsch, like that of Gellner, would
seem to indicate that such must be the inevitable outcome.

To draw such a conclusion, however, may be to apply
the ideas of Deutsch and Gellner too mechanically. It
is interesting to compare the experience of Hyderabad
in Andhra with that of Bangalore in Karnataka. The
situation of Hyderabad and the related Telengana dispute have some points of correspondence with Deutsch's
model. As the state capital, Hyderabad has received
an influx of job hunters from all regions of the state
and this circumstance has inspired hostility among the
people of the Telengana region leading to a demand for
a separate Telenganan state, in which employment may be
more securely reserved for local people. Although the
contribution of language is unclear and the role of
other attributes more prominent the situation approxi-
mates to that delineated by Deutsch. Although similar
ingredients of tension are seemingly present in Bangalore, with its Tamil community entrenched in a Kannada
state, there has been no visible conflict. It may be
that the different experience of the two cities could
be explained within the terms of the Deutsch model by
reference to the relative rates of urbanization or it
could be that the model needs modification. In any
event our attention is usefully directed towards cities
with distinct ethnic communities which stand in a
similar situation.

Deutsch's theory of community and society and his
stress on the rate of assimilation has provided the
main theoretical foundation for the most interesting
book yet written on the subject of political identification in India: Paul R. Brass, *Language, Religion and
Politics in North India*, London 1974. In this volume
we shall return again and again to the ideas and
conclusions of this fertile work and it may be helpful
at the outset to comment upon Brass's position. His
book contains studies of three agitations: the Maithili
movement in north Bihar; the Urdu movement in Uttar
Pradesh (UP); and the Sikh movement in the Punjab. Why,
he asks, did no Maithili state emerge? Why did Urdu

decline? and why was a Sikh state formed in the Punjab?
He finds the answer in the predominance of religion
over language as a mode of political identification in
north India: no religious cleavage reinforced the Maithili agitation; Urdu became identified with Islam and
eventually suffered from the communal tag; and the
Sikhs successfully masked their agitation for an
essentially religious state in the garb of a demand for
a linguistic unit. In each of the latter two cases
language was made to conform to the basically religious
cleavage. 'Language', he writes, 'has not been a
barrier in fact to communication between religious
groups, but it has been turned into a symbolic barrier
by political elites seeking to advance the interests of
their religious communities' (p.22). In this statement
is enshrined the most significant of three modifications
to Deutsch's theory which he propounds, namely that
politics and political organizations play a crucial
role in the creation of group identities. Such is
indeed also the principal message of another important
book upon this subject: Jyotirindra Das Gupta, *Language
Conflict and National Development*, Berkeley 1970. Das
Gupta places his emphasis upon language rather than
religion but he declares that 'linguistic cleavage is
politically generated cleavage' (p.265). Lastly,
readers of Ram Gopal, *Linguistic Affairs of India*,
London 1966, will be struck by his account of the
formation of the linguistic states and the evidence
which he brings forth to show how the demands were the
product of political interests rather than the ebulli-
tions of primordial loyalties. In each interpretation
the overriding impression is of manipulation and those
who have followed this essay with sufficient assiduity
will have little difficulty in perceiving the connexion
with an essential element in the argument of Elie
Kedourie. As the role of political organization is
emphasized so the political imperatives of group
loyalties fade until they seem to be no more than convenient instruments for designing man; only the moral
condemnation is fashionably absent. By introducing the
factor of political organization into Deutsch's argument, these writers have brought in a Trojan horse which
threatens to destroy the framework which they wished to
supplement; they have not only undermined the determinism of the natural theorists but that of the modernizing
theorists as well.
 The third modernizing theory which we may consider is

that propounded by Anthony Smith: *Theories of Nationalism*, London 1971. Smith greatly develops one feature
of Gellner's explanation, namely the dynamic role of
the state in fostering changes in political identification. During the eighteenth century, Smith argues,
there developed what he terms the scientific state, the
product of advances in science and technology and distinguished not merely by centralization but also by
interventionism: the scientific state claims that it
alone can adequately provide for the needs of its
citizens and fully develop their potential. Its desire
to integrate its citizens is more easily accomplished
through the medium of a common language, but by
promoting this instrument the state creates linguistic
minorities which feel themselves excluded from the body
politic. More significantly, for the purposes of
Smith's theory, the claims of the scientific state bring
it into conflict with traditional religion. Traditional
societies, he contends, had a cosmic world view which
was of vital importance to the members of these
societies. The scientific state's challenge to this
Weltanschauung sets up a crisis of authority, or, as
Smith phrases it, a problem of dual legitimation. To
give one's allegiance to the scientific state means to
consent to secularization, that is the de-institution-
alization of religion. Faced with this prospect the
intellectuals divide into three groups: the trad-
itionalists who reject the scientific state, the
messianic universalists who welcome it, and those who
attempt to formulate a compromise through the device
of providential intervention, by asserting that God
works in the world through the scientific state. This
third path inevitably leads to the eventual secularization of the religious community and subsequently to its
politicization. In this way nationalism is born. At
this point of evolution the providentialists are rejoined
by the assimilationists who have been rejected by the
cosmopolitan world with which they sought to identify,
rather in the manner set out by Kedourie.

Overloaded with abstractions as it may seem to be in
this concise exposition, the Smith theory yet has much
to offer to the student of South Asia. In particular
the emphasis upon the role of the state is most
important. Too often theories of nationalism concentrate upon changes in the social, economic or intellectual climate, underlining such factors as urbanization,
industrialization, social and physical mobility, and

excluding political change except in the form of
changes in political organization - the spread of democracy and the growth of parties and other vehicles of
political ambition - that is, political changes principally concerned with the way in which power is manipulated. But the most striking feature of political
development during the last two hundred years has been
the way in which political power has been created and
concentrated in the hands of the state. In traditional
societies power was diffused among many groups; in
modern societies it is concentrated in the state
organization which has taken over a mass of functions
previously exercized by a variety of groups. There is
a world of difference between 10,000 single-cell
batteries which cannot be coupled together and one
10,000 volt machine. For one thing the latter can kill.
More importantly the larger machine can perform functions which are beyond the capacity of the smaller
batteries. In traditional societies it mattered little
to most people who controlled the government, what was
their religion, or in what language they conducted.
their affairs, for the functions of government were
limited to the conduct of war, the construction and
maintenance of a few public works, the incomplete
administration of the criminal law, and the collection
of the small number of taxes required for these
purposes. Most decisions affecting the mass of the
population of traditional states' were taken by the
small groups to which loyalties were given and with
which their members identified. It was the gradual
transfer of these decisions to the state which progres-
sively politicized the bulk of the population and led
to a struggle to control the state, a struggle in
which numbers were to exercize an unprecedented influence. It was the decision taken by the Habsburg and
Ottoman governments to modernize their structures,
that is to enlarge the operations of government, which
provoked the national agitations which in turn contributed to the eventual destruction of their empires.
  It is a paradox of modern history (if an obvious one
once it is stated) that as the power of the modern
state to coerce its citizens increases so does the
opposition to its activities among those who are unable
to identify with it. In every state in which multiple
political identification exists in considerable measure
there is a heightening tension and various factors may
decide the issue either way: whether the national state

17

is consolidated or whether it is divided. It is characteristic of the relative blindness of historians to the dynamic role of the state that students of Indian nationalism have usually failed to relate its development to the activities of the British Indian governments and studies of the post-independence period have paid insufficient attention to the potent part played by the central government. Most commonly the initiative has been considered to reside in the challenging group and the government has been seen as an institution contributing merely by its reactions. From this generalization, some exceptions may be made.

Certain writers have emphasized the role of government in reshaping ideas of political identity in South Asia. At the core of Francis Robinson's *Separatism Among Indian Muslims* (London 1974) is the significance of the part played by the British government both through its perception of Muslims as a group and through its ability to vary the conditions of government employment in the United Provinces. C.J. Baker (in *The Politics of South India 1920-1937*, London 1976) emphasizes administrative changes in the Madras Presidency - first the greater impact of government upon society from the end of the nineteenth century and second the loosening of government control during the 1930s - and places them in the foremost rank of the factors which reshaped concepts of political identity in southern India. Turning to the post-independence period Rajni Kothari (*Politics in India*, Boston 1970) claims that the outstanding feature of recent Indian political development is the creation of a centre and that the expanding role of government has brought about major changes in the social structure. 'Governmental-ism', as he terms it, results in a reshaping of political identity although he does not see in this development a threat to Indian unity. New ethnic identities are not created, but old identities are restated in political terms. Once so stated they are able to accommodate one another through the normal processes of political bargaining; indeed, by impli-cation they are formed as bargaining counters. 'Contrary to certain prevalent notions on the "identity crisis" in societies that have not developed an over-riding national identity, we have found that it is through the political articulation of particularistic identities that a more stable pattern of integration becomes possible.' (p.247) Recent accounts of the

Tamil movement have tended to confirm this view which
we may characterize as the political scientist's greater
harmony theory, somewhat less felicitously expressed
than it was by Nehru but clothed in a comfortingly
scientific habit.

Accounts of the operation of government upon society
commonly simplify the relationship and treat it as one
between two levels only, the interplay between a
variety of groups on the one hand and government on the
other. Even in relatively homogeneous structures such
as that of the United Kingdom the merits of this mode
of analysis seem questionable for in such structures we
may distinguish the representation of several levels,
for example, the United Kingdom, Britain, Scotland,
and the Orkneys. In such heterogeneous structures as
the USSR and India the difficulties posed by the
simple model seem much greater. Awareness of political
identity cannot be merely an index of the relationship
between government and a single community but must
embrace the relationship between that community and
several layers of government. Thus the creation of
linguistic states in India (which may be represented in
one sense as the product of the desire of certain
groups to establish new governmental systems in which
they would be majorities) necessarily created minorities within the new states to whom the state governments appeared as hostile forces threatening their
cultural identities (or more precisely their ability,
as members of a particular cultural group, to share
in the bounty of government to their own satisfaction)
and to whom districts, or even smaller political arenas,
appeared as possible refuges which might be fortified
against the blast of state intervention, and to whom
the central government appeared as a possible protector.
Nor did the process end at that point for yet smaller
minorities reversed the relationship and looked to the
state governments as potential allies against the larger minorities. The Indian political system began to
resemble a gigantic game of leapfrog. The bargaining
possibilities of so complex a situation are ample. It
should not, however, be supposed, as seems to be
implied in the argument of Rajni Kothari, that ethnic
communities, when politicized, necessarily trade under
their real names. Certainly in the Middle East the
contrary practice is the rule, and cultural minorities
habitually hide behind more respectable ideological
devices. We may consider one characteristic model.

In traditional and in modern societies it is usual
for a group to capture the power and patronage of the
state and to use them to secure for itself a privileged
position. In modern societies the situation differs
from that in traditional societies in two ways: the
power and patronage is larger and its deployment affects
other groups more drastically; and under the conditions
of democracy it is commonly a group which identifies
itself as the majority which takes control of the state.
It has been the general experience that when this
happens the economic, social and political eminence
formerly enjoyed by minorities is substantially dimin-
ished and that when these minorities define themselves
in cultural terms a new system of political identities
and national conflicts is created. This situation may
be disguised by ideological terms in two ways. First,
it is not unusual that a previously less favoured
majority comes to power under a socialist, not an
ethnic banner, for the reason that the demand that
state power should be used to redress an imbalance
between cultural communities normally involves an
increase in state power, which may be conveniently
presented as a demand for socialism. Second, minorities may also espouse a socialist creed because its
universalist claims offer the prospect that the
minority may escape from the disabilities inherent in
its identification as an ethnic minority. Historically,
universalist ideas, with their common accompaniment of
doctrines of human and minority rights, have been the
peculiar hallmark of certain minorities, notably of
those which could not consolidate their identity in a
territorial area which could offer a more obvious
refuge than did liberal ideology. The popularity of
socialist ideology in certain states undergoing the
process of modernization may be partly attributed,
therefore, to its suitability for masking fundamental
conflicts. In practice, it could be argued that by
accelerating the increase of state power socialist
principles serve to inflame the differences between
communities. It is an interesting reflection that the
most successful examples of political stability in
plural societies have included Switzerland, and, until
recently, Lebanon. In both states the government has
deliberately abstained from taking an active part in
modernization and has kept its demands to the minimum.
In Lebanon the state found itself ultimately unable to
sustain this role when it came under increasing pressure

to intervene to correct inequalities and imbalances within society and its intervention eventually brought it into the arena of inter-group conflicts and contributed to its seeming present collapse, although the major cause of that event lay outside Lebanon.

The lesson for states bent upon modernization is a sombre one. To hold back from intervention is to provoke action to compel intervention; to intervene is to provoke the politicization of groups which will deny the legitimacy of the state itself. Yet the state can also enlist powerful forces in its own support: its control of the army and of investment; the great patronage at its disposal which may be used to create interests devoted to its continuance; and its almost exclusive access to international support.

Before discussing the international factor it may be interesting to review the policy of the Government of India since independence in the light of the above remarks. The central government possesses two aspects: first as the body principally concerned to maintain the unity of India, and second as an all-India bazaar, where various groups strike their bargains. Its policies have reflected both aspects. On the one hand it has created and maintained all-India institutions in administration, economic planning, law, communications and military forces, and has asserted the primacy of all-India politics. On the other it has made substantial concessions to regional forces, for example in the formation of linguistic states, in the devolution of powers in certain fields, and in the languages of administration. Its ideology has reflected the same ambivalence: a socialist doctrine concealed ethnic divisions and the failure to implement it avoided inflaming them. Curiously, however, its doctrines seemingly prevented it from making use of one weapon at its disposal. Mainly on the grounds of economic efficiency the centre resisted demands for the subdivision of existing states, although there would appear to be reason to suppose that the unity of India might be more easily maintained if a strong centre confronted constituent elements which were too small to survive in independence.

In considering the role of the international factor in influencing relations between cultural groups it is noteworthy that, while it is neutral towards changes of government, the climate of international politics is strongly hostile to changes in state boundaries. In

Africa the international system has operated to defend
the integrity of Nigeria, the Congo, the Sudan and
Ethiopia against the efforts of those who sought to
break those states into new political units, just as in
the nineteenth century it helped to preserve the Ottoman empire. More rarely, and usually under exceptional
circumstances, has the international system been sympathetic to changes in state boundaries. The most
obvious example is the partition of the Austrian and
Ottoman empires at the end of the first world war.
More recent examples include the partition of Palestine
and the division of Pakistan. In general we may conclude that the international system supports existing
states through a variety of means - international aid,
diplomatic pressure and even military aid - but that
the examples of its willingness to intervene, under
certain circumstances, to produce a contrary result
is sufficient to induce cultural groups to take the
international system into consideration when shaping
their policies.

The desire to enlist aid from the international
system may influence the selection of cultural criteria
for membership of an aspiring nation, or, at least, the
presentation of those criteria, for it is evident that
certain criteria may attract support from particular
states when other emblems would fail. Thus a tribal
group in Rhodesia would be more likely to attract
support from socialist countries if it could present
itself as radically disposed, or from capitalist
countries if it could show itself to be of a conservative inclination. And the white community does not
present itself as white but as the defender of civilization. It is not only the culture which people think
they possess which is significant but also that which
others deem them to possess. Nations, like individuals,
need to appear to be respectable if they are to flourish. This point, argued here in relation to the
operation of the international system, is, of course,
equally applicable at other levels of political
activity, and is central to Paul Brass's thesis concerning the role of language and religion in northern
India.

The second point at which Smith's theory offers
rewarding insights to students of South Asia is his
treatment of religion. One weakness of much writing on
the subject of the politicization of religion is the
common assumption that religion is the same phenomenon

in the traditional society as it is in the modern;
that confronted by a new challenge men instinctively
identify with the familiar group and try to bring it
into the political arena. Such an assumption takes no
heed of the fundamental difference between the role of
religion in the traditional and in the modern society,
a difference summed up in the word secularization.
From the viewpoint of traditional society, religion is
not primarily a matter of personal belief; pre-eminently
it is the system which legitimizes certain functional
institutions, primarily concerned with law and education, which ramify into many other areas of social life
so that men whose status is derived from their position
in religious systems often become the articulators of
social and other grievances. The secularization which
accompanies the process of modernization is not so
much the passing of personal belief - that misunder-
standing is an unfortunate legacy of the Darwinian
controversy - but principally the transfer of their
social functions from the religious institutions to
the state. One natural consequence of this transfer is
the politicization of the religious community, whether
this takes the form of an attempt to obstruct the
transfer or of a bid to share in the decisions now to
be made by the state. Secondly, more subtly and more
doubtfully, the loss of religion's former social functions gives to personal belief a greater importance
than hitherto and it is this element which becomes a
powerful unifying factor among religious adepts. It
is no accident that the emergence of religiously-based
political movements, from the Sarekat Islam in Indonesia
to the Muslim Brotherhood in Egypt, coincides with the
progress of secularization. Such movements play a
crucial role in modernization. The Muslim Brotherhood
had the appearance of an anti-modernizing force but it
contrived to swallow the camel of modernization while
objecting to the trimmings, accepting the growth of
state power while opposing dance halls, preferring to
manipulate symbols rather than to challenge the essence
of the process, relying upon the power of personal
belief rather than upon the institutional structure and
functions of traditional religion. In this way religion
plays a novel role in mobilizing people from the traditional into the modern society - the Muslim Brotherhood was essentially an urban movement - and one which
is interestingly displayed in the history of Egypt
during the last hundred years. In that period we can

observe the alternate predominance of secular and
religious ideologies as components of Egyption nationalism. Each phase of secularism can be seen as a phase
of consolidation; each phase of religiosity can be seen
to coincide with the political assimilation of another
large group moving from the traditional into the modern
society. There is a seeming paradox that in the most
active phases religion seemed to predominate, in the
periods of consolidation it was secularism - the
pattern is only superficially distorted during the
Nasser period. It could be argued that religion is the
most efficient mobilizer of men from the traditional
society but that it is too deficient an ideology to
sustain indefinitely the activity of the modern state -
only a secular ideology is suitable for this object
and the religious ideology is discarded when it has
served its purpose. Even religious movements which
begin with the flattest rejection of modernity and the
most uncompromising assertion of the traditional values
perform a similar role in preparing men to accept
modernization. The Wahhabis of Arabia, the Mahdiyya
movement in the Sudan and the Sanusiyya in Libya all
begän with an affirmation of traditional Islam but
ended by forming governments of a character unknown to
the early Muslim period. Through the device of the
Ikhwan the Wahhabi movement eventually accomplished a
major modernizing revolution in effecting a profound
alteration in the economy and political allegiances of
the tribal peoples of eastern Arabia.

It will be noted that the examples chosen are all of
Muslim movements. Partly no doubt this is the consequence of greater familiarity with them. But partly
the frequent occurrence of such movements in Islam
seems to suggest two distinctions which may repay
further study in the course of an examination of the
relationship between religious identification and
nationalism. The first distinction concerns the
difference between revealed religions and others. Movements similar to those which have been discerned in
Islam may easily be demonstrated to have existed in
Judaism and Christianity. In the former the Zionist
movement is pre-eminent; in the latter the use of
religious loyalty as a mode of political identification
may readily be shown to have played a considerable role
in eastern Europe and in Russia during the nineteenth
century, and the Philippines, Ethiopia, Lebanon, Uganda
and Ireland in the twentieth. Judaism, Christianity

and Islam have certain attributes which make them more
adaptable for politicization than are other religions.
The consciousness of being a community chosen by God to
receive and transmit an important message inculcates in
them a natural introspection: the community, its history and its future become the objects of rapt and
exclusive contemplation and the fate of other communities which have not been chosen by God becomes of
little consequence. Revelation, therefore, fosters a
peculiar and enduring concept of community and one
denied to religions which lay no claim to such an
experience. Further, the acts of writing down the
revelation, of studying and discussing it inspire an
intellectual activity which creates a body of material
which in turn forms the basis of law, the subject of
education, and a prescription for behaviour. There
emerges a class skilled in the interpretation of this
material and the leadership provided by this class, and
its dominance over law and education, serves to bind
the community more closely together, and thereby creates
a platform for the further enlargement of its functions.
It was the retention or abandonment of the Sharia which
respectively distinguished the Algerian Muslim and the
évolué, and it was religion which was the basis of the
Algerian national movement during the war with France.
Of course, at this point the distinction between
revealed and non-revealed religions begins to lose
some of its force for other religions also have
writings to which peculiar veneration is accorded and
which have their interpreters and their systems of law
partly derived from such writings. Nevertheless, divine
ordinances have a status to which other writings, no
matter how highly regarded, cannot aspire.

The second distinction relating to the operation of
religion as a mode of political identification concerns
the difference between religions which are characterized
by a high degree of organization and those which are
not, a difference only partly corresponding to that
between revealed and non-revealed religions. Thus most
Christian sects have usually possessed a high degree of
organization while Judaism, at least during most of the
last two thousand years has not. Within Islam there
are marked variations but in the absence of a necessary
priesthood no degree of organization which approaches
that of the Roman Catholic church. Among non-revealed
religions on the other hand the monastic organization
characteristic of Theravada Buddhism and the new

religious associations which it was able to throw up
afforded a basis for political movements which contributed to the formation of Burmese, Sinhalese and
Thai nationalism. In China on the other hand it is
difficult to envisage how religion could provide a
focus for political identification (except among
minority groups), for Confucianism is too diffuse to
perform that function, while ancestor reverence tends
only to reinforce the loyalties of the traditional
society. It is noteworthy that, apart from the Muslim
movements of the north-west and the Buddhist-based
movement in Tibet, the movement in which religion
played the most obvious part - that of the Taipings -
drew its religious identity from Christianity. But
plainly, in the role and organization of secret
societies there is room for much modification of these
casual remarks.

The position of Hinduism in relation to this discussion is one which requires the most detailed consideration. As noted above, Hinduism appears at first
sight to lack the attributes of revelation and organization which it is suggested may have assisted the
adherents of other religions to use those religions as
vehicles of political assertion. The generally
secular formulation of Indian nationalism under the
direction of its Hindu leaders may seem to confirm that
view. But this may be a superficial opinion. The
several advantages of a secular presentation need not be
rehearsed here and an examination of the secular formulations of early Bengali nationalists reveal that they
made certain fundamental assumptions about the Hindu
identity of India; these assumptions, as mentioned in
the early part of this paper, became more explicit
subsequently. The rise of Hindu communalism affords an
interesting parallel with that of movements such as the
Muslim Brotherhood; like them it can be seen as a response to secularism, not so much a movement of the
religious community into the political arena as the
widening of that arena to embrace the community's own
cherished customs.

Consideration of the question of the significance of
organization raises the problem of whether Hinduism is
more properly to be regarded for our purposes as a
single religion or as a number of groups whose identity
is founded upon religion through its legitimation of
the caste system. It has been suggested by James Manor
that caste groups are really social groups and that the

26

term religious group should be reserved for groups
identified by doctrine, symbol, etc.[4] The problem is
an interesting one for it reveals an important distinction brought about by the process of modernization. In
traditional societies religious groups were social
groups and their doctrines and rituals may be regarded
as mere appurtenances of that social identity rather
than as the principal distinguishing features of the
community. It is only when social functions are
stripped away that the surviving doctrinal elements
assume major importance as the main visible signs of
membership in the community. Somewhat hesitantly I
would suggest that we may disregard the problem here,
however, on the grounds that caste identification
fulfills a function similar to that of religious
identification during the process of the transition
from tradition to modernity; indeed one may discern a
tendency for caste groups to become more like religious
groups during the process of modernization, for as
their social functions decline they emphasize rituals
as a means of preserving their identity. In terms of
caste, Hinduism may be declared to be highly organized
and as caste organizations have proliferated it has
become more organized. The relationship of caste
organization to political identification is one which
has been widely studied in recent years and it is
unnecessary to survey the conclusions of that discussion here.

In considering the implications of the modernizing
theories I have moved on to discuss additional points,
notably the role of the state and the function of
religion as an emblem of political identification. At
this point it will be appropriate to extend this consideration to the other component in the relationship
under study, namely language. Paul Brass observes a
phenomenon for which he offers no real explanation:
that while in most transitional situations, including
that in south India, it is the linguistic community
which becomes the basis of political identification,
in northern India it is the religious community, and
the linguistic cleavage has tended to adapt itself to
this more fundamental division. This apparent discre-
pancy may be explained in a variety of ways. First,
it could be claimed that Brass has misinterpreted the
true situation in northern India. But while it may be
that Brass has exaggerated the possibilities of Maithili
becoming the basis of a strong, politically conscious,

linguistic community, his interpretation of the situation in UP and the Punjab is confirmed by other writers. Second, it could be asserted that the Sikhs and the UP Muslims are unique communities and that their experience need not lead to a major modification of the general theory which gives primacy to linguistic communities. Third, it could be argued that languages may be arrayed along a spectrum which would include overlapping areas of toleration within which differences between languages were insufficiently great to generate political identification on that basis. Thus it has been suggested that the reason why speakers of Kannada have been less prone to espouse linguistic nationalist presentations than those of Tamil, Telugu and Malayalam is that Kannada is nearer to Sanskrit and therefore to Hindi. Observation suggests, however, that much slighter linguistic differences than that which obtains between Kannada and Hindi have been associated with separate political identities. As Deutsch's Swiss example illustrates, the question of linguistic relationships is exceedingly complicated - perhaps too complicated to be accommodated within a spectrum. A fourth possible line of argument is that Islam, or revealed religions in general behave differently from others in situations of cultural clash during a period of modernization. Or lastly, it might be possible that the experience of northern India could actually reinforce a general theory of political identification, less European in its basis than that of Deutsch, in which religion and language each play a part at different stages. The outlines of such a theory were adumbrated above and here it may be rephrased in a more extended form.

It is not true that the linguistic community is the usual basis of political identification. As mentioned above, religion has played a major role in political identification in all the revealed religions and in Buddhism, and a prominent part in Hinduism. In modernizing situations it is common for religion, the main emblem of the traditional society, to become the midwife of the modern. The politicization of religion is an important phase in the development of transition. It is not, however, an essential one, for the role of religion in the transition must depend upon its role in the traditional society; in some cases religion cannot form an appropriate foundation for political identification and another base is chosen. Commonly, however, the distinction between religion and language is one of timing. In the earliest stages of modernization it is the religious community which is threatened and there-fore forms the initial vehicle for participation in the political arena. For each new contingent mobilized to the modern society religion retains its importance as a vital adaptive mechanism. But at later stage in the process it is language which comes to predominate as the focus of political allegiance. The explanation is simple: in the traditional, largely non-literate society language is of little importance; in the modern society literacy, education and employment, particularly in the greatly enlarged public sector, mean that language is a matter of much greater consequence.

A further factor which may have postponed the emer-gence of linguistic nationalism in South Asia was the facility with which the early nationalist leaders could employ English. For them there was little advantage in espousing a linguistic cause which could only increase the competition for the places to which they aspired. And the possession of good English was a necessary attribute for anyone who sought to bargain with a British government. Only when a larger, humbler, poorer group, less comfortable in English, was added to the national struggle did language become more promin-ent and, even so, the durability of the early leaders often ensured that it remained a subordinate issue until well after independence was achieved. And what is true of English at the higher levels is true of other languages at subordinate levels; thus Urdu was readily employed by the elites of all communities in the Punjab until 1947.

The sequence of first religion then language, is often obscured by the actions of people and especially of governments. Brass observes that in India informal rules do not permit religious opposition to government but opposition based upon linguistic grounds is permis-sible within certain limits, that is, short of a demand for secession. One effect of these rules is that religious groups disguise their true nature by depict-ing themselves as linguistic groups. Governments themselves may also find it convenient to adopt a similar subterfuge. Thus the Turkish national movement which led to the creation of the Republic of Turkey is usually depicted as the work of the Turkish people, that is a group primarily identified by language. In fact it was the work of a mixed group of Turks, Kurds

and Albanians held together by a common desire to
defend Islam against the inroads of the Christians,
especially the Greeks. Both at the time and subsequently, however, its leaders found it desirable to
obscure this essentially religious inspiration. Partly
this was because a Muslim movement would imply the
continuance of the Ottoman Caliphate; partly because a
Muslim movement would be likely to spread into other
former Ottoman lands and thereby provoke a reaction
from Britain and France which might strip from the
nationalists all that had been gained; partly because
if Turkey were to find a place in the system of international relations she would be more acceptable as a
linguistic than as a religious state. Further, once
the religious minorities, the Greeks and the Armenians,
had been eliminated from Turkey there was no further
obstacle to a secular posture; minorities could be
tolerated when they no longer existed. Finally, it
was the ambition of the new rulers of Turkey to pursue
a modernizing policy and for that purpose a linguistic
identity was much more suitable than a religious
nationalism; it was difficult to legitimize an interven-
tionist policy by reference to an ideology inextricably
wedded to minimal government. In the true Muslim state
it was the Sharia, the law of God, not the government
which was the true ruler and the Sharia was an inadequate basis for a modernizing state. Such was also the
discovery of Pakistan after 1947. A state which justified its existence solely through Islam might have been
expected to do what Maulana Maududi demanded, namely to
adopt the Sharia as the basis of government. The
rejection of this course was the inevitable concomitant
of the Pakistani decision in favour of modernization, a
decision which was itself partly the consequence of the
need to defend the new Islamic homeland. The Pakistani
experience indeed summarizes the dilemma of Muslim
states in the modern world: to survive as Islamic states
they had to shed the essence of that which made them
Muslim. And it was the decision to modernize which
encouraged the growth of linguistic identity which in
turn led to the break up of Pakistan. The attempt to
reinforce a religious identity by the extension of Urdu
failed; Urdu was rejected in Sind and in East Bengal,
where it served only to enhance the distinctiveness of
the Biharis.

Finally it may be useful to place this discussion of
the role of language and religion in political identifi-

cation in a wider context. If language and religion
have been the principal emblems of political identification in South Asia they have not been the only ones.
Nor have cultural groups identified by language and
religion always exhibited a related political identity.
Some factors which may have influenced the outcome have
been mentioned already, such as the rate of urbanization, the progress of industrialization, the pressure
of government, and the international factor. Here I
propose briefly to survey some others.

A major factor must be the advent of democracy.
Democracy creates the most favourable conditions for
the formulation and expression of political identity.
The electoral process encourages groups to identify
themselves politically so that they may exert a greater
influence both within constituencies and within parlia-
ments. No doubt the questions of the formal reservation of seats for Muslims and for scheduled castes
played a part in consolidating their political identities. But most of all democracy emphasizes numbers:
only within a democracy do the concepts of majorities
and minorities have any real political meaning. It
is the question of numbers which lies at the heart of
our second factor.

A significant factor in political identification is
the relative compactness of the community. No other
feature explains so well the different political arti-
culations of the two leading Christian communities in
nineteenth-century Syria. The smaller, more compact
Maronite community saw its best chance in the creation
of an autonomous Lebanon; the larger, more diffused
Greek Orthodox community became wedded to the notion
of a Greater Syria. Numerous as the Muslim/Urdu
community is in India it forms a majority in no sizable
area and cannot consolidate its identity through any
obvious administrative rearrangement. Its cultural
identity is politically unhelpful to it, and it is
obliged to seek a universalist solution which protects
minority rights. The concept of the territorial area
and its definition has also played a major part in the
enunciation of national aims in Sri Lanka. By emphasizing its island nature the Sinhalese ensure that they
remain a majority; for the Tamils on the other hand
more suitable areas would be smaller - a divided island;
or larger - a Dravidistan in which they could regard
themselves as a majority. To redefine the territorial
area of political action is the dream of all national-

ists: if only there were a Kurdistan for the Kurds or a Baluchistan for the Baluchis or a united Ireland for the Catholics of Northern Ireland.

A third factor must be the influence of example. Without proceeding to the lengths of Kedourie in his assertion that nationalism in Asia and Africa is a mere copy of that in Europe we can observe that the examples of European nationalism did serve, historically, as a source of inspiration to South Asian nationalists, and also that even within South Asia political identification has proved infectious. Without the example provided by their Indian fellows the history of the Tamil community of Sri Lanka must have been different; and the story of the spread of Muslim political identification from its stronghold in the United Provinces affords many insights of a similar nature.

As a corollary of this last point one may note the role of immigrants in forming political identity. Commonly minorities are quicker to become conscious of the political implications of their cultural identity than are majorities. Members of a politicized minority who have found their position to be intolerable and who have left their former area of habitation have exerted powerful influences upon the perception of political identity among related communities. Such a role was played in the development of Turkish nationalism by Turkish immigrants from the Tsarist Empire, among Ottoman Armenians by disgruntled members of the Russian Armenian community, among Albanians by Albanian emigres in Italy, in Pakistan by Muslims from UP, and in Orissa by a minority of Oriyans outside the borders of the state.

Of the theories which have been considered in this essay the first seems to me to have little or no analytical value but it possesses some historical importance deriving from the commitment made to it by so many nationalist leaders, and its persistence deserves some study, like all myths which perform a significant function. The second theory also repays investigation for it has exercized considerable influence upon writings on nationalism in South Asia. At one level it forms the basis for most Indian interpretations of the emergence of Pakistan and at another the notion of political manipulation is firmly embedded in the arguments of the most recent writers on political identification. It is however a theory to be used with caution, for its extended use inevitably eliminates the commonality on which our concepts depend; each situation becomes wholly unique. The third theory has also had considerable historical importance in fuelling national feeling, although it offers no especial insight into the roles of language and religion, tending as it does to direct our attention away from communities founded on these bases and towards those founded on the basis of occupation or of class. Most valuable for our purposes are likely to be the fourth group of theories, those based upon modernization, each of which can be employed to illuminate some feature of the political landscape of South Asia. These modernizing theories provide useful explanations of the timing of changes in political identification, and between them go a long way towards explaining why, in the circumstances of the transition from tradition to modernity, it should have been groups defined by religion and language which have emerged as the primary objects of political identification, rather than groups identified by race, history, kinship, region, occupation, or by other criteria.

Yapp, 'Language, Religion and Political Identity: A
General Framework'

1. I have taken this quotation from the essay by
Dagmar Bernstorff, below p.144.
2. Government of India, Ministry of Home Affairs,
*The Fourteenth Report of the Commissioner for Linguis-
tic Minorities in India*, Delhi 1972, Para.965.
3. In his recent article on *Nationalism* in the
Encyclopaedia Britannica Year Book 1978, pp.24-9,
Kedourie gives greater weight to the process of
modernization (notably the increase in the power of
the state) in the development of nationalism in Europe.
4. Below, p.176.

ELITE GROUPS, SYMBOL MANIPULATION AND ETHNIC IDENTITY AMONG THE MUSLIMS OF SOUTH ASIA

Paul R. Brass

1

The study of the processes by which ethnic groups and nations are formed has been beset by a persistent and fundamental conceptual difference among scholars concerning the very nature of the groups involved, namely, whether they are 'natural', 'primordial', 'given' communities or whether they are creations of interested leaders, of elite groups, or of the political system in which they are included.[1] The primordialist argues that every person carries with him through life 'attachments' derived from place of birth, kinship relationships, religion, language, and social practices that are 'natural' for him, 'spiritual' in character, and that provide a basis for an easy 'affinity' with other peoples from the same background. These 'attachments' constitute the 'givens' of the human condition and are 'rooted in the non-rational foundations of personality.'[2] Some go so far as to argue that such attachments that form the core of ethnicity are biological and genetic in nature.[3] Whatever differences in detail exist among the spokesmen for the primordialist point of view, they tend to unite upon the explicit or implicit argument that ethnicity, properly defined, is based upon descent.[4] Since, however, it is quite obvious that there are very few groups in the world today whose members can lay any serious claim to a known common origin, it is not actual descent that is considered essential to the definition of an ethnic group but a belief in a common descent.

There are some aspects of the primordialist formulation with which it is not difficult to agree. Even in modern industrial society, let alone in pre-modern or modernizing societies, most people develop attachments in childhood and youth that have deeply emotive significance, that remain with them through life either consciously, in the actual persistence of such attachments in the routines of daily life, or embedded in the unconscious realms of the adult personality. Such

35

attachments also often provide a basis for the formation of social and political groupings in adult life
for those for whom they have a continuing conscious
meaning in their daily lives. Even for those persons,
particularly in modern societies, who have been
removed from their origins or have rejected their
childhood identifications, such attachments may
remain available in the unconscious to be revived by
some appeal that strikes a sympathetic psychic chord.

It is difficult, however, to travel much further
than this with the primordialists. First of all, it
is clear that some primordial attachments are variable.
In multilingual developing societies, many people
command more than one language, dialect, or code.[5]
Many illiterate rural persons, far from being attached
emotionally to their mother tongue, do not even know
its proper name. In some situations, members of
linguistically diverse ethnic communities have chosen
to change their language in order to provide an
additional element in common with their group members.
In other situations, ethnic group members have deliberately shifted their own language and educated their
children in a different language than their mother
tongue in order to differentiate themselves further
from another ethnic group.[6] Finally, many people, if
not most people, never think about their language at
all and never attach any emotional significance to it.

Religious identification too is subject to change -
and not only by modern cosmopolitan man engaged in
enlightened spiritual quests. Shifts in religious
practices brought about under the influence of religious
reformers are common occurrences in pre-modern, modernizing, and even in post-industrial societies. Sometimes such shifts are clearly designed to promote
internal solidarity and external differentiation from
other groups.[7]

Even one's place of birth and kinship connections
may lose their emotional significance for people or be
viewed negatively. A psychoanalyst might argue that
these attachments at least pursue men through life and
must always remain as potential sources of affective
involvement with others. Yet, millions of persons
have migrated by choice from their native places in
both modern and traditional societies and, while many
have retained an emotional attachment to their place of
origin, many have chosen to assimilate to their new
society and have lost any sense of emotional identifi-

cation with their homelands. For those who do not
migrate, one's place of birth identifies a person, but
a sense of identity based on attachment to one's
region or homeland usually does not become a politically significant matter for those who remain there
unless there is some perceived discrimination against
the region and its people in the larger society.
Moreover, even the 'fact' of one's place of birth is
subject to variation. A person is born in a particular
village or town, but one is not born in a 'region', for
a region is itself an artificial construct. A person
may be born in Savannah, Georgia, and not consider
himself a 'Southerner'. It is also possible obviously
for 'Southerners' to be born out of their region.
Insofar as kinship connections are concerned, the
range of genuine kin relationships is usually too
small to be of political significance. Fictive kinship relationships may extend the range of some ethnic
groups rather broadly, but their fictive character
presumes their variability by definition. Consequently,
even 'the facts of birth' are either inherently of no
political significance or are subject to variation.[8]

As for the argument that it is not place of birth or
kinship or mother tongue or native religion that
defines ethnicity but a belief in a common descent that
draws on one more of these attachments, it must be
conceded that the argument stated in this general form
is not without force. Many ethnic communities do
explicitly proclaim or implicitly assume that the
underlying basis of their unity is shared descent. It
is not at all difficult to find a broad spectrum of
such communities. Broad as the spectrum may be,
however, it will still not suffice to encompass all the
culturally-defined collectivities whose members lay
claim to special privileges because of some shared
cultural features and who are united internally by their
attachment to them, unless we define common descent so
broadly as to include shared historical, linguistic, or
religious experiences. In the latter case, however, we
do nothing more than redefine descent to equal shared
cultural features.

There are two more serious objections to the primordialist point of view on ethnicity. One is the
assumption that sometimes accompanies it that the
recognition of distinct primordial groups in a
society is sufficient to predict the future development
out of them of ethnic communities or nations. This

assumption, which is associated principally with the
early European ideologists of nationalism, is no
longer widely held even by their primordialist des-
cendents, for it is clearly an untenable proposition.
A second point of view is more widely held, namely,
that ethnic attachments belong to the non-rational
part of the human personality and, as such, are
potentially destructive of civil society.[9] This
notion suffers from two defects. One is that it
ignores the possibility that an ethnic identity may be
felt or adopted for rational as well as affective
reasons to preserve one's existence or to pursue
advantage through communal action. The second is the
assumption that primordial attachments are more dangerous to civil order than other kinds of potential conflicts, presumably because of their highly emotive
character. However, there is no empirical evidence to
warrant the view either that primordial conflicts have
produced more disruption in civil societies than economic, class conflicts or that the former conflicts are
less amenable to compromise than the latter.

While many primordialists will concede that some
aspects of culture are changeable and that the
boundaries of ethnic groups may be shifted in the
course of social and political movements that promote
their interest, they stand firm on one point, namely,
that ethnic groups properly so-called are groups based
on distinctive cultures or origin myths or patterns
of exchange with other groups that have core features
that persist through time.[10] Even this bedrock position of the primordialists poses problems for the
student of comparative ethnic movements. For one
thing, while some ethnic groups do draw upon old and
rich cultural heritages with a persisting core, many
movements create their cultures after-the-fact, as it
were. If, on the one hand, there are groups such as
the Jewish people whose social and political identities
have undergone innumerable transformations while a
core culture has been retained and transmitted over
the millenia by the rabbinate steeped in the Talmudic
tradition and by ordinary believers following their
daily 'self-defining routines',[11] there are sufficient
examples of other groups whose core cultures are less
easy to identify, but that have nevertheless formed a
basis for cohesive and sometimes successful ethnic and
nationalist movements. The mushroom growth of ethnic
political movements in the United States in recent

times provides at least a few examples of the latter
sort that are more than ephemeral in nature.[12]
A second difficulty with the bedrock primordialist
position is that, even where there is a persisting
core culture, knowledge of its substance may not be of
much use in predicting either the development or the
form of ethnic movements on behalf of the cultural
groups in question. Certainly a knowledge of the core
religious cultures of orthodox Judaism or of traditional Islam in India would have suggested that the
least likely possibilities would have been the rise of
a Zionist movement or of the movement for the creation
of Pakistan for the traditional keepers of those
cultures, the rabbinate and the ulema, have consistently argued that a secular national state is incompatible with either religion. Of course, both the
rabbinate and the ulema have been largely responsible
for the persistence of Jewish and Islamic communities
wherever they have persisted, but they are communities
differently defined and bounded than are Israel and
Pakistan.
Do these criticisms of the primordialist perspective
then mean that any cultural content should be removed
entirely from the concept of ethnicity? Is ethnicity
to be seen from the extreme instrumentalist point of
view as the pursuit of interest and advantage for
members of groups whose cultures are infinitely malleable and manipulable by elites? Are 'ethnic conflicts'
merely 'one form in which interest conflicts between
and within states are pursued'[13] and ethnicity 'a
communal type of organization which is manipulated by
an interest group in the course of its struggle to
develop and maintain its power'?[14] And is culture
change part of 'a bargaining process' that can be
understood best in terms of a market model by which
ethnic group leaders and members agree to give up
aspects of their culture or modify their prejudices for
the right price?[15] The statements just cited come from
a literature that tends to treat cultural factors in
ethnic movements as epiphenomenal. Abner Cohen in fact
has written about groups that create cultural markers
for purposes of internal communication with each other
in secret societies and dominant cliques.[16]
The fact that new cultural groups can be created for
purposes of economic and political domination, however,
does not mean that the primordialist perspective is not
relevant to our understanding of ethnic groups with

long and rich cultural heritages. In other words, one
possible route toward reconciling the perspectives of
primordialists and instrumentalists may lie in simply
recognizing that cultural groups differ in the strength
and richness of their cultural traditions and even
more importantly in the strength of traditional institutions and social structure. The persistence over
time, for example, of religiously-based communal
institutions among Jews and Muslims wherever they are
found means that these cultural groups always form
potential bases for ethnic movements. However, the
mere persistence of the core religious traditions of
such groups as these offers no prospect for predicting
whether or when ethnic movements will arise among them
and whether or not such movements will be effective in
mobilizing their members. Such cultural persistence
suggests only that it is likely that the groups can be
mobilized on the basis of specific appeals and not
others and that, when ethnic appeals are made, the
pre-existing communal and educational institutions of
the groups will, if made available for the purpose,
provide an effective means of political mobilization.
In short, the values and institutions of a persisting
cultural group will suggest what appeals and symbols
will be effective and what will not be and may also
provide traditional avenues for the mobilization and
organization of the group in new directions. Nevertheless, the leaders of ethnic movements invariably select
from traditional cultures only those aspects that they
think will serve to unite the group and that will be
useful in promoting the interests of the group as they
define them. When they do so, moreover, they affect
the self-definition of the group and its boundaries,
often to such an extent that the ethnic community or
nationality created out of a pre-existing ethnic group
may be a very different social formation from its
progenitor. Or, in the case of groups that have had
a sense of identity and community even before ethnic
mobilization takes place and that contain elites whose
traditional right to define the group and its boundaries are well-established, ethnic mobilization led
by others than the traditional elites will introduce
into the group conflicting definitions of its essence
and extent.

Consequently, whether or not the culture of the
group is ancient or is newly-fashioned, the study of
ethnicity and nationality is in large part the study

of politically induced cultural change. More precisely,
it is the study of the process by which elites and
counter-elites within ethnic groups select aspects
of the group's culture, attach new value and meaning
to them, and use them as symbols to mobilize the group,
to defend its interests, and to compete with other
groups. In this process, those elites have an advantage whose leaders can operate most skilfully in
relation both to the deeply-felt primordial attachments of group members and the shifting relationships
of politics.

2

The differences of viewpoint between primordialists
and instrumentalists have also found expression among
South Asia specialists in their efforts to interpret
and explain ethnic and nationality movements there.
The differences have been most pronounced in discussions of the origins and development of Muslim separatism and the Pakistan movement. From the primordialist
point of view, which was also the view of the leaders
of Muslim separatism, Hindus and Muslims constituted
in pre-modern times distinct civilizations destined to
develop into separate nations once political mobilization took place. The differences between the two
cultures were so great that it was not conceivable that
assimilation of the two could take place and that a
single national culture could be created to which both
would contribute. The contrary view is that the cultural and religious differences between Hindus and
Muslims were not so great as to rule out the creation
of either a composite national culture or at least a
secular political union in which those aspects of
group culture that could not be shared would be relegated to the private sphere. From this point of view,
Muslim separatism was not pre-ordained, but resulted
from the conscious manipulation of selected symbols of
Muslim identity by Muslim elite groups in economic and
political competition with each other and with elite
groups among Hindus.[17]
This issue has recently been joined again in an
exchange between Francis Robinson and me.[18] Although
Robinson and I agree on many aspects of the Muslim
separatist movement, an apparent difference persists
concerning the relative weight to be assigned to the
pervasiveness of Islamic values, to the strength of

Muslim religious institutions, and to the extent to
which a Muslim identity existed in the nineteenth
century as constraining factors on the possibilities
for Hindu-Muslim cooperation and on the freedom of
Muslim elite groups to manipulate symbols of Muslim
culture in the political process. Robinson argues
that 'the religious differences' between Muslims and
Hindus in the nineteenth century, before social
mobilization began, 'were fundamental' and that some
of those differences, such as on idol worship, on
monotheism, and on attitudes toward the cow 'created
a basic antipathy' between the two communities 'which
helped to set them apart as modern politics and self-
governing institutions developed in town, district
and province.' The Muslims of Uttar Pradesh (UP),
primed by these fundamental religious differences,
already conscious of themselves as a separate community, and aware that they were a minority, 'feared
that the Hindu majority would not only interfere with
their religious practices such as cow-sacrifice, but
also ... would discriminate against them' on such
matters 'as education and employment.'[19] In short,
Hindus and Muslims in nineteenth-century India were
separate religious communities predisposed towards, if
not necessarily pre-ordained as, separate national
groups. If it was not a foregone conclusion that
Hindus and Muslims would go separate ways politically,
it was unthinkable that the separate identities of
either group could be subordinated or assimilated to
the other.

Robinson's argument is not entirely inconsistent with
the model developed in *Language, Religion and Politics
in North India* which, although it emphasized the roles
played by elite groups in manipulating cultural symbols
to create political identities, did not ignore either
pre-existing cultural values or inter-group attitudes
as factors influencing the ability of elites to manipulate particular symbols. In fact, the model developed
in *Language, Religion and Politics* did not take off
from an extreme instrumentalist perspective or from the
assumption that either elites or the groups whose
interests they claim to represent are cultural blank
slates. Rather, it began with the following question:
Given the existence in a multi-ethnic society of an
array of cultural distinctions among peoples and of
actual and potential cultural conflicts among them, what
factors are critical in determining which of those

distinctions, if any, will be used to build political
identities? In the model developed in *Language,
Religion and Politics*, the factors emphasized were the
roles played by particular elite groups, the balance
between rates of social mobilization and assimilation
between ethnic groups, the building of political organizations to promote group identities and interests,
and the influence of government policies. However, it
was not assumed that the pre-existing cultures or
religious practices of ethnic groups are infinitely
malleable by elites.

Nevertheless, it is an important and not well-
explored question to consider to what extent and in
what ways the pre-existing values, institutions, and
practices of cultural groups with long and rich heritages constitute primordial attachments that constrain
elites who manipulate symbols of group identity for
political purposes. In the remainder of this essay,
this question will be explored with specific reference
to three elements involving Hindu and Muslim traditional cultural values, institutions, and communication in South Asia in the last century - attitudes
toward cow protection and cow sacrifice, the role of
the personal and family law components of the Sharia
in Muslim life, and the attitudes of Hindus and Muslims
towards the Hindi and Urdu languages. In this section,
the issue will be taken up by considering separately
each element of traditional culture and its use by
elites in politics. In the following section, the
extent to which elites are able to alter the definition
of a group's boundaries by manipulating sets of
symbols will be analysed.

Consider first the different attitudes of Hindus and
Muslims towards the cow. As Robinson points out, 'Hindus revered the cow, the Muslims ate it.'[20] Moreover,
Muslims sacrificed cows at certain religious festivals
such as Bakr-Id.[21] The cow, therefore, was always a
potential symbol of group identity for Hindus and of
group conflict between Hindus and Muslims. However, it
is also important to recognize that the symbol of the
cow has had differential import for Hindus and Muslims.
For orthodox Hindus, it is simply mandatory to avoid
the killing of kine. It is not, however, mandatory for
Muslims to eat kine. It is a disputed matter whether
or not cow sacrifice is essential to Muslim religious
ritual.[22] These 'objective' cultural parameters
clearly limited and constrained the freedom of movement

of Hindu and Muslim elites in the late nineteenth and twentieth centuries in South Asia, but it did not confine them completely. Hindus might have ignored the fact that Muslims slaughtered cows for both dietary and ritual purposes - except insofar as cow slaughter was flaunted before them - but many chose in the 1880s and 1890s to form cow protection societies and to demand passage of laws to prevent cow slaughter. Muslims might have avoided cow slaughter and, thereby, made a grand concession to Hindu sentiment without violating their own religious susceptibilities. In fact, Abd al-Bari, the fiery *alim* of Firangi Mahal offered to stop Muslim cow slaughter during the early days of the Khilafat and non-cooperation movements[23] and the Muslim League, in its 1919 meeting, passed a resolution recommending the substitution of 'the sacrifice of other animals in place of cows.'[24] The predominant leaders of the Indian National Congress attempted to restrain the leaders of the cow protection movement and tried to prevent them from demanding laws to prevent cow slaughter, even though the cow protection movement had considerable support among Congressmen in the northern provinces.[25] Moreover, even the most militant cow protectors used an economic argument for the prevention of cow slaughter which, however transparent a cover it may seem for religious sentiment, always kept open the possibility that Hindus and Muslims could reach an agreement on secular grounds concerning an issue of profound religious import.[26] That the issue was not settled on terms such as these was not because of its primordial character, but because several elite groups among both Hindus and Muslims found it useful as a convenient symbol in their efforts to build internal unity and in their conflicts with each other. The cow was a symbol that could be used equally by orthodox Hindus defending traditional religious practices, by revivalist Hindu leaders attempting to reform them, by Hindu political leaders who wished to promote a specifically Hindu form of Indian nationalism,[27] and by Muslim religious and political elites who feared Hindu dominance and found anti-cow slaughter movements useful as an example of how Muslims would be oppressed under a representative system in which Hindus would be in a majority.

John McLane has suggested that the political significance of the cow in Indian politics should not be over-emphasized and that it is not possible to separate

controversy over the cow slaughter issue from other
issues of elite conflict over access to education,
government employment opportunities, and political
representation with which it was 'intertwined'.[28]
Moreover, he has argued that, although the cow protection movement of the 1880s and 1890s had a great
impact on Hindu-Muslim relations and precipitated a
chain of riots in 1893, the disappearance of the cow
protection movement thereafter 'suggests that popular
sentiment was not broad or adamant and that Hindu
leaders regarded the alienation of Muslims and the
government as too heavy a price to pay for any possible benefits'for its continuance. He suggests further
that 'the issue of cow slaughter was more symbolic than
substantive', that it 'was not central' to the persisting substantive issues of Indian politics, which
concerned 'the distribution of political power' under
the constitutional structures devised under British
rule in India.[29] It would be more precise to say that
the cow protection issue was not central to the
political elites who dominated the leading political
organizations of Indian nationalism and Muslim
separatism. It was central to the Hindu religious
leaders, revivalist and orthodox, and it later became
a useful symbol for Hindu communal organizations
committed to a Hindu definition of Indian nationalism,
such as the Hindu Mahasabha and the Jan Sangh. It was
also a persistent irritant in Hindu-Muslim relations
in municipal politics in the towns of the United
Provinces in the late nineteenth and early twentieth
centuries.[30] After independence, the constituent
assembly of India acknowledged Hindu sentiment on the
matter by including in the directive principles of
state policy an article containing a mandate for the
state to prohibit cow slaughter. This mandate has
since been implemented by most state governments in
India. Moreover, as late as 1966, a movement was
launched by Hindu revivalist groups, supported by the
most prestigious orthodox gurus associated with the
holiest sanctuaries of Hinduism, in support of the
demand that the government of India impose a ban on
cow slaughter throughout the country. The movement
culminated in the largest mass demonstration ever
witnessed in the post-independence period on the
streets of Delhi, but the government refused to accept
the demand.
      The cow, therefore, may be seen as a primordial

attachment for Hindus, to which religious reformers and
Hindu nationalists in the late nineteenth century
attached new meaning as a symbol of Hindu communal identity, and which secular political leaders of the time
either avoided because they could not control its use
or used provocatively in constructing catalogues of
grievances against their opponents from the rival
community. Differences in Hindu and Muslim attitudes
toward the cow, therefore, provide an example of the
intrusion into politics of a symbol that had primordial
meaning for Hindus and that served to threaten the
religious and political position of Muslims in India.
The cow protection movement brought Hindu and Muslim
religious sentiments into direct conflict, even though
the issue was of less religious significance for
Muslims than for Hindus. Moreover, Hindu sentiment
toward the cow was such that it limited the freedom of
action even of the secular leaders of the Congress.
Elites were therefore constrained on this highly
emotive issue, although a few Hindu leaders took
independent action on it in opposition to the primordial feelings of Hindus in hopes of political cooperation with Muslims, and Muslim religious and political
elites offered to defer to Hindu sentiment on the
matter.

The issue of Muslim personal law provides a somewhat different example of a symbol of great religious
significance to Muslims and with no religious significance to Hindus, but which has brought Muslims in
India into conflict with secular nationalists, both
Hindu and Muslim. It is a religious obligation for
Muslims to adhere to the body of laws that make up the
Sharia and that includes the 'personal law' relating
to marriage, divorce and inheritance. However, the
application of the law is often a complex matter that
may involve the intervention of clerical authority.
Muslims must be taught some of the most important laws
of Islam from an early age, but ordinary Muslims can
hardly be expected to know more than a fraction of the
body of prescriptions and proscriptions contained in
the Sharia. The interpretation and application of the
Sharia is one of the principal mechanisms by which the
ulema maintain their control over Islamic society.
While an orthodox Muslim would not think of violating
the more evident and established principles of the
Sharia and while he would revere the law, the Sharia
means most to the Muslim clerics.

In Muslim-majority societies undergoing secularization, the Sharia invariably emerges as a symbol of conflict between the ulema and the secular political elites, who wish to establish a centralized state for which they consider a modern legal system essential. In former colonial societies with large Muslim populations and in societies such as contemporary India, where Muslims are in a minority, the issue naturally acquires a different significance, for the modernizing elite will then be predominantly non-Muslim and will, therefore, be attacked for interfering with the religious rights of Muslims. This, of course, has been the case in India both under British rule and since independence where any attempt to discuss the formulation of a uniform civil code has been sure to call forth the nearly unanimous opposition of the ulema.

The British did impose a secular system of criminal and procedural law in India and they abolished the *qazi* courts that had previously enforced Muslim law, but they did not develop a uniform civil code for personal and family law.[31] On the contrary, both Hindu and Muslim personal law were formally recognized and were applied in the government courts.[32] Although the constitution of independent India established as one of the directive principles of state policy the passage of a uniform civil code, that directive has been carried out only with respect to non-Muslims under the Hindu Code Acts of 1955-56.

Neither the British nor the leaders of post-independence India were willing to antagonize the ulema on the matter of reform of Muslim personal law, for it is believed that the ulema have succeeded in imparting to most Muslims the feeling that any tampering with the personal law would amount to an attack on Islam. The fear that the ulema would be able to mobilize the mass of Muslims in India in opposition to any efforts to reform their personal law has enabled them to hold hostage both the secular Hindu political elites and all Muslim political leaders who seek to represent Muslim interests. During the nationalist period in India, when the Congress and the Muslim League vied for the support of the Muslim public, Congress leaders succeeded in forming a political alliance with the Jami'yat-al-ulama-i-Hind, founded in 1919 for 'the exclusive purpose of safeguarding the "Shari'ah".'[33] For its part, the Muslim League, many of whose leaders were secular

politicians opposed both to the rigid application of
the Sharia and to the continued hold of the ulema over
the Muslim masses, nevertheless felt obliged to include
in its demands protection for Muslim personal law.

In this case, therefore, the issue, however much
the Sharia is seen as essential to Islam, does not
involve conflict with Hindus as such. It is a symbol
that Muslim religious elites use to constrain Muslim
political elites who, in turn, have often found it
useful as a symbol in their conflicts with Hindu elites
for political influence in the Muslim community. Since
Muslim adherence to the Sharia does not impinge upon
the religious feelings of Hindus and does not endanger
Hindu-Muslim relations, the secular political elites in
modern India have been able to avoid a confrontation
on this issue with Muslims. Whereas, on the issue of
cow protection, many otherwise secular-minded Hindu
elites felt constrained to support cow protection
legislation in the Constitution of India and in state
legislation after independence, they have been negatively constrained on the question of a uniform civil
code. The strategy followed in India since independence has been to use secular Muslims to speak on behalf
of modernization of the Muslim personal law, but to
avoid any action on the issue that would endanger Hindu-
Muslim relations. In effect, a tacit bargain has been
struck in modern India whose terms are that Muslims
will not be permitted to violate Hindu feelings by
slaughtering cows, while the Muslims retain the right
to have a separate system of civil laws.[34] This
bargain could have been struck at any time before
independence had it not served the interests of Hindu
religious elites and Muslim political elites to keep
the issues alive. It was not struck because Hindu
revivalists found the symbol of the cow invaluable in
uniting Hindus, because the Muslim political elites
found the cow protection issue useful to demonstrate
the dangers of Hindu majority rule, and because both
Hindu and Muslim political elites found the issue of
the Sharia valuable in recruiting the support of the
ulema in their conflicts with each other for political
influence.

A third major symbol of Muslim identity and Hindu-
Muslim conflict, particularly in the north Indian
states of UP and Bihar, is the Urdu language. The
adoption of Urdu as a symbol of Muslim identity by
Muslim political elites in north India from the late

nineteenth century onwards illustrates several points
concerning the uses made of cultural symbols by
political elites.[35] One point illustrated by the use
of Urdu as a symbol of Muslim identity is the way in
which elites attach new value to symbols for purposes
of promoting identity and differentiating one group
from another. In the nineteenth century in north
India, before the extension of the British system of
government schools, Urdu was not used in its written
form as a medium of instruction in traditional Islamic
schools, where Muslim children were taught Persian and
Arabic, the traditional languages of Islam and Muslim
culture.[36] It was only when the Muslim elites of north
India and the British decided that Muslims were backward in education in relation to Hindus and should be
encouraged to attend government schools that it was
felt necessary to offer Urdu in the Persian-Arabic
script as an inducement to Muslims to attend the
schools. And it was only after the Hindi-Urdu controversy developed that Urdu, once disdained by Muslim
elites in north India and not even taught in the Muslim
religious schools in the early nineteenth century,
became a symbol of Muslim identity second only to
Islam itself.[37]

A second point revealed by the Hindi-Urdu controversy in north India is how symbols may be used to
separate peoples who, in fact, share aspects of
culture. It is well known that ordinary Muslims and
Hindus alike spoke the same language in the United
Provinces in the nineteenth century, namely Hindustani,
whether called by that name or whether called Hindi,
Urdu, or one of the regional dialects such as Braj or
Awadhi. Although a variety of styles of Hindi-Urdu
were in use in the nineteenth century among different
social classes and status groups, the legal and
administrative elites in courts and government offices,
Hindus and Muslims alike, used Urdu in the Persian-
Arabic script. When the Urdu-speaking elite divided
politically on the question of script, however, that
the division was communicated and transmitted to the
mass of the people. As more and more government
schools were set up, it became a critical question,
therefore, for Urdu and Hindi spokesmen to insist that
Hindus had the right to be taught through the medium of
Hindi in Devanagari script and that Muslims had the
right to be taught through the medium of Urdu in
Persian script because their languages and cultures

were inseparable. Moreover, leaders of the Hindi movement and of the Urdu movement set out to separate the
two languages through Sanskritization and Persianiza-
tion of its two forms.[38] In this way, the literary
elites of the United Provinces deliberately chose to
emphasize and even to create linguistic differences
rather than to emphasize and enhance the linguistic
elements held in common by Hindus and Muslims alike by
such devices, for example, as developing a common
vocabulary and teaching both scripts.

A third point is that the choice of a symbol often
has a material basis, arising out of elite competition
for economic advantage. Urdu became a symbol of
Muslim identity in north India when the British,
partly because of the demands of Hindi supporters,
moved to either replace Urdu with Hindi as the language
of administration in the northern provinces or to
admit Hindi on an equal basis with Urdu. The Muslim
elites in north India rose up to defend Urdu because
the replacement of Urdu by Hindi or even its admission
to equality threatened the advantage that Muslims
traditionally held in government employment, particularly in the United Provinces. It should be especially emphasized in this regard that the adoption of
the Devanagari script presented only a slight difficulty for Muslims, whereas the maintenance of Urdu
in Persian-Arabic script raised much greater difficulties for Hindus. It is a relatively small matter
for a Hindustani-speaker to learn to read and write
the language in Devanagari, which is a quite simple
script, but it requires a much greater educational
investment to learn and maintain the Persian-Arabic
script. The defence of Urdu, therefore, could not
have arisen out of a fear that Muslims would acquire
an undue burden by the need to learn the Devanagari
script but out of a desire to maintain the rather
heavier burden on Hindus of acquiring proficiency in
the Persian-Arabic script to qualify for government
jobs.

A fourth point is that the same symbol may be used
at different times for contrary objectives. When the
demand was made to admit Hindi in Devanagari script as
an official language in the North-Western Provinces
and Oudh, along with Urdu in Persian-Arabic script,
Muslims argued that Urdu was not their language only,
but the common possession of Hindus and Muslims alike
and that it should be retained as the sole official

language for this reason and for its alleged technical
advantages over Hindi. The argument that Urdu is the
language of both Hindus and Muslims continues to be
made up to the present by its defenders. Moreover,
the argument has some historical validity. However,
Urdu has also often been used as a symbol by Muslim
elites to separate themselves from the Hindus. When
Hindu leaders refused to withdraw their demands for
official recognition of Hindi and for its use in the
educational system and when its use threatened the
material interests of Muslim elites, many Muslims began
to argue that Urdu was the special language of Muslims,
that its cultural heritage was expressed through it,
and that it was nearly as much a part of Muslim
identity as Islam itself.

The final point illustrated by the Muslim adoption
of Urdu in Persian-Arabic script is the tendency for
ethnic groups in conflict to separate themselves
from each other by multiple symbols and to seek to
make those symbols congruent. In the early nineteenth
century, Muslims and Hindus had different religious
traditions and practices and, insofar as they were
educated at all, they were taught Persian or Arabic,
if they were Muslims, Hindi or Sanskrit, if they were
Hindus. In the different dialect or language regions
of north India, however, Muslims and Hindus alike
spoke the language of the region in which they lived.
In other words, they may have used different languages
to communicate with their deity, but they used a
common language to communicate with each other. In
the course of the Hindi-Urdu controversy, however, as
Hindi and Urdu were developed as alternative regional
standard languages taught in all government schools
in the different dialect regions of the north, Hindi
in Devanagari script became the language of Hindus and
Urdu in Persian script the language of Muslims. The
functions of language in the north thereby became
transformed from their traditional uses for ritual
communication with a deity or for ordinary discourse
into symbolic links among members of the same ethnic
group, barriers to communication between members of
different religious groups, and additional marks of
identity and separateness for such groups.

The changes over the past century in both Muslim
and Hindu attitudes towards the Urdu language and the
several different symbolic uses to which it has been
put by Muslim elites in their competition with Hindus

demonstrate that 'primordial' attachments may be
subject to substantial variation for the sake of
political and economic interests. Hindus and Muslims
in north India had the same 'given' mother tongues.
The religious and political elites of north India
and the British authorities, however, made decisions
about official languages and scripts and about media
of instruction in the schools that, over time, have
affected the ways in which ordinary Hindus and Muslims
feel about their language and how it should be used.
In fact, the two languages, Hindi and Urdu, have
also diverged in the past century. Initially, however, the language controversy was principally a
struggle over scripts. The Persian-Arabic and Devanagari scripts, however, are not 'givens'. They are
cultural transmissions, with religious significance
because they are the scripts used to decipher the
religious texts. But they did not have to become
symbols of group identity. They became symbols of
identity because elite groups, with the aid of government, promoted them as such in their conflicts with
each other.

3

The three examples given above illustrate the interrelationship among a group's cultural symbols, the
interests of specific elite groups in relation to
particular symbols, and the freedom of action that
elites have or do not have to manipulate such symbols
in the political process. However, in order to perceive fully the nature of the relationship between the
ethnic identity of a cultural group and the actions of
its elites, it is necessary to consider how sets of
symbols are used to define the boundaries of a group.
It is important to recognize beforehand, however, that
at no time in the history of any cultural group is
there likely to be anything like unanimous agreement
on defining what it means to be a member of a particular cultural group. Moreover, any definition that
acquires a high degree of consensus within a community
at a particular point in its history is likely at
some time to be subject to redefinition as a consequence of either internal conflicts of interest or
ideology within the group or as a consequence of
external changes that affect segments of the group
differentially.

Insofar as the Muslims of India are concerned, two
features of their historical development as a community
are particularly relevant here. One is that, when the
British arrived, the Muslim community of India or of
any part of India was much less of a social fact than
it is today. Secondly in the course of the social and
political development of the Muslim community in the
nineteenth and twentieth centuries, the symbols used
to define its boundaries have varied depending upon
the elites who have done the defining. With regard to
the social reality of the Muslim community in India
before the arrival of the British, Hardy has described
it as 'unified at best by a few common rituals and by
the beliefs and aspirations of a majority - not the
totality - of its scholars.'[39] Titus has pointed out
that Muslims in India have always been divided along
sectarian lines, some of them sharply antagonistic,
and has described in detail several Muslim groups
whose religious practices were quite similar to those
of Hindus.[40] Seal has remarked that the Muslim community in the nineteenth century 'was not homogeneous.
Language, caste and economic standing worked together
to divide Muslim from Muslim no less than Hindu from
Hindu.'[41]

In what sense, then, was there a Muslim community
at all in India in the nineteenth century? There was
certainly a community of Muslim believers, united by
a common relationship to a deity, by a belief in the
prophethood of Muhammad, by a recognition that the
Quran was the ultimate source of religious authority,
and by participation in common worship. Many, but not
all Muslims were guided by the Sharia, there was a
considerable diversity of religious practices, rituals,
and beliefs at the mass level not recognized or condemned outright by the orthodox ulema, Muslims spoke
different languages, and they did not have a common
origin, some being descendants of invaders from the
Middle East, others being indigenous converts. In the
early nineteenth century, then, there was at most a
Muslim community of believers, with only a limited set
of beliefs and religious practices held in common, but
not a Muslim political or speech community.

During the late nineteenth and twentieth centuries,
however, elites within the Muslim religious community,
in their efforts to adjust to the extension of the
British imperial system in India and to new sets of
relationships with other religious groups, began to

define the Muslim community in different ways. The British authorities materially assisted this process for all elite groups involved in it by treating the Muslims of India as an official category for purposes of census enumeration, distribution of government appointments, political representation, and education. One such elite group, itself internally diverse in some ways, was the ulema. They set about through movements of religious revival, through the establishment of networks of educational institutions, and through political action to unify the Muslim community, to educate the Muslim masses in Islamic beliefs and rituals and to persuade them to avoid non-Islamic religious practices, and to seek governmental recognition for a legal definition of the Muslim community in India as well.[42]

Muslim revivalism arose initially out of the need felt by the ulema to combat the threats of Christian missionaries to convert Muslims, of western education to subvert them, and of the imperial state to loosen their control over the faithful by introducing a modern legal system. Although Muslim revivalism was directed initially against the alien rulers, it brought Muslims into conflict with Hindu revivalists who were engaged in a similar enterprise and who resented Muslim proselytization as much as Christian missionary activity. The conflict between the two revivalisms led to a sharpening of the religious boundaries between Hindus and Muslims to the extent - which, to this day is far from complete - that each side succeeded in convincing its followers to relinquish ritual practices and forms of worship held in common.

Thus, the ulema did not accept Muslim religious identity in the form that they found it in the nineteenth century, but worked to impart to the Muslim masses an understanding and a practice of Islam more in line with what the ulema considered to be proper for the faithful. In doing so, the ulema who led the 'traditionalist revival' were also concerned with defending their definitions of Islamic propriety from the reformist interpretations of the modernists in Islam, particularly of Sayyid Ahmad Khan and the Aligarh movement, who had by the end of the nineteenth century also become a threat to the control of the ulema over the Muslim community.[43] Religious revivalism had a dual impact on the Muslims as a religious community in that it both solidified the relationship between

the clerics and the masses[44] and separated the faithful more clearly from non-Muslims. The ulema also
set about to extend the enforcement of the Sharia
among Muslims who had not been fully subject to it.[45]
For the ulema, then, the Muslims of India constituted
both a religious and a legal community. Such a
definition of the Muslim community is, of course,
exactly in conformity with orthodox Islam,[46] but it
did not exist in nineteenth-century India as fully
as the ulema wished and it had, therefore, to be
enforced.

It is important to recognize that the conception of
the Muslim community held by the ulema in the nineteenth century did not include a definition of the
Muslims of India as a political community in the
modern sense of the term, that is, as a self-determining entity with the right to have a state of its own
and the authority to make its own laws. Such a
definition would have then been considered contrary
both to the orthodox teachings of Islam concerning the
universality of the Muslim community and concerning
the duty of Muslims to follow the Sharia rather than
man-made law. It was not until the second decade of
the twentieth century that some of the ulema began to
articulate a different conception of the 'Muslims as
forming a political community ... capable of combining
in common enterprises because its members share the
values of Islam.'[47] However, that conception did not
include the idea that the Sharia could be applied or
interpreted 'by popular decision and collective will.'[48]
That task was to remain the prerogative of the ulema.
Moreover, insofar as any of the ulema in India articulated a modern conception of 'territorial nationhood',
it was not to apply to the Muslims as a separate people
but to India as a whole,[49] in which the Muslims after
independence were, it was hoped, to constitute a
'largely self-governing' religious community.[50]

Although the elimination of non-Islamic religious
practices prevalent among Indian Muslims and the
protection of the Sharia were the more prominent goals
of the ulema who became active in politics and social
movements, particularly in the Jami'yat-al-ulama
formed in 1919,[51] they also played a part through the
Jami'yat and through their educational network in
promoting the spread of the Urdu language among Muslims
and its use as an additional symbol of Muslim identity.
An Urdu strongly infused with Arabic and Persian words

was the medium of instruction at the leading ulema-
dominated school at Deoband in UP and at its affiliated madrasahs spread throughout north India.[52]
Although Arabic, not Urdu, was the language used by
ulema in Kerala, in the north and in Hyderabad, the
ulema found that a Persianized-Arabicized Urdu was
the most useful vehicle both to provide access to
traditional Islamic literature and to communicate with
ordinary Muslims. In its 1926 conference, the Jami'yat-
al-ulama passed a resolution demanding that the 'Urdu
language and Urdu script be declared as the accepted
National Language and the accepted National Script'
of India.[53] In the post-independence period, as Urdu
lost some of its hold in the government schools in
the north, the ulema rushed to the defence of Urdu,
which came to be seen as part and parcel of Muslim
'social and cultural identity and their spiritual
inheritance.'[54]

For the ulema, then, the Muslim community of India
has been defined primarily in religious and legal terms.
The primary symbol of Muslim identity for the ulema,
however, is Islam itself, in which adherence to the
Sharia is an indispensable aspect. Urdu has also been
included in the ulema's definition of the Muslim
community but as a secondary symbol only, used defen-
sively in conflict with Hindus. However, while the
ulema would exclude from the Muslim community those
persons who blatantly violate the Sharia, they would
clearly not exclude non-Urdu speakers.

For the Muslim political elites who founded the
Aligarh movement and the Muslim League and who led
successfully the movement for the creation of Pakistan,
the values attached to the several potential symbols
of Muslim identity in India were quite different.
Moreover, from the beginning, the definition of the
Muslim community articulated by the modernizing Muslim
elites associated with Sayyid Ahmad Khan and the Aligarh
movement was a political one. In contrast to the
ulema, who attached most value to symbols of Muslim
identity that not only separated Muslims from non-
Muslims but isolated Muslims from contamination by
alien religious and legal influences and preserved the
influence of the ulema within the Muslim community,
the modernist elites were initially interested in
using the community as a base for the exercise of
influence in the wider society. The Muslim aristocrats and government servants who founded the various

institutions associated with the Aligarh movement moved
in the same spheres as and had similar interests to
those of their Hindu counterparts. As landlords, they
wanted to retain control over their tenants, who were
both Hindu and Muslim. As government servants, they
wanted to ensure that they and their children would
continue to have favoured access to the best jobs in
government.

Whereas the interests of the ulema required only the
striking of a bargain whose terms were that the personal law provisions of the Sharia would not be
tampered with or replaced by secular laws in return for
which the ulema would not resist the authority of the
imperial state in other respects, the interests of
the Muslim aristocrats and government servants required
active collaboration with the British authorities. The
terms of the bargain worked out in the last decades of
the nineteenth century and the first two decades of the
twentieth between the modernist Muslim elites and the
British were that the British would recognize the
existence of a Muslim community in India, with the
Muslim aristocrats and government servants as its
spokesmen, would concede to those spokesmen a separate
political arena in which they would not have to compete
with non-Muslims, would grant extra representation to
those spokesmen in a proportion beyond the actual
population of the community they were to represent, and
would help the Muslims to maintain their advantage in
government employment. In return, the Muslim landlords
and government servants were expected not only to avoid
opposing government but to provide positive support
for it and opposition to its detractors.[55]

The primáry symbols of Muslim identity used by the
privileged Muslim classes in the late nineteenth
century were political and historical. They argued
that the Muslims of India had been the rulers of the
country until the British arrived,[56] that their
previous tradition of rule gave them an historical and
political importance far beyond the mere numbers of
the Muslim population of the country, and that they were,
therefore, entitled to a continued and more than proportionate share in political power under British rule.
The Muslim elites and their historiographical and
literary apologists looked back to the great days of
Muslim expansion and political power not only in India
but in the Middle East, Africa, and Europe for inspiration. For these Muslim elites, as for the ulema, the

Urdu language became a secondary symbol of Muslim
identity only when it came under attack by Hindu
revivalists, with the support of the British government. Since, however, it was through the Urdu
language that the Muslim elites in the nineteenth
century preserved their privileged access to government jobs, recognition of Hindi by the provincial
governments in north India, particularly in the North-
Western Provinces and Oudh, threatened the social
political position of the Muslim minority in the
Hindu majority areas and upset the Muslim-British
bargain.

It is noteworthy that the Sharia does not appear as
a prominent symbol of Muslim identity for the Muslim
landlords and government servants. Although the
landed Muslim classes had a specific interest in the
application of the Muslim law of *wakf* in such a way
that they could put their properties into a trust for
the use of their descendants, they did not like those
aspects of Sharia that restricted their abilities to
dispose of their properties to persons of their
choice.[57] Islam itself was but a secondary symbol for
the Muslim political elites of the nineteenth century.
Although Sayyid Ahmad Khan did, on occasion, defend
Islam from the attacks of Christian missionaries, he
was not interested in launching an Islamic counter-
offensive, but rather in 'demonstrating the basic
similarity between Islam and Christianity', [58] which
fitted well with his persistent design for a collaborative alliance between the British and the Muslims of
India. Nor were the nineteenth-century political
elites even seriously engaged in defining the
boundaries of the Muslim community. Rather, they
accepted the British official recognition of the existence of a Muslim community, which involved their
enumeration in the decennial censuses and frequent
reports and inquiries into the conditions of this
community and its alleged backwardness in relation to
Hindus. The Muslim elites of the nineteenth century
were concerned principally to use the data provided
by the British concerning the backwardness of the mass
of Muslims, with whom the leaders had little contact,
as an argument for preserving their own privileges.

Although Sayyid Ahmad Khan was concerned to promote
Western education among the Muslims so that they would
be in a better position to qualify for high government
office, he did not feel that education alone qualified

a man for a position of importance in the realm. Such
distinctions were to be reserved for persons 'of high
social position' and 'of good breeding', not for men
'of low caste or insignificant origin'.[59] Nor did he
favour competition with the Hindus, particularly with
the despised Bengalis, but he urged the Muslims to
educate themselves so that they might be eligible to
be selected to serve the Raj. He proposed, in effect,
a collaboration between the former ruling nations and
classes of Hindustan, among whom he sometimes included
the Rajputs, with the then ruling nation, the British.

After the First World War, however, the secular
Muslim elites became more diversified and middle-class
professionals and professional politicians became more
prominent in Muslim politics. At the same time, as the
franchise was extended to larger numbers of people
under the Montagu-Chelmsford reforms and later the
Government of India Act, 1935, it became necessary, if
Muslim leaders were to substantiate their claim to
represent their community, for them to engage in
political mobilization of the people in whose abstract
name elite benefits had been previously sought. Moreover, the diversification of elites within the Muslim
community itself led to intra-communal elite competition for the right to speak for the community.

Robinson has described the initial impact on Muslim
politics of elite diversification and increasing
pressures for political mobilization during the
Khilafat movement of 1919-1920. During this movement,
the newer groups of middle-class professionals and full-
time politicians joined in an alliance with the ulema
in a campaign whose central symbol was a pan-Islamic
one.[60] Most members of the traditional Muslim elite
groups and the secular-oriented Muslim leaders such as
Jinnah refused to have anything to do with this movement, the former because it involved a challenge to
government and their collaborative relationship with
it, the latter because it involved an emotional merging
of religion and politics.

In the decades after the Khilafat movement, however,
the secular political leadership of the Muslim League
dominated Muslim politics and sought to achieve for the
Muslim community in India the kinds of goals that had
been set by the Aligarh movement leaders, most of which
concerned satisfactory political representation. The
famous Fourteen Points drafted by Jinnah in· 1929
contained twelve points that focused on matters of

political representation, including such questions as
the proportion of seats to be allotted to Muslims in
legislatures and cabinets, maintaining or extending
the number of Muslim-majority provinces, and the
retention of separate electorates. Only two of the
fourteen points specifically mentioned religious or
cultural matters. Point seven demanded full religious
liberty and point twelve demanded constitutional
'safeguards for the protection of Muslim culture and
for the protection and promotion of Muslim education,
language, religion, personal laws and Muslim charit-
able institutions.'[61] The issue of the Sharia, of
such central and overwhelming importance to the ulema
and considered by many others than the ulema to be
essential to any definition of the Muslim community,
is relegated to two words in a long sentence without
any specific mention of the nature of the 'safeguards'
to be sought. It is also noteworthy that Urdu is not
mentioned specifically in the Fourteen Points. In
Jinnah's later statements and in various resolutions
and manifestoes of the Muslim League, protection of
Urdu was sometimes mentioned. However, it is clear
enough from the infrequent attention given to the
Urdu issue in his own speeches and writings that the
language issue was not his primary concern.[62] As for
the Sharia and the ulema, Jinnah hardly ever referred
to the former and occasionally criticized the latter,
some of whom he described as 'that undesirable element
of Maulvis and Maulanas' from whose political clutches
the Muslim League had freed the Muslim masses.[63]

Jinnah's definition of the Muslim community was a
political one, rather than a religious-legal or
linguistic one. Although, therefore, it was entirely
different from the definition used by the ulema, it
also moved away from the historical-political definition of the early leaders of the Aligarh movement.
The Muslim community for Jinnah was not an abstract
historical-political entity but a contemporary political
force. Safeguards and weightage in representation for
Muslims were now sought not because of the historical
importance of the Muslim community in India but because,
though they were a minority, they were also a separate
people with distinct interests. They could not,
therefore, be treated like the shifting minorities in
a representative system who could be voted down on one
issue, but would have a chance to prevail on other
issues. On the contrary, the Muslims of India

represented a permanent and persisting political interest and could not be treated only as a minority.

Jinnah's political methods were also entirely different from those of the Muslim political elites of the nineteenth century. Collaboration with the British authorities could not provide the necessary safeguards for Muslims, especially as India moved closer to self-government. What was required was unity, solidarity, and organization. After the formation of Congress governments in six provinces in India in 1937 and the unwillingness of the Congress to cooperate with the Muslim League on its terms in those provinces, Jinnah's call for Muslim unity and solidarity became his principal theme. The Muslims, Jinnah insisted, should follow the Muslim League as its 'only authoritative and representative organization'[64] and should pursue 'one single definite uniform policy'.[65] Only by organization and unity could the Muslim minority protect its 'rights and interests' against what Jinnah saw as 'a permanent Hindu majority.'[66]

It was a short step from this position ideologically, but rather a larger one rhetorically, to the position articulated by Jinnah after the failure of the Muslim League to achieve its political goals in India in the 1930s and the passage of the Pakistan resolution of 1940, namely, the idea that the Muslims of India constituted a self-determining political community, a nation in the modern sense of the term. The differences between Hindus and Muslims in India were now seen as not merely religious differences, but as entirely different ways of life and thought. Hindus and Muslims in India were distinct peoples, with 'different religious philosophies, social customs, literatures,' and histories.[67] As such, it was unthinkable that they could live as a mere minority in a Hindu-dominated country. Rather, they must have a state of their own in which they would establish their own constitution and make their own laws.

Once the state of Pakistan was founded, however, Jinnah reverted to a position much more consistent with his secular political orientation, namely, that the differences between Hindus and Muslims were matters of personal religion only, which did not prevent their cooperating together as citizens of the same state.[68] His death in 1948, however, meant that others in Pakistan had to face up to the fundamental contradiction

between the secular political conception of a modern
Muslim state and the religious-legal conception of it
held by the ulema. Others too had to face the contradictions posed by the fact that north Indian Muslims
who had taken the lead in Muslim separatism had for
decades been promoting the view that Urdu was the
language of the Muslims, a position vehemently denied
by the Bengali majority in the new state. These
contradictions have so far proved to be irresolvable.
The first contributed to the prolonged difficulties
in reaching a consensus on a constitution for Pakistan,
the second to its disintegration. The persistent
problems of maintaining national unity in Pakistan in
the face of linguistic and cultural diversities
suggest that a satisfactory definition of the boundaries of the Muslim nation is yet a long way off.

4

In the preceding pages, the relationship between elite
interests and three Hindu and Muslim cultural symbols
in South Asia in the nineteenth and twentieth
centuries have been discussed. It remains to consider
what the discussion suggests about the relationships
between these 'givens' of Hindu and Muslim existence
in north India and the symbols used by religious and
political elites.
   In some senses, all three of the symbols discussed
can be considered primordial attachments - the cow, the
Sharia, and the Urdu language. For the orthodox Hindu,
the prohibition against killing and eating beef is
inseparable from his religion and his whole moral
outlook on life. It is, therefore, inconceivable
that any Hindu politician could expect to be effective
in mobilizing support by proposing that the prohibi-
tions against cow slaughter be discarded as super-
stitious.[69] It is also evident that the cow is always
potentially a symbol that can be called up by Hindu
religious or political elites to mobilize large numbers
of Hindus either to build internal unity or to engage
in action directed against Muslims. To say that the
cow is always potentially available as a mobilizing
symbol, however, does not mean that any Hindu politician or religious leader who uses it at any time is
bound to succeed. It does mean, though, that if government or the Muslims flaunt Hindu sentiment by permitt-
ing open or too evident slaughtering of cows, Hindu

religious leaders are likely to rise up and mobilize
Hindus in protest. Does this mean that Hindu-Muslim
conflict was inevitable in Hindu-majority India and
that Muslims must submit to Hindu sentiment on the
issue? The strength of Hindu feeling on cow protection
and the relatively much smaller significance of cow
slaughter for Muslims surely dictated that the terms of
any political accommodation between Hindus and Muslims
would involve limitations on Muslim freedom to
slaughter cows. In the pre-independence period, the
symbol of the cow was also available to those Muslim
leaders who wished to provoke Hindu-Muslim conflict
by using it to protest against Hindu oppression of
Muslims. It would be nothing but folly for any Muslim
politician in India to so use it in post-independence,
post-partition India.

The Sharia has been used as a symbol of Muslim
identity in a manner similar to the use of the cow by
Hindus. It has been a central symbol for the Muslim
religious elites, the ulema, but only a secondary
symbol for the secular Muslim political elites. The
ulema have fought to protect the personal law portions
of the Sharia and their right to interpret those
provisions against the inroads of the state and the
desires of other Muslims who are not ulema to reform
the personal law. The success of the ulema in using
the Sharia as a symbol of Islam has meant that the
state and secular Muslim leaders are constrained from
attempting to reform the Muslim personal law by a mass
public opinion that has been socialized to believe that
it will be un-Islamic to do so.

Unlike the symbol of the cow for the Hindus, however,
the Sharia is a divisive symbol within the Muslim
community itself. One would be hard put to find many
Hindus who think it important to slaughter cows,[70]
but many secular Muslims consider it essential to
modernize the Sharia and to adopt a uniform civil law
administered by the state. This division within the
Muslim community and the fact that the Sharia is not
a divisive symbol in Hindu-Muslim relations made
possible political bargains before independence
between Hindu and Muslim elites, that is, between the
secular Hindu political elites and the ulema, to
undercut the hold of secular Muslim elites over
Muslim public opinion. After independence, however,
in the changed political contexts of India and Pakistan, the Sharia has become a potential symbol of

conflict between the ulema and the secular political
elites in both states. The hold of the Sharia over
Muslim public opinion in South Asia then has become a
'given' of religious belief, but the use of the Sharia
as a symbol of conflict or cooperation between elites
nevertheless varies according to political circumstance.
In other words, political context and elite interests
determine the political significance of this religious
symbol.

The most variable symbol discussed here is also the
most 'primordial' of the three. Surely, one's mother
tongue is second only to one's family relationships as
a 'given' and surely it is acquired sooner and more
instinctively than feelings of reverence for a
religious symbol such as the cow or than respect for
a complex body of laws such as the Sharia. Yet,
despite the high degree of shared features in the
spoken languages of Hindus and Muslims in north India,
both sides have claimed as their true language one of
the two regional conflicting standard languages,
Hindi or Urdu, and alternately argued either that one
is merely a version of the other or that the two are
entirely different languages. In the late nineteenth
century, the predominantly Muslim, Urdu-speaking elite
argued that Hindi was but a dialect of Urdu less
effectively written in the Devanagari script than in
the Persian-Arabic script and that therefore Urdu in
the latter script should be retained as the sole
official language of the North-Western Provinces and
Oudh. After independence, the predominantly Hindu
elites in the same province have argued that Urdu is
but a variant of Hindi and that therefore there is no
need to grant official recognition and status to it,
that only Hindi should be recognized as the official
language of the state. Yet, throughout the long
history of the Hindi-Urdu controversy, many of the
spokesmen for both sides have taken the quite different
view that the two languages are entirely distinct,
that Hindi is the proper language of Hindus and Urdu
the proper language of Muslims, and that a threat to
either language is equivalent to a threat to the
religion of the respective community. Sometimes, in
fact, the argument that one language is but a
variant of the other has been made for political
purposes only by people whose true feelings are that
each language is identified with one of the two
communities.

The three examples suggest the following generalizations concerning the relationships among elites,
symbols, and primordial attachments. First, although
the 'givens' of human existence and of long-persisting
cultural communities may constrain the free manipulation of cultural symbols by elites, they do not prevent
entirely their manipulation or even alteration of
their meaning. It is after all a different proposition
to say, 'Hindus revere the cow', than it is to say,
'Those who revere the cow are Hindus.'

Second, when primordial symbols are brought forth
into the political arena, it is likely that a particular elite stands to gain from their use. Far be it
from any non-Muslim to deny the religious significance
of the Sharia for Muslims. Yet, when the Sharia is
brought forth as a political symbol, it is certain
either that the ulema are concerned about a threat to
their authority in Muslim society or that secular
Muslim elites are using it for advantage against
perceived threats from a rival elite to their control
over the Muslim community.

Third, the cultural 'givens' may make their appearance in the political arena in a dramatic way at one
time or another and then may disappear for long
periods because it is in no one's interest to bring
them forth as central symbols. Such has been the
case with the cow protection issue, which has occupied
the centre of the stage only twice in modern Indian
history - once in the late 1880s and early 1890s, and
then again in 1966. In between, there was no loss of
Hindu reverence for the cow, and its symbolic uses did
not cease., but no great movements were launched in its
defence.

Finally, the existence of primordial attachments,
even of contradictory attachments held by rival communities, does not mean that bargains cannot be struck
over them based on agreements to respect each others'
feelings and to keep them out of politics. Hindus
revere the cow and Muslims are brought up to eat it,
but dietary habits are changed more easily than
religious beliefs. Consequently, Muslims may change
their primordial attachment to eating beef for the sake
of the Hindu primordial attachment to the sanctity of
the cow, particularly if Hindus agree not to tamper
with those attachments that Muslims value more than the
Hindus, such as the Sharia. Now, this particular
bargain, though not an explicit one, surely exists

tacitly in contemporary India. It is at least certain
that the ulema will not rise up in a body to defend
cow sacrifice as long as there is no interference with
the Muslim personal law.

An examination, one by one, of the use of specific
cultural symbols and the attachment of new value to
them by religious and political elites does not take
us to the heart of the process of identity formation,
which involves the manipulation of a multiplicity of
symbols and attempts to define a group in terms of
sets of symbols. It is in the ways in which symbols
are combined and the emphasis given to particular
symbols in relation to others that the boundaries of
communities are established or break down. It has
been shown above how, in the history of Muslim separatism, three different elite groups used the same sets
of symbols, but emphasized and combined them in
different ways, thereby arriving at different definitions of the Muslim community in India. The Muslim
landlords and government servants in nineteenth-
century north India were interested in establishing
the historical importance of the Muslim community in
India and the right of its elites to occupy ruling
positions in public life. Therefore, for the nineteenth-century Muslim political elites, the central
symbols were historical ones, with religion and
language secondary.

For the ulema, religion and law, with the two
defined as inseparable, were the primary symbols, with
Urdu again a secondary symbol. The Muslim community
was defined in terms of religious beliefs, ritual
practices, and adherence to the Sharia. Muslims need
not seek political sovereignty or domination in multi-
communal India. It was sufficient, if not ideal,
that they constitute a religiously and legally autonomous community guided by the ulema.

For the secular political elite of middle-class
professionals and politicians who dominated the Muslim
League in the 1930s and 1940s, however, it was not law
that mattered but political power. For this elite,
the Muslim community was defined in political terms,
that is, as a self-determining nation, distinctive in
religion, history, philosophy of life, literature, and
language from the Hindus, but unfortunately a minority.
During the drive for Pakistan, Jinnah went nearly to
the point of defining the Muslims of India as those
who followed the Muslim League. No one else, he

insisted, had the right to speak, politically at least, for the Muslims of India. Those who remained outside the League were classed into two categories - those yet to be organized and those who were 'careerists' and betrayers of the cause of Muslim unity.

For all three elite groups in the north and even for Jinnah, the Urdu language at some point also became an important symbol, but always a secondary one. Nevertheless, it proved to be the proverbial double-edged sword. For, while Urdu was a convenient symbol to reinforce the sense of separateness of north Indian Muslims, it was resisted vehemently by the Bengali political elites, by Sindhi-speakers, and by other language-group leaders in post-independence Pakistan.

The game of symbol selection and symbol manipulation, therefore, is clearly one that requires considerable skill and that is not always played successfully. Elites are indeed limited and constrained by the cultures of the groups they hope to represent. Some symbols are emotionally powerful, but may be dangerous to use - not only because their use threatens civil disorder, but because their use will benefit one elite group rather than another. Other symbols may be useful for conflict with a rival community, but potentially divisive internally. The great dilemma constantly faced by political elites who manipulate symbols of identity among peoples with rich cultures is that political mobilization of the community against its rivals requires unity and solidarity, which in turn requires that sets of symbols be made as congruent as possible. However, since most cultures are internally diverse, the search for additional symbols of unity often leads to internal discord rather than to the desired solidarity and cohesion.

Where in all this does the idea of ethnic groups as descent groups fit? It is simply irrelevant to the case of Muslim separatism in north India, unless the notion of descent is defined so broadly as to include a sense of a separate history. Unless one is willing to stretch the notion of descent to this extent, the only option for those who insist upon including descent in the idea of ethnicity is to exclude from its scope cases such as that of the Muslims of India. However, we will then be placed in an analytically difficult position for there is no *prima facie* case to be made for the idea that processes of identity-formation among

groups for whom an origin myth is a central symbol are
any different from those among groups for whom it is
not.

A final point remains to be taken up, namely, the
notion that, whatever changes take place in the
boundaries of ethnic groups, there remains a cultural
core that persists through time. If this argument is
applied to the Muslim case, it has an evident, but
superficial relevance. For, while it is certainly
true that Islamic symbols have been important to all
groups who have sought to establish the existence of
a Muslim community or nation in India and while it is
also true that some of those symbols remain relatively
constant - in form, if not always in meaning - the
ethnic community or nation for whom they are a constant
has not yet been established. The Quran, the prophet
Muhammed, the Sharia are constants for Muslims everywhere, at least wherever Islam and the ulema have a
strong hold, but the Muslims of the world are neither
an ethnic community nor a nation. Muslim political
elites in India in the nineteenth and twentieth
centuries attempted to argue that the Muslims of the
subcontinent formed a distinct nation and they had a
grand, but ephemeral success. It proved to be ephemeral because beyond the core of Islamic symbols, all
other symbols proved to be divisive and could not be
made congruent with the religious ones. In fact,
Islamic symbols, whose 'unifying power'[71] has indeed
been often demonstrated, have been repeatedly used by
political elites in different contexts in South Asia
in pursuit of competitive advantage against rivals
from other communities and as a base for achieving
political power, but their repeated use has not yet
established a firm basis for a Muslim nation anywhere
in South Asia. Rather, there exists on the Indian
subcontinent a multiplicity of Muslim ethnic groups,
communities, and potential nationalities, congruent in
both religion and language, but nowhere defined by
descent.

Brass, 'Elite Groups, Symbol Manipulation and Ethnic
Identity among the Muslims of South Asia'

Several friends and colleagues were kind enough to
read two earlier drafts of this chapter and to provide
detailed criticisms and suggestions. I am very
grateful to Charles F. Keyes, Daniel S. Lev, Francis
Robinson, David Taylor, Muna Vakil, and Malcolm Yapp,
whose comments have aided me substantially in revising
those earlier drafts. In many cases, I have made
changes in text and footnotes that would not have
occurred to me otherwise. Since I could not always be
sure, however, that my revisions would satisfy those
who made the suggestions, I have limited my acknow-
ledgments to them here, for the most part. I absolve
my colleagues from responsibility for any remaining
errors or deficiencies and for the arguments presented.

  1. Malcolm Yapp has contrasted the arguments of
those theorists of nationalism who see it as a 'natural' phenomenon with those who see it as 'unnatural'
in chapter 1 of this volume. Judith A. Nagata has
made a similar comparison between two groups of
scholars of ethnicity whom she labels 'primordialists'
and 'circumstantialists' in 'Defence of Ethnic
Boundaries: The Changing Myths and Charters of Malay
Identity', in Charles F. Keyes, ed., *Ethnic Change*,
unpublished manuscript submitted to University of
Washington Press. Joshua A. Fishman contrasts the
work of those who approach the study of ethnicity
from the subjective, internal point of view of the
actors themselves with what he calls the 'objectivist,
externalist' school in 'Social Theory and Ethnography:
Neglected Perspectives on Language and Ethnicity in
Eastern Europe', in Peter Sugar, ed., *Ethnicity in
Eastern Europe*, Santa Barbara, forthcoming, chapter 2.
In this paper the two perspectives will be referred to
as 'primordialist' and 'instrumentalist'. The latter
term refers to a perspective that emphasizes the uses
to which cultural symbols are put by elites seeking
instrumental advantage for themselves or the groups
they claim to represent.
  2. The quotations are, of course from Clifford
Geertz, 'The Integrative Revolution: Primordial Sentiments and Civil Politics in the New States', in

Clifford Geertz, ed., *Old Societies and New States: The Quest for Modernity in Asia and Africa*, New York 1967, pp.108-110 and 128.

3. Fishman, 'Social Theory and Ethnography', takes this view. An extreme statement of the position may be found in Pierre L. van den Berghe, 'Race and Ethnicity: A Sociobiological Look', *Ethnic and Racial Studies* 1, 4 (October 1978), forthcoming.

4. See especially Fishman, 'Social Theory and Ethnography'; Charles F. Keyes, 'Towards a New Formulation of the Concept of Ethnic Group', *Ethnicity* 3, 3 (September 1976), pp.202-213; and E.K. Francis, *Interethnic Relations: An Essay in Sociological Theory*, New York 1976, pp.6-7.

5. See, for example, Joshua A. Fishman, 'Sociolinguistics and the Language Problems of the Developing Countries', in Joshua A. Fishman et al., eds., *Language Problems of Developing Nations*, New York 1968, p.3, and John J. Gumperz, 'Some Remarks on Regional and Social Language Differences in India' and 'Language Problems in the Rural Development of North India', in University of Chicago, The College, *Introduction to the Civilization of India: Changing Dimensions of Indian Society and Culture*, Chicago 1957, pp.31-47.

6. All the situations mentioned in this paragraph have occurred among different language groups in north India. For details, see Paul R. Brass, *Language, Religion and Politics in North India*, London 1974.

7. The conversion of untouchable Hindu castes in India to Buddhism is a case in point. See Owen M. Lynch, *The Politics of Untouchability: Social Mobility and Social Change in a City of India*, New York 1969, chapter 5. Another well-known example is the Black Muslim movement in the United States.

8. Keyes, 'Towards a New Formulation', pp.204-205, takes a rather different view on 'the facts of birth' than the one presented here.

9. See especially Geertz, 'The Integrative Revolution'.

10. Fishman, 'Social Theory and Ethnography', is especially insistent on this point. See also Keyes, 'Towards a New Formulation', p.210.

11. Fishman, 'Social Theory and Ethnography'. Even for the Jews, however, there have been important internal divisions of attitude and feeling towards some aspects of the core culture. For an interesting analysis of the ways in which the meanings of persistent

Jewish cultural symbols have been reinterpreted at
different times and in different cultural contexts,
see Pearl Katz and Fred E. Katz, 'Symbols as Charters
in Culture Change: The Jewish Case', *Anthropos* 72
(1977), pp.486-496.

12. Even if, for example, one accepts Martin
Kilson's view that 'black ethnicity' in the United
States has 'lacked until recently the quality of
authenticity - that is, a true and viable heritage,
unquestionable in its capacity to shape and sustain
a cohesive identity or   awareness', blacks have, in
fact, adopted or created new cultural symbols and
used them to build a political cohesiveness and
identity of greater strength than that of other
groups with more 'authentic' cultural traditions.
'Blacks and Neo-Ethnicity in American Political Life',
in Nathan Glazer and Daniel P. Moynihan, eds., *Ethnicity: Theory and Experience*, Cambridge, Mass., 1975,
p.243.

13. Nathan Glazer and Daniel P. Moynihan, 'Introduction', in ibid., p.8.   .

14. Abner Cohen, 'Variables in Ethnicity', in
Keyes, *Ethnic Change*.

15. Michael Banton, 'The Direction and Speed of
Ethnic Change', in ibid.

16. Abner Cohen, *Two-Dimensional Man: An Essay on
the Anthropology of Power and Symbolism in Complex
Society*, Berkeley 1974, pp.98-102 and 106-110.

17. I have contrasted these opposing points of
view and presented my own in Brass, *Language,
Religion and Politics*, chapter 3.

18. Francis Robinson, 'Nation Formation: The Brass
Thesis and Muslim Separatism', and Paul R. Brass,
'A Reply to Francis Robinson', in *Journal of Commonwealth and Comparative Politics* 15, 3 (November 1977),
pp.215-234.

19. Francis Robinson, *Separatism Among Indian
Muslims: The Politics of the United Provinces' Muslims, 1860-1923*, London 1974, p.13.

20. Ibid.

21. Ibid., pp.77-8.

22. Ibid., pp.285 and 299 and John R. McLane,
Indian Nationalism and the Early Congress, Princeton,
N.J. 1977, p.279.

23. Robinson, *Separatism Among Indian Muslims*,
p.299. Abd al- Bari's offer was not without precedent
in Indian Muslim history. Akbar, whose memory

admittedly is not revered by pious Muslims, prohibited
cow slaughter during his reign. Vincent A. Smith,
Akbar the Great Mogul: 1542-1605, 2nd ed., Oxford 1919,
p.220, cited in McLane, *Indian Nationalism*, p.277.
Emperor Bahadur Shah also prohibited cow slaughter
during the Mutiny of 1857: ibid., p.278.

24. A.M. Zaidi, ed., *Evolution of Muslim Political
Thought in India*, Vol. II, *Sectarian Nationalism and
Khilafat*, New Delhi 1975, p.217.

25. McLane, *Indian Nationalism*, pp.280, 304-305.
However, McLane argues that the Congress officially
kept silent on the cow protection issue and on the
participation of Congressmen in Hindu communal
activities, when a more forthright and outspoken
stand against both was called for 'to allay Muslim
fears': p.330.

26. Ibid., pp.285-288. The merging of religious and
economic arguments for cow protection has been a persistent feature in the cow protection movement. See,
for example, the detailed economic arguments for cow
protection presented in Thakur Das Bhargava, *Cow in
Agony*, Bombay 1958. The author, who also supports
cow protection for cultural and religious reasons,
reaches the conclusion on economic grounds 'that there
are no useless cattle in India which cannot justify
their existence and sufferance to reach full physical
age'; p.16.

27. McLane, *Indian Nationalism*, pp.275, 280, 282-4.

28. Ibid., pp.272-3 and chapters 9 and 10, passim.

29. Ibid., p.326.

30. See, for example, Robinson, *Separatism Among
Indian Muslims*, pp.56, 81-2. However, even in the
municipalities, Robinson's work suggests that where
Hindu-Muslim political alliances existed, as among the
landlords in eastern UP, the cow slaughter issue was
not permitted to intrude into politics: p.79.

31. Tahir Mahmood, *Muslim Personal Law: Role of the
State in the Sub-continent*, New Delhi 1977, pp.3-4,
62-3.

32. Ibid., chapters 1 and 2.

33. Ziya-ul-Hasan Faruqi, *The Deoband School and the
Demand for Pakistan*, Bombay 1963, p.68.

34. Muhammad Ismail, the Kerala Muslim League leader,
suggested a formal and explicit bargain of this sort in
the Constituent Assembly of India in December 1948:
Mahmood, *Muslim Personal Law*, p.95.

35. See Brass, *Language, Religion and Politics*,

pp.127-38 for the background of the Hindi-Urdu controversy in UP and for further illustration of some
of these points.

36. William Adam, *Reports on the State of Education
in Bengal (1835 and 1838), Including Some Account of
the State of Education in Bihar and a Consideration of
the Means Adopted to the Improvement and Extension of
Public Instruction in Both Provinces*, edited by
Anathnath Basu, Calcutta 1941, pp.290-1.

37. Robinson also notes the shift of Muslim attitudes from dislike for Urdu to the identification of
Urdu as 'a symbol of Muslim power and influence' and
the attachment to it of 'an almost religious significance'. He suggests that this shift occurred 'in the
second half of the nineteenth century' but that it
predated the Hindi-Urdu controversy. If so, the
latter controversy certainly intensified the new
feelings of attachment of Muslims to the Urdu language.
The dimensions of the shift, however, can hardly be
doubted. Sayyid Ahmad Khan who later became a great
proponent of Urdu criticized the British education
policy in 1858 for its neglect of Arabic and Persian
and its attention to Urdu and English, which, he
wrote, had 'tended to strengthen the idea that Government wished to wipe out the religions which it found
in Hindustan!' *Separatism Among Indian Muslims*, pp.70,
91, 98.

38. These remarks are based on the work of Jyotirindra Das Gupta and John J. Gumperz, 'Language
Communication and Control in North India', in Fishman,
Language Problems of Developing Nations, esp. p.157.
Francis Robinson has, however, suggested in a personal
communication to me that Urdu was already Persianized
in the nineteenth century. Even so, the commonalities
between Hindi and Urdu were sufficient to make it a
matter of choice what kind of Hindi-Urdu - or Hindi and
Urdu - was to be taught in the schools and used at the
elite level for administrative and literary purposes.
Robinson argues further that, in fact, a de-Persianiz-
ation of Urdu took place in the nineteenth century. I
do not have the competence or knowledge to judge
whether Robinson's or Das Gupta and Gumperz's observations are more accurate, but the point is that Hindi
and Urdu can be used as one common language or as two
separate languages, as vehicles of common communication or as separate expressions of the distinctive
cultures of Hindus and Muslims. Some elites among both

Hindus and Muslims in the nineteenth century chose the
latter course.

39. P. Hardy, *The Muslims of British India*, Cambridge 1972, p.2.

40. Murray T. Titus, *Islam in India and Pakistan:
A Religious History of Islam in India and Pakistan*,
Calcutta 1959, chapter 5 and pp.170 ff. Cf. Bernard S.
Cohn who has remarked that, 'at the folk level', there
has been 'little functional difference between Hindus
and Muslims', *India: The Social Anthropology of a
Civilization*, Englewood Cliffs, N.J. 1971, pp.66-7.
See also David M. Mandelbaum, *Society in India*, Vol.
II, *Change and Continuity*, Berkeley 1970, pp.413, 527,
546-9 for a survey of the anthropological literature
on Hindu-Muslim similarities and differences in Indian
villages with respect to social and religious
practices. Hardy too has noted the observance of
common festivals, celebrations, and worship by Hindus
and Muslims in town and country in Mughal times in *The
Muslims of British India*, pp.19, 27.

41. Anil Seal, *The Emergence of Indian Nationalism:
Competition and Collaboration in the Later Nineteenth
Century*, Cambridge 1971, p.300.

42. Most of the religious societies formed to
defend Islam in the late nineteenth century against
perceived Christian missionary and Hindu attacks
adopted explicit goals of unifying the Muslim community.
The Anjuman-i-Himayat-i-Islam, founded in Lahore in
1885, for example, established as one of its goals
'the creation and preservation of friendly feelings
and concord between the different sects of Islam'.
The goals of educating the masses to a common understanding of proper Islamic beliefs and practices were
also clear in the missionary activities of some of the
societies which were designed to reach 'ignorant
Muslims' as much as or more than non-Muslims; ibid,
p.351. The Jamiyat-al-ulama was quite explicit in its
goals of persuading 'all the Muslims of India to give
up the unnecessary, useless and wasteful practises
and ceremonies which are against the commands of God
and His Prophet'. A.M. Zaidi, ed., *Evolution of Muslim
Political Thought in India*, Vol. III, *Parting of the
Ways*, New Delhi 1977, p.686. The Jami'yat also of
course took the lead in demanding governmental enforcement of Muslim personal laws and in opposing any
legislation on matters of personal and family law
perceived not to be in conformity with the Sharia:

Mahmood, *Muslim Personal Law*, pp.27-31, 52-5, 83-5, and passim.

43. Aziz Ahmad, *Islamic Modernism in India and Pakistan, 1857-1964*, London 1967, chapter 5.

44. Aziz Ahmad has remarked that one of the objectives of the Deoband seminary was 'to re-establish contact between the 'ālim and the average Muslim': ibid., p.104.

45. Mahmood, *Muslim Personal Law*, p.21.

46. See Peter Hardy, *Partners in Freedom - and True Muslims: The Political Thought of Some Muslim Scholars in British India, 1912-1947*, Lund 1971, p.15.

47. Ibid., p.23.

48. Ibid., p.31.

49. Ibid., pp.37-8.

50. Ibid., p.41.

51. See, for example, the statement of the goals of the Jami'yat, given in Faruqi, *The Deoband School*, p.68.

52. Faruqi, *The Deoband School*, p.36.

53. Zaidi, *Evolution of Muslim Political Thought*, Vol. III, p.692.

54. S. Abul Hasan Ali Nadwi, *Muslims in India*, translated by Mohammad Asif Kidwai, Lucknow n.d., p.133.

55. It was not only with Muslims and Muslim landlords that such a bargain existed, but with other collaborators with the British authorities as well, including Hindu landlords. Reeves has described how the government of the United Provinces instigated the collaborating landlords there in 1920-1 to join in an 'anti-non-cooperation movement' by forming *aman sabhas* to provide 'vocal support for the government and open denunciation of the non-cooperators'. Peter D. Reeves, 'The Politics of Order: "Anti-Non-Cooperation" in the United Provinces, 1921', *Journal of Asian Studies* 25, 2 (February 1966), p.266.

56. 'What is this nation of ours?' asked Sayyid Ahmad Khan in 1887. 'We are those who have ruled India for six or seven hundred years.' Speech delivered at Lucknow on 28 December 1887, reprinted in A.M. Zaidi, ed., *Evolution of Muslim Political Thought in India*, Vol. I, *From Syed to the Emergence of Jinnah*, New Delhi 1975, p.42.

57. In the 1890s, the Privy Council restricted the rights of Muslims to establish *wakfs* that were clearly meant principally for the benefit of descendants rather than as charity for the poor. See Asaf A.A. Fyzee,

Outlines of Muhammadan Law, 2nd ed., London 1955, pp.
254-66 and Zaidi, *Evolution of Muslim Political
Thought*, Vol. I, pp.300-20. In 1913, Jinnah sponsored
the successful passage in the Imperial Legislative
Council of the Wakf Act, which restored the right of
Muslims to place their properties into trusts, the
income from which would go to descendants. Zaidi,
op.cit., p.429 and Hector Bolitho, *Jinnah: Creator
of Pakistan*, London 1954, p.53. Mahmood, however,
claims that the Muslim landlords opposed the more
general application of Sharia inheritance provisions
that would have prevented them from excluding women
from inheritance or bequeathing their properties to
adopted sons: *Muslim Personal Law*, pp.26 and 30-1.

58. Rafiq Zakaria, *Rise of Muslims in Indian
Politics: An Analysis of Developments from 1885 to
1906*, Bombay 1970, p.236.

59. Sayyid Ahmad Khan, speech of 28 December 1887,
in Zaidi, *Evolution of Muslim Political Thought*, Vol.
I, p.34.

60. Robinson, *Separatism Among Indian Muslims*,
chapters 8 and 9.

61. Cited in Khalid B. Sayeed, *Pakistan: The
Formative Phase, 1857-1948*, London 1968, p.73.

62. *Some Recent Speeches and Writings of Mr.
Jinnah*, edited by Jamil-ud-Din Ahmad, Lahore 1942,
passim.

63. Ibid., p.42.

64. Ibid., pp.87, 104.

65. Ibid., p.30.

66. Ibid., p.41.

67. Muhammad Ali Jinnah, Presidential Address at the
All-India Muslim League, Lahore Session, March 1940, in
ibid., p.153.

68. Jinnah's inaugural address in the Pakistan Constituent Assembly, August 1947, cited in Mahmood,
Muslim Personal Law, p.174.

69. Such suggestions are reserved only for the most
ignorant Western journalists commenting sanctimoniously
on the Indian scene. The most sanctimonious such
advice ever seen by this author appeared in an article
by Oriana Fallaci, 'Indira's Coup', *New York Review
of Books* 22, 14 (18 September 1975), pp.14-21, which is
so noteworthy for its total lack of understanding of
Indian society, its cultures and peoples that it
deserves to be exposed and condemned openly. Fallaci
comments ignorantly at p.15 on the issue of cow

slaughter as follows: 'There exists no politician in India daring enough to attempt to explain to the masses that cows can be eaten.' The especial stupidity of the comment, of course, lies not only in the fact that Fallaci thinks a politician who proposed such a thing would be 'daring' rather than insane, but in her belief that the masses are not aware that cows can be eaten.

70. Some Hindus do, of course, eat beef, but there is no serious movement among Hindus to legalize cow slaughter.

71. Robinson, *Separatism Among Indian Muslims*, p.356.

ISLAM AND MUSLIM SEPARATISM

Francis Robinson

There would appear to be a tendency amongst Muslims to
organize in politics on the basis of their faith.
Where Muslims predominate, organizations take the form
of Islamic political parties such as the Muslim
Brotherhood of Egypt or the Jama'at-i-Islami of
Pakistan, whose aim has been to ensure that state and
society run as far as possible along what they consider
to be Islamic lines. Where Muslims form a minority,
there frequently springs up a demand that Muslims
should be organized as a separate political community,
either as a separate nation state or as a state within
a state. One excellent example outside South Asia is
the Moro liberation movement of the Muslim Filipinos,
but there is no shortage of examples within South Asia:
there is the demand of the Moplah community of Kerala
in 1947 for the foundation of a Moplastan within the
Indian Union;[1] there is the formal request made by the
Majlis-e-Ittehadul-Muslimeen of Andhra Pradesh to the
Indian government in the late 1960s that a separate
state for all Indian Muslims should be carved out on
the east coast between Vishakhapatnam and Madras;[2] and
there is the most striking example of this phenomenon,
the campaign of the All-India Muslim League which led
to the foundation of Pakistan as an Islamic state in
1947. Of course, the formation of religious political
parties is not restricted to Muslim societies; it is a
feature of societies whose faiths have a strong ideological content. So alongside the Jama'at and the
Muslim Brotherhood we must set the Christian Democratic
parties of Europe and Latin America. But the formation
of separatist movements on the basis of religious con-
fession, the assertion of a political identity on the
basis of religion, which on occasion in modern times
threatens to become a national identity, does seem to
be an especial characteristic of Muslims. It is a
characteristic which requires explanation.

One example of Muslim separatism, that of the Muslims of the United Provinces who were at the heart of
the drive to create Pakistan, has received more
scholarly attention than most examples. In his book
Language, Religion and Politics in North India, Paul
Brass has explained the phenomenon thus: there was

little in the objective differences between Hindus
and Muslims, and not much more in their revivalist
movements to make their separation inevitable. What
was crucial was the process of 'symbol selection'; and
the fact that Muslim elites chose divisive rather than
composite symbols. 'Muslim leaders in north India in
the late nineteenth century', Brass writes, 'did not
recognize a common destiny with the Hindus, because
they saw themselves in danger of losing their privileges as a dominant community...' So they chose to
emphasize 'a special sense of history incompatible
with Hindu aspirations and a myth of Muslim decline
into backwardness'.[3] According to Brass, if Muslims
organize on the basis of their faith in politics, it
is because Muslim elites perceive it to be the most
effective way of keeping or gaining political power.

If this somewhat baldly stated argument, which
implies that Islam is epiphenomenal, stands up in the
case of the UP Muslims, we should have a useful starting point from which to examine other examples of
Muslim separatism. But it does not. Brass, in his
important attempt to elevate the political process to
the status of an independent variable in the fashioning of political identity, has made his Muslim elites
far too free to choose a separatist path deliberately
as the best way of protecting their material interests.
When UP Muslims emphasize Islamic historical symbols of
disunity as opposed to Indian historical symbols of
unity, he does not allow that these may have been
symbols they preferred. When they parade the so-called
myth of Muslim backwardness, he does not make room for
the element of truth in the claim. Similarly he gives
little weight to the way in which the choices of
Muslim politicians may have been restricted by the
preference of Muslim society, by competition from an
increasingly assertive Hindu revivalism, and by the
moulding influence of the imperial system of political
control and the framework it created for political
action. The realm in which politics is autonomous has
been made far too large.[4]

In his essay included in this volume Brass seems to
have gone some way to meet this criticism. He acknow-
ledges the role of the colonial government in encouraging Muslims to organize as Muslims in politics: the
British always being prepared to accept rather than to
ignore the divisions of the societies they ruled.[5]
Implicit in his analysis of the use of the cow as a

symbol is an acceptance of the way in which Hindu
revivalism not only limited the options of the UP
Muslim elite but also those of Hindu elites.[6] Then
Brass, in distancing himself from those he terms the
'extreme instrumentalists' who hold that cultures
are infinitely malleable and manipulable by elites,
suggests a further constraint of sorts. He recog-
nizes that 'cultural groups differ in the strength and
richness of their cultural traditions and even more
importantly in the strength of traditional institutions and social structure' so 'the persistence ... of
religiously-based communal institutions among Jews and
Muslims wherever they are found means that these
cultural groups always form potential bases for ethnic
movements.' This means 'it is likely that the groups
can be mobilized on the basis of specific appeals and
not others and that, when ethnic appeals are made, the
pre-existing communal and educational institutions of
the groups will, if made available for the purpose,
provide an effective means of political mobilization.
In short, the values and institutions of a persisting
cultural group will suggest what appeals and symbols
will be effective and what will not be and may also
provide traditional avenues for the mobilization
and organization of the group in new directions.'[7]
We may conclude, though Brass does not, that the rich
resources for mobilization and organization which
existed amongst the Muslims of north India may well
have acted as an incentive to Muslim elites to
organize on the basis of religion in politics. And an
incentive to take one form of action as opposed to
another is usually regarded as something of a restric-
tion on an individual's freedom to choose.

The prime purpose of Brass's essay, however, is to
analyse a further constraint on the freedom of elites
to select and manipulate symbols. He is concerned to
consider 'to what extent and in what ways the pre-
existing values, institutions and practices of cultural
groups with long and rich cultural heritages constitute
primordial attachments that constrain elites who manipulate symbols of group identity for political
purposes'.[8] And after analysing elite use of the
symbols of the cow, the Sharia and the Hindi and Urdu
languages over the last hundred years, he concludes
that 'elites are indeed limited and constrained by
the cultures of the groups they hope to represent'.[9]
So implicitly as well as explicitly considerable

constraints on the freedom of elites to manipulate
symbols are acknowledged. The realm in which politics
are autonomous has been greatly reduced. This is an
important step forward.

However, when he concludes that elites are constrained by the cultures of the groups they wish to
represent, Brass admits much more than he seems to
realize. The argument which he uses with respect to
symbols surely applies no less to all the ideas which
might go to form the culture of a group. These
represent the range of possible actions. And thus
Brass's argument falls into line with Quentin
Skinner's recent contribution on the role of ideas in
political action. Concerned to demonstrate the
dynamic relationship between professed principles and
actual practice in seventeenth- and eighteenth-century
English politics, Skinner argues that men in pursuing
their interests are limited by the range of concepts
available to legitimize their actions, and that this
range of concepts is in turn limited by the prevailing
morality of society.[10] Thus, in explaining Muslim
separatism, account must be taken of the ideological
framework within which the Muslim elites of north
India operated. This would seem to make Brass's
development of his original thesis a stride rather than
a step forward.

Nevertheless, there is yet one more constraint of
central importance which Brass does not seem to take
into account. His elites seem to stand apart from
their societies and their cultural traditions. They
manipulate, they choose within their cultural framework
apparently at will and only according to their political
interests. Their rational pursuit of power is
constrained only by the cultures of the groups they
hope to lead and not by their own culturally determined
preferences and beliefs. That this approach is
unsatisfactory has already been indicated,[11] but the
point would appear to need emphasizing. It is not just
the masses but the elite who understand and pursue
their interests within the frameworks of ideas they
possess for understanding the world. Moreover, on
occasion these ideas may act as a motivating force; in
the mysterious dialectic between ideas and reality
there are times when ideas are not just legitimizers of
action taken for other reasons but also a prime force
in directing the deeds of men. In our context, of
course, it is Islamic ideas and values in their

particular north Indian form which inform the assumptions and penetrate the consciousness of the UP Muslim elite. Nor does it matter whether we deal with the acknowledged holy man whose life consists of learning, prayer and fasting or the man in a suit whose visits to the mosque are rare; few if any will escape something of the moulding force of their culture's religious base. If for the holy man the Islamic vision of the world will be all-embracing, its power is often still strong in apparently secular men who have often merely made the transition from 'religiousness' to 'religious-mindedness',[12] while even the highly secularized usually carry with them some of the assumptions and preferences of the particular religious culture from which they have sprung.[13] Islamic ideas and values, then, both provide a large part of the framework of norms and desirable ends within which the UP Muslim elite take their rational political decisions, and act on occasion as a motivating force. Here is a further constraint on the autonomy of politics.

This essay will examine the Islamic tradition for ideas which might encourage political separatism; it will see, necessarily somewhat impressionistically, what parts of this body of ideas were received in northern India and how they developed there; it will then consider their role in influencing the politics of the Muslim elite of the UP. This last endeavour involves problems of method. Using the Skinnerian or Brass technique all we need do is to show that the Muslim elite profess particular ideas in order to suggest their impact on political action. As necessary legitimizers of action they will place limits on the range of possible actions elites can perform. Thus far matters are relatively uncontentious. The problems arise when we confront the question of ideas as a motivating force. It is hard to know the springs of human action. All the historian can do is to suggest what might have been the case and stand by his judgement, which is no doubt an unsatisfactory method for the political scientist, but it is part of the historian's craft and he should uphold it. The best method of investigating motive forces is through extensive exercises in biography. We do not have room for such exercises here, assuming that enough information was available in the first place; all we can do is to use our judgement, based on what we know of the lives of the men concerned and of what others thought of them.

Frequently we shall give weight to a man's reputation for faith. It seems reasonable to do so when in Islam no distinction is made between religion and politics and when, indeed, religio-political ideas are derived from the very word of God to whose guidance the believer submits in all things. For the faithful such ideas will have something of a commanding force. This is not to say that the faithful will be moved in all things and at all times by Islam. They are after all human. Nevertheless, their strivings as humans will be motivated in part at least by their desire to fulfil their vision of the word of God.

The particular aspect of the Islamic tradition which bears on the tendency of Muslims to organize on the basis of their faith in politics is the emphasis it places on the idea of community. Being part of the Muslim community is a central part of being a Muslim. The Islamic era begins not with the birth of Muhammad, or with the first revelation of the Quran, but with the Hijrah, the point when Muhammad and the Muslims left Mecca for Medina. This was the point when the Muslims of the tribe of Quraish opted to place their loyalty to Allah before the ties of kinship. Now the *umma*, the community of believers, was advanced as the best of all communities. It was an especial favour granted by God to the Muslims, a charismatic community. The charisma can be seen at work in the major role of *ijma*, or consensus of the community, in the maintenance and development of the Sharia; 'my community', declared Muhammad, 'will never agree on error'. Muslims believe that it is through belonging to this community that their lives become significant.[14]
However, in forsaking the lesser community of the tribe for the greater community of the Islamic *umma*, Muslims did not leave all their tribal values behind. Some came to play a part in the new solidarity, most notably the tribal sense of *asabiyya*, or the brotherhood of those who belong,[15] which has been a value most strikingly manifest in Islamic history. We see it continually underpinning the idea of the equality of all believers. We see it in the career of the fourteenth-century traveller Ibn Battuta who was able to cross the world from Tangier to China, from Sumatra to Mali, be received as a brother by Muslims wherever he went, and frequently gain employment. We see it now in

the immense interest of Muslims in Indonesia in the
break-up of Pakistan,[16] and in the partisan support
for the Arab states from Muslim Filipinos,[17] or for
that matter from Muslims throughout the world, whenever the Arab states go to war with Israel.

This sense of community is fostered by the key
rituals of Islam. All confess their faith with the
same formula. They acknowledge one book, and with
minor differences follow one law. All pray in basically the same way and are urged to pray communally
whenever possible, while the last act of prayer itself
commemorates the community as the Muslim turns to his
neighbour on either side in performing the salam.
When Muslims give alms, and the mandatory requirement
is often about one-fortieth of his income a year, it
is to support the community. No one who has lived
with Muslims in the month of Ramadan can fail to feel
the powerful sense of community generated in the
joint experience of hardship. The performance of the
Haj, the fifth pillar of the faith, represents the
ultimate celebration of the community. All focus on
Mecca and the Ka'aba. All on reaching the land of
pilgrimage don two white sheets, the *ihram*, in recognition of the equality of all men before Allah. They
camp in their hundreds of thousands on the Plain of
Arafat, and though they speak with many different
tongues, and come from the four corners of the earth,
as they live through the first thirteen days of the
month of Zu'l-Hijja they experience the reality of the
community as never before. Of course, but a fraction
of the Muslims perform the Haj in their lifetimes, but
there are many who wish to, and know its meaning.

The sense of community is also fostered by the
distinctive qualities of Islamic society and culture
derived at various removes from the central requirements of the faith. There is, for instance, the cust
custom of keeping women in strict social segregation
from men. There is the use of the Arabic script for
writing whatever local language the Muslim uses, a
practice which has helped create 'Islamic' languages
out of almost identical 'non-Islamic' ones. There
are the typically Islamic decorative patterns, most
notably the arabesque. Then there is the classical
literature ranging from devotional and legal works
through to belles lettres in prose and verse 'which
have been carried wherever Muslims have gone, and
transmitted from generation to generation, have formed

the common background of literary culture shared
among all Muslims of cultivation, those who maintained
the norms of Islamic society'. Everywhere Islam went,
writes Marshall Hodgson, 'there has been a continuous
pressure toward persuading all Muslims to adopt like
standards, like ways of living based on the Islamic
ideals prevailing at a given time ... everywhere
Muslims are noted for their keen consciousness of the
world Muslim community ... and maintain in the most
diverse geography not only the essential distinctive
Islamic rites ... but also, to some degree, a sense of
a common cultural heritage.'[18]

Further insights into the meaning of the community
are offered by Muslim attitudes to non-Muslims. The
latter were divided into two categories. There were
kafirs, pagans, polytheists, atheists, who must be
brought by holy war under the authority of the true
faith. There were *dhimmis*, Jews and Christians,
peoples of the book, who were allowed to live as
tolerated minorities within the *umma*. Of course, they
suffered disabilities. They were not, for instance,
allowed to play a part in the running of the community,
or to convert others to their faiths. But they were
allowed to keep their religion, and they could if they
wished become Muslims. In time the distinctions
between *dhimmi* and Muslim became stronger. The
dhimmi communities who contributed so much to the
working of the early Islamic state and the intellectual
development of Islam came increasingly to be seen in a
hostile light, being recognized only to be rejected
and their beliefs refuted. This process, which also
signified the increasing mental isolation of the *umma*,
reached its peak in the *millet* system of the Ottoman
state. The *millet* was any religious group of *dhimmi*
status. They were allowed to administer their own
personal law and to manage their own education. Copts,
Greeks, Armenians, etc. thus had their own identity
under the law. Fundamental attitudes to non-Muslims
seemed to lead inexorably to the creation of separate
legal and social orders, and hence to suggest a
separate political order as well.[19]

More flows from the Muslim attitude to non-Muslims
than their desire to assert and maintain their distinctiveness. Also implicit is their sense of superiority.
When they made themselves a separate community, as they
fled from Mecca to Medina, the Muslims did so in the
knowledge that their's was God's path and that their

fellow-tribesmen turned away from it. 'You are the best nation raised up for men', Muhammad told them, 'you enjoin good and forbid evil and you believe in Allah.'[20] This sense of superiority was further boosted by the consciousness that Islam was historic-ally final amongst religions. Muhammad's revelation was perfect because it brought to mankind the principles which made further revelation unnecessary. This feeling should never be forgotten either in assessing Muslim responses to the challenges of history or in understanding their relationships with men of other faiths.

Clearly associated with the superiority of the community has been its relationship with political power. It has been forged in the successful assertion of power, and the exercise of power brought a large part of the civilized world to submit within its first hundred years. 'Islam did not speak from catacombs ... it saw the way of truth as passing always through thrones.'[21] And reasonably so, because from the earliest days the possession of power had ensured that Muslims would be able to follow their faith. Moreover, the use of this power was as much a matter for God's concern as the observance of the fundamentals of the faith. 'To Allah belongs whatever is in the heavens and whatever is in the earth' declared the Prophet.[22] Church and state in the charismatic community were indivisible. So history and belief encouraged men to feel that Islam could be Islam properly only in conjunction with political power.

The symbol of the charismatic community was the Caliph (Khalifa), or successor of Muhammad. He was believed, for long in practice and always in theory, to be the divinely ordained head of the community. His task was on the one hand to lead the community in submission to God, to be the Imam, the model whom Muslims should follow. Thus he acknowledged his subservience to God's law, the Sharia. On the other hand, he was to use his power to create the conditions in which the Sharia would be preserved and put into effect, which in the long run meant enabling the ulema to guard and interpret the law. Until the end of the Ummayyad Caliphate in 750 A.D., the political sway of the Caliphs of Islam matched the spread of the community of believers. But from this time onwards power in the Islamic world was dispersed amongst many rival Caliphs and Sultans. Yet 'The Caliphate did not cease to symbolize what it failed to embrace. It stood for the fundamental axiom of Islamic existence, namely that the state is the sign and surety of the faith and the faith is the ground and seal of the state.'[23] That the *umma* and power should go hand in hand has always been a belief with astonishing emotive appeal for Muslims. 'Might', declared Muhammad, 'belongs to Allah and His Messenger, and the believers.'[24]

This was the ideal. Our problem is to assess the impact of the ideal on north Indian Muslims. We need to see it flowing into their minds, interacting with reality and forming their actions. In doing so it is important to remember that, although we can comprehend the ideal in its entirety, intellectually that is though not emotionally, it is unlikely to have been perceived thus by most Muslims. Theirs will have been an understanding, and perhaps an emphasis, on part of this body of ideas: on relations with non-Muslims perhaps, or the sense of brotherhood, or the feeling of superiority; some sort of understanding of the whole will have been reserved for few. Nevertheless, whether understanding was fragmentary or more complete, it helped to shape the Muslim's apprehension of the real world contributing both to the framework within which he made his rational political decisions and indicating the ends which he ought to pursue. In South Asia one of the hardest aspects of the real world which Muslims had to take into account was the fact that they formed a small minority in a population that was Hindu and polytheistic, *kafir* by the strictest tenets of their faith. This fact should never be forgotten because it raised in an acute fashion the problem of the relationship between the community of believers and power. Muslim attempts to cope with this problem offer us continuing insight into the enduring appeal of the ideal of the charismatic community.

Our primary concern is to assess the influence of the ideal that Muslims should form a distinct religio-political community during the rapid political mobiliza-tion of north India over the last hundred years. Nevertheless, we should understand the potency of this ideal somewhat better if we learn something of its impact on Indian Muslims in earlier centuries, and how that impact had varied with Muslim fortunes. Clearly, almost from the time that Muslims first entered India

it had not been possible for them to live as true
members of the *umma*; that possibility had finally
disappeared with the loss of effective control by the
Abbasid Caliphate in the ninth and tenth centuries and
the rise of regional rulers. All the same, the
writings of Indo-Muslim historians from the thirteenth
to the eighteenth centuries make it clear that they
saw the history of Islam in India as a direct continuation of universal Islamic history. The ideal was
reconciled with reality by means of the 'pious sultan'
theory. The ulema agreed that the central test of
whether Muslims were living as Muslims ought to live
was not whether they lived beneath the writ of the
Caliph of Islam but whether they lived beneath the law
of Islam. The local sultan was to fulfil the role of
the Caliph, and, providing that he enforced the Sharia
through *qazis*, or merely providing that he did not
commit apostasy or force Muslims to go against the
Sharia, he was not forcibly to be resisted. Thus the
'pious sultan' theory coped with the problem of the
unity of the *umma*. But there was a second and rather
more serious problem, that of the relationship between
Muslims and non-Muslims, which in India bore so
heavily on the relationship between Islam and power.
Medieval Muslim regimes in India could not survive
without Hindu support; they needed Hindu taxes, man-
power and political authority. The problem of reconciling ideal with fact, of bending the Islamic vision
of the *umma* to embrace a tolerance of, if not the
equality of, the polytheistic Hindu, was hard. Sometimes the problem seems just to have been ignored, at
others Hindus were given the status of *dhimmis*, and
subjected to the *jizya* tax, while at others, and most
notably under Akbar, whose expanding empire came to
depend so much on Rajput support, they were treated as
equals. The ideal was distorted greatly beneath the
weighty logic of power.[25]

Not all were prepared to accept such a distortion.
There was a fairly continuous undercurrent of dissent,
particularly from members of the ulema. Most notable
was the Mahdawi movement of Syed Muhammad of Jaunpur
which, beginning in the Lodi period, laid upon each
individual Muslim the duty of seeing that the Sharia
was put into effect in its entirety. There was also
the Naqshbandi Sufi order which came to widespread
influence under the Mughals and propagated a hostile
attitude to Hindus. Indeed, whenever Muslim rulers

found themselves in difficulties there seems to have
been a demand for the strict application of the Sharia
to Hindu-Muslim relationships. It was almost as though
Muslims felt that it was because their rulers had
lapsed in this respect that they were in trouble. It
was to this sentiment that Aurangzeb appealed when,
confronted by his rebellious Hindu subjects, he
reimposed the *jizya* in 1679. By the beginning of the
eighteenth century, Muslim writers who a hundred years
before had written of rebellious Hindus as *mardud* or
rejected of God, now wrote of them as *kafirs*.[26]

As Muslim power declined in the eighteenth century,
as Hindus, Sikhs and Christians acquired increasing
sway and Muslims found themselves cut off from the
foundations of their culture in the central Islamic
lands, the Muslims began to fear for the future of
Islam in India. Their reaction was to distinguish
between Muslim and non-Muslim yet more rigorously, to
purify Islam of its Hindu accretions, and if necessary
to use force to achieve these ends. When possible,
and sometimes when impossible, Muslims tried to unite
their vision of Islam with power. Shah Waliullah
dominated this process in the eighteenth century. He
aimed both to consolidate Islam intellectually within
India and to free it from Hindu accretions. Moreover,
he was a man of action, inviting, first, petty Muslim
princes to wage jihad against the Hindu powers to save
the *Dar al-Islam*, and when they failed turning to Ahmad
Shah of Afghanistan for aid. For Waliullah, Indian
Muslims were a community within India, but one in need
of a Sultan because it was in danger of becoming 'a
people without any knowledge of Islam or paganism'.[27]

The movement of Sayyid Ahmad Shahid (Barelvi) drew
inspiration directly from Waliullah just as it drew
support directly from his grandchildren. Sayyid Ahmad
aimed to create an ideal Muslim community where
individual and social life could follow unhindered the
tenets of Islam. So in 1826-7 following the example of
the Prophet, he fled from pagan-dominated India to
establish his ideal state on the North-West Frontier.
His followers waged jihad first against the Sikhs and,
after the annexation of the Punjab, against the
British, being active right down to World War One. In
the same vein there sprang simultaneously in Bengal the
peasant rising of Dudu Miyan, inspired by Barelvi, and
the Fara'izi movement of Haji Shariatullah, inspired by
Arabian Wahhabism. Both Bengali movements gained much

support from peasant economic grievances, but the
important point was that their solution was to strive
to realize their vision of the Islamic ideal. There
were similar strivings elsewhere, ranging from the
scholarly movement of the Ahl-i Hadiths with its
austere interpretation of the Sharia to the extraordinary jihad waged by some Sunni ulema of Awadh in
1855 against the Shia government with the object of
putting a stop to the large concessions which had been
made to Hindus and Hinduism.[28]

Thus, whenever the protective umbrella of Muslim
power was lifted, or Muslim rulers obeying the
exigencies of power in a largely Hindu society
appeared to betray the Islamic ideal, there were
Muslims who retreated to first principles. Their
examination of these was likely, almost paradoxically,
to drive them to try and reunite Islam with power. Not
all Muslims subject to the growing influence of what
has been termed 'shariat-mindedness' were likely to
follow its directions to their conclusion. Such an
outlook had obvious limitations for those who wished
to survive somehow under the British, or in Hyderabad,
or in Awadh up to 1856 where a universalistic Persian
Shi'i culture arguably reached its peak in India.
Nevertheless, versions of the ideal, much stimulated
by increasing contact with Wahhabi Arabia and much
circulated by those members of the ulema who were
quick to seize the opportunities offered by the Raj's
religious neutrality and the growth of the press, had
been powerfully asserted since the mid-eighteenth
century. Muslims of the elite knew of them, and knew
their import.

It would appear that Brass wishes us to believe
that these ideas had no force amongst the UP Muslim
elite as they led their community into modern politics.
Their thoughts, all of a sudden, owe nothing to their
past. Versions of the Islamic ideal, or the fragments
of it they receive, carry no weight. The elite, we
are asked to accept, have disentangled their faith,
and the political values it generates, from their
political thinking. As they select and manipulate
symbols, if this is what they do, their prime consideration is how best to serve their material interests.
Islam does not help to mould their apprehension of
their interests and commands no end they wish to seek.
It is merely a tool, and no more. Thus Muslims who
write about the history of Islamic civilization rather

than that of the Mughals, who move to defend Urdu
rather than let its cause go by default, who direct
their thoughts to men of their faith rather than to
the Indian nation, are made to do so not because it
might have been religious instinct, or at least
cultural preference, but because, from a choice of
possibilities, they saw these policies as the best
mobilizers of support for their interests. Of course,
it is improbable that we shall ever have the privilege
of entering the minds of the UP Muslim elite which
existed during the one hundred years before 1947, but
it seems unlikely that Islamic ideas and values which
were so significant in the past played no part in
influencing the direction of their thoughts and in
motivating particular actions.

Take, for instance, Sayyid Ahmad Khan. His role as
the protagonist of Muslim elite interests, as the
founder of Muslim separatist politics, is well known.
There is his attempt to rehabilitate the Muslims in
British eyes after the Mutiny; there are his educational projects designed initially to benefit the Urdu-
speaking elite but after the language question was
raised quickly re-directed to benefit primarily
Muslims; there is his political leadership which during
the last thirty years of the nineteenth century taught
Muslims that their best chance of preserving their
strong position in north India lay in allying with the
British. Throughout he fought hard to preserve the
Muslim elite position in education, in jobs, and in
the developing representative system of government.
Nor did he allow any pan-Islamic loyalties to hinder
this purpose. Though he, like most Indian Muslims, was
sensitive to the international brotherhood of Islam,
when it seemed that Indian Muslims might make much of
their loyalty to the Turkish Caliph after the Russo-
Turkish war of 1877-8, he was adamant that loyalty was
owed to the British first of all.[29] The British
filled the role of 'pious sultan'. Considering
Muslims in India, he seemed at first to regard them as
a *qaum* or nation within the Indian *qaum*,[30] but faced
with the realities of Indian nationalist politics from
the mid-1880s he made it clear that the Muslim *qaum* was
the *qaum*.[31]

It is tempting to interpret, as many have done,
Sayyid Ahmad's politics, his concern for the Indian
Muslim *qaum* before all other considerations, entirely
in terms of the material interests of the north Indian

elite. But if we place his politics in the context of
his whole life and work, the picture seems somewhat
different. Though many detested his approach to Islam,
no one who knew him seems to have doubted his faith.
They could not because it was awe-inspiring. 'Man
cannot forget God', he declared, 'God himself pursues
us so tenaciously that if we want to leave him, He does
not leave us.'[32] Before the Mutiny, when his bio-
grapher Hali described his piety as 'terrifying', most
of his writing was on religious subjects. After the
Mutiny almost all his intellectual energy, greatly
informed by the insights of the Naqshbandis, of Shah
Waliullah and of Sayyid Ahmad Barelvi, was devoted to
trying to resolve the conflict between religion and
science,[33] indeed his endeavour to reinterpret Islam in
the light of western learning played a central role in
his life.[34] 'Today', he told an audience in Lahore in
1884, 'we are, as before [i.e. when Islam came into
close contact with the world of Greek ideas] in need of
a modern *'ilm al-kalam* by which we should either refute
doctrines of modern sciences or undermine their foundations, or show that they are in conformity with the
articles of Islamic faith.' If we did not 'reveal to
the people the original bright face of Islam. My conscience tells me ... I would stand as a sinner before
God.'[35] Islam had to be defended against the preju-
diced ignorance of western orientalists; but, much
more important, it had to be interpreted so that young
Muslims could imbibe modern science and remain Muslims.
Sayyid Ahmad saw the world as a Muslim. This fact
defined for him his nation, his first allegiance. And
he was, according to Nazir Ahmad, 'intoxicated with
love of his nation'.[36] As a Muslim, the conditioning
of his Mughal heritage apart, he believed it was his
duty to make his people strong. 'The more worldly
progress we make, the more glory Islam gains' was his
motto according to one student of his ideas.[37] If he
thought primarily in terms of the Indian Muslim nation,
it was because it was his life's work to persuade
Muslims to come to terms with the realities of the
present, two of which were the political fragmentation
of the *umma* and British power in India.

  Most of Sayyid Ahmad's supporters were also men of
deep faith. And for the most part they supported him
in spite of what they regarded as his dangerous
innovations in attempting to accommodate Islam to
western rationalism. Two of these whom, no doubt,

Brass has in mind when he talks of the UP Muslims
emphasizing 'a special sense of history incompatible
with Hindu aspirations' were Altaf Husain Hali and
Shibli Nu'mani. Hali's *Musaddas*, an epic poem describ-
ing the rise and splendour of Muslim achievement and
its decline, was first published in 1879. So great
was its impact that it became a kind of Muslim
national anthem, parts of it usually being recited to
inaugurate sessions of Muslim social and political
organizations. And, although the work was commissioned
by Sayyid Ahmad and had an impact which was far greater
than anyone could have imagined, it was an outpouring
of faith as much as it was calculated and successful
propaganda. 'I was wholly given to religious
fanaticism', says Hali of himself in the early 1870s,
'and was prey to dogmas and orthodoxy. I considered
the Muslims the very cream of creation....'[38] Moreover
the poem was in harmony with the Indo-Muslim historical
tradition which saw the history of Islam in India as a
continuation of universal Islamic history, and
suggested too that the only history fit for study was
that of Muslims. Shibli Nu'mani, poet, theologian,
but primarily historian, shared this outlook, which
was bolstered in his case by wide travel in the Ottoman
empire and, despite all his professions of detachment,
a desire to demonstrate the superiority of Islam.[39]
Turning to Sayyid Ahmad's political successors we have
a similar picture. Viqar al-Mulk, who played a leading
part in Muslim separatist politics from 1901 till his
retirement from the secretaryship of Aligarh College
in 1913, greatly increased the Islamic content of
education and daily life at the College, and according
to Shaukat Ali, 'his example inspired us with respect
for the grandeur of the Muslim life...'.[40] Muhsin al-
Mulk, the leading figure in the Muslim deputation to
the Viceroy of 1906 and in the foundation of the All-
India Muslim League, was profoundly interested in
religious questions,[41] and declared his distinctly
Islamic attitude to earthly matters in *Tahzib al-
Akhlaq*: 'our worldly affairs cannot be independent of
our religion. This applies to our politics as well'.[42]

For the ulema, of course, the indivisibility of
politics and religion was an axiom. Although many seem
tacitly to have accepted that the pious sultan theory
might apply to the British, the penetration of the
modern state into their world and their growing
realization that the control of that state was being

devolved on Indians raised for them in new form the
problems of the relationship between Islam and power
and their relations with Hindus. They needed a new
theory to reconcile ideal with fact. Shibli outlined
the direction the ulema should take in his opening
address to the *Nadwah al-ulama* in 1894. He attacked
the idea that religion could be separated from the
rest of the community's affairs. The concerns of the
ulema, the guardians and interpreters of the Sharia,
were not just regulations concerning prayer and fasting
but every aspect of Muslim life. 'The national life',
he declared, 'is in the ulama's right of ownership ...
and they alone have or can have absolute sway ... over
it.'[43] Shibli's hopes for the reassertion of the
control of the ulema over Muslim affairs, which of
course meant that Muslims would be subject to the
Sharia, came to nothing. The idea, however, lived on.
It was the object of two associations founded by the
ulema of Firangi Mahal in 1910, the *Majlis-i-Islah* and
the *Majlis Muid-al-Islam*.[44] It was most powerfully
expressed in the addresses of the ulema of Deoband and
of the *Muid-al-Islam* to Montagu and Chelmsford in 1917,
which government described as 'a nakedly impracticable
demand for the predomination of priestly influence'.[45]
Moreover, it was actually given concrete form during
the Khilafat movement, through which members of the
ulema came to have for three years great influence on
Muslim and even on Congress politics.[46] By 1921 some
members of the ulema were setting up organizations to
administer the Sharia. In Bihar, for example, a
system of religious courts was established in the
districts, each headed by an Amir-i-Sharia, which were
subject to a provincial court headed by an Amir for the
province,[47] and this organization was still working in
1924.[48] Thus both in word and in deed the ulema demonstrated their view of the kind of community in which
Muslims should live: the only true 'Home Rule' for
Muslims, declared Abd al-Bari of Firangi Mahal, would
be the enforcement of the Sharia.[49] This did not
necessarily mean that Muslims need fall out with non-
Muslims, but as power was being redistributed in
India in the years before 1947 there was an attraction
in the thought that the Sharia might be supported by
the full force of state power.

For almost all the ulema the ideal source of power
for Muslims lay in the Caliph of Islam. During the
modern Ottoman period, the Sultans had arrogated this

position to themselves. Of course, that they should
provide the conditions in which the Sharia could be
enforced throughout the Islamic world was impossible.
Nevertheless, the Indian ulema, in common with Muslims
in other countries where they were in a minority,
tended to be powerful supporters of the Ottoman claim
to the universal Islamic Caliphate and were concerned
that the Sultans should have the power to maintain this
claim; and in offering their support expressed their
sense both of Muslim brotherhood and of the significance of the Islamic *umma* of which the Caliph was
symbol and focus. Such ideas were strong in the Shah
Waliullah school, particularly after his grandson
Muhammad Ishaq migrated to the Hijaz, and they became
strongly associated with the ulema of Deoband and the
Nadwah al-ulama.[50] But such ideas or sympathies seemed
to be no less strong amongst those members of the ulema
who owed little to Shah Waliullah, like the Firangi
Mahalis, who were in the forefront of the Khilafat
movement.[51] In the late nineteenth century the pan-
Islamic sentiments of the ulema were stimulated, as
the Christian powers encroached increasingly on the
central Islamic lands, as learned Indian Muslims
travelled more frequently in the Ottoman territories,
as Sultan Abd al-Hamid's sedulous propaganda had some
effect, and as Jamal al-din al-Afghani's ideas began
to hit their mark. These feelings reached a new
intensity as the Ottoman empire came under the final
assault before and during World War One. They launched
Abu'l Kalam Azad's *Al-Hilal*, instinct with the ideas
of Afghani. They spurred the foundation of organizations such as the Anjuman-i-Khuddam-i-Ka'aba to
protect the Holy Places of Islam, and the attempts of
Mahmud al-Hasan of Deoband and his followers to
persuade Ottoman armies and frontier tribesmen to
attack British India through the Khyber Pass. These
feelings reached their peak in the Khilafat movement
which was primarily designed to prevent the allied
dismemberment of Turkey after World War One. British
India was declared *Dar al-harb* and thousands of poor
Muslims fled to Afghanistan. Many of the ulema
launched themselves into the mainstream of Indian
politics and for some years diverted them in their
direction. And all was reinforced by Abu'l Kalam
Azad's caliphal theory which insisted that 'no nation
or community lives ... without a political centre ....
The only possible political centre for Islam in the

twentieth century is the Ottoman Caliphate with all
its imperfections .... The Ottoman Caliphate
possesses the only sword which Muslims have for the
protection of the Religion of God ... and it is not
only the sense of brotherhood of Muslims but also the
recognition that the Ottoman Caliphate is the last
independent Muslim power that inspires the devotion
of Indian Muslims to it.'[52]

The pan-Islamic vision of the ulema, and their
concern actively to defend the institutions of their
faith beyond the frontiers of India, found an echo
amongst many young western-educated Muslims. Two
strands seemed to be uppermost in their minds: one was
the sense of *asabiyya*, the sense of fellow-feeling with
all those who bore the impress of Islamic civilization;
and the second was the lingering concern that Islam
should have power, and if an Islamic empire bounding
the *umma* was impossible in contemporary conditions,
the Turkish Caliph should at least wield enough power
to protect the heartlands and holy places of the faith.
When the young men were first moved in the years before
World War One, the sense of *asabiyya* seems to have been
the predominant strand. For instance, Hasrat Mohani
was imprisoned for a newspaper article criticizing
British educational reforms in Egypt. Iqbal, sailing
past Sicily, bemoaned the end of Muslim civilization
in that island many centuries before. Muhammad Ali
made clear his concern over the fate of Morocco,
Tripoli, Persia as well as Turkey. And his feelings
were extraordinarily strong; when in 1912 he heard
that 'the Bulgarians were only 25 miles from the walls
of Constantinople - from Constantinople, a name that
had for five centuries been sacred to every Muslim as
the centre of his highest hopes', he contemplated
suicide.[53] After World War One the pan-Islamic feeling
of the western-educated came to focus on preserving the
Ottoman Caliphate, and the emotive concern that Islam
should be linked with some kind of temporal power came
uppermost. By this time changes had taken place in
some at least of the western-educated. They grew
beards, replaced their western suits with more 'Islamic'
dress, began to read the Quran and discovered Islam.
Thus the pursuit of a secularized pan-Islam drew men
back to their faith. At the same time they built up
close relations with the ulema, leading to the
foundation of the Khilafat organization, which ran the
greatest mass movement India had yet seen. After

Ataturk's abolition of the Turkish Caliphate in 1924,
which brought the movement in large part to an end, the
pan-Islamic vision remained with some at least of the
western-educated, most notably the Ali brothers. As
there was no longer any element on which their lingering desire to unite Islam and power could focus, their
sense of *asabiyya* came to the fore again. They
supported the Arabs against the Jews during 1929-30
over the Wailing Wall affair. They supported a plan
to establish a pan-Islamic university in Jerusalem,
which they envisaged perhaps as an Aligarh for the
umma. And so it was in symbolic tribute to the sacrifices of Indian Muslims for pan-Islamic causes that the
Grand Mufti of Jerusalem arranged in January 1931 for
Muhammad Ali to be buried in the enclosure of the Aqsa
mosque. Thus the pan-Islamic drives of Indian Muslims
came to focus on Zionist settlement in Palestine which
to this day they see not only as a stake thrust by the
West into the Islamic heartland but also as a symbol
of the shadow cast by the West over the Islamic vision
of history.

The pan-Islamic feeling, which for some years was
prominent in Indian politics and for a moment engulfed
them, illustrates the latent force amongst Indian
Muslims of Islamic ideas, and the emotional drives
they derived from them. The material interests of
various leaders were to some extent served by the pan-
Islamic movement: they found occupations commensurate
with their self-esteem, they found an income, their
newspapers paid, they became the greatly admired
leaders of their people, they acquired power. But it
was not primarily for reasons such as these, and in
some cases it was not at all, that men like Hasrat
Mohani, Muhammad Ali, Abu'l Kalam Azad or Mahmud al-
Hasan gave of themselves so freely and spent years in
captivity. It was not for these reasons that they
indulged in politics which had little bearing on the
fate of Indian Muslims. Above all things they wanted
to do something for Islam; they wanted to assert
their visions of Islam. Common to most of their
visions were the various key ideas associated with
the Muslim sense of community. There was a belief in
the reality of the *umma* and in the importance of
Islamic brotherhood and the obligations it brought
with it. There was belief in the superiority of
Islam, which caused an uproar when Muhammad Ali
announced that a Muslim of low character was superior

to any non-Muslim be he Mahatma Gandhi himself.[54] And
there was an overwhelming feeling that the Ottoman
Caliphate should have power, that the *umma* should have
a powerful political centre which was the nearest even
these visionaries could come to unifying Islam with
power in the modern world. If ever Islamic ideas
created the frame within which men apprehended reality
and acted on it, it was here. Pan-Islamism ignored
the realities of great power conflict, the conflicting
ambitions of Turks and Arabs, the existence of nation
states, but most of all the situation of Muslims in
India.

Considering the UP Muslim elite in the years between
the end of the Khilafat movement and the creation of
Pakistan we are hampered, somewhat surprisingly, by a
lack of biographical evidence about many leading men.
No one can be placed quite so completely in the context
of his life as Sayyid Ahmad Khan or Muhammad Ali,
while even where there is evidence it is often of a
secondary kind and, one senses, subject to the requirements of the polemic which surrounds the emergence of
Pakistan.

Let us turn first to the ulema, who are convention-
ally, but quite incorrectly, regarded as opposing
Muslim separatist politics as a group. Those of the
ulema who did so were primarily those of the Deoband
school closely associated with the Jami'yat-al-ulama-i-
Hind. Until the 1937 elections they followed a course
largely parallel with that of the Muslim League, being
concerned to protect Muslim interests as they saw them
against the power of the majority, by which they meant
protecting the Sharia. And they were prepared to
support the League, and other Muslim organizations so
long as they worked in harmony with the Congress. But,
when the League refused to cooperate with the first
Congress government formed in the UP after the 1937
elections, the Jami'yat opposed it, and the ulema from
the Jami'yat were prominent in Congress battles for
Muslim seats from the Jhansi by-election of June 1937
to the memorable struggle for Liaqat Ali Khan's
Muzaffarnagar constituency in 1946. They were
implacable enemies of the League in word and deed.

The point which concerns us is how did the ulema of
the Jami'yat reconcile their support for Indian
nationalism with the tendencies to political
separatism inherent in basic Islamic ideas? The
answer is that they did not in any realistic sense.

98

They were nationalist only in so far as they wanted
to rid India of the British. They saw the Hindus as a
force given by God to help them in this task.[55] In
everything else they followed the separatist tendencies
of their faith. In independent India they were not
going to be subject to the Indian Penal Code, but to
the Sharia; they were not going to participate in an
Indian education which might breed a sense of a common
culture and common purpose, but they were going to
continue to educate and be educated in Islam.[56] In the
laws they observed and the values they cherished
Muslims were to be a separate people in the Indian
nation, or, as Husain Ahmad Madani put it, a *millat* in
the Indian *qaum*.[57] The sense of Muslim distinctiveness
persisted as strongly as ever. If they had to accept,
temporarily, that they would have to deal with Hindus
on an equal footing, their sense of the superiority of
Islam, of its historical destiny, came through in
their belief that, although the non-Muslim could no
longer be made to submit by force, nevertheless, when
he saw the quality of the life lived by Muslims, he
would freely choose the way of Islam.[58] This
represented some considerable feat of re-interpretation,
but it was nothing to the change they envisaged in the
relationship between Islam and power. Whatever
happened in independent India, they could not expect
the state machinery automatically to enforce the Sharia.
They knew that the Sharia would only be observed if
Muslims wished it to be, if they saw it as a moral
imperative - without state sanctions.[59] Thus the
community lost some of its charisma. It existed less
because God commanded it than because Muslims willed
it. Muslims submitted no longer because of His
awfulness and the power of His earthly authorities but
through internal struggle and feats of will. God was
no longer above but in the heart. It is tempting to
suggest that the Jami'yat made it possible for Muslims
to live in a Hindu-dominated India by pulling God out
of the heavens and placing him within man. The final
meaning of accepting the political weakness of
Muslims seemed to be acknowledging the weakness of God
to command.

It is not hard to see why so many Muslims should
have found the position of the nationalist ulema
unattractive. Their use of the principle of *ijtihad*
seemed to deny so much of what many Muslims thought
central to their faith. Fighting for a community

which seemed to depend less upon the will of God than
upon the will of Muslims had none of the appeal of the
struggle for the Caliphate, and, as events turned out,
none of the emotive appeal of Pakistan for all the
attempts of the nationalist ulema to show how little
the western-educated leadership of the Muslim League
would respect the Sharia. Large numbers of the ulema
supported the League, indeed we may well learn, when
more work is done and our understanding of the period
is less shrouded by the mists of propaganda, that the
balance of opinion amongst the learned men of Islam
favoured the Muslim League and Pakistan.[60] Certainly,
members of the ulema from a wide range of schools gave
the League active support. Foremost, from the
extremely influential Firangi Mahal family, were Maulana Inayatullah, principal of the Madrassa Nizamiyya,
and Maulana Jamal Miyan, son of Abd al-Bari, leading
member of the family and eventually Joint
Secretary of the Muslim League. There were many
influential Deobandis. Maulana Mazhar al-din, for
instance, who helped to found the organization which
broke away from the Jami'yat-al-ulama-i-Hind, the
Jami'yat-al-ulama-i-Hind (Kanpur).[61] There was Mufti
Muhammad Shafi,[62] the chief Mufti of Deoband, and
Shabbir Ahmad Usmani,[63] a leading scholar of *hadith*,
and Zafar Ahmad Thanvi who, it would appear, practically
wrested Sylhet from the Congress single-handed in the
referendum of 1947.[64] But most important was Maulana
Ashraf Ali Thanvi, a leading Sufi with many followers
and a scholar whose handbook on the requisites of
Islam, *Bihishti Zewar*, was and remains an exception-
ally popular guide to correct behaviour. He resigned
from the management committee of Deoband over its
pro-Congress stance and eventually came out publicly
in support of the League.[65] A third school, the
Barelvis, gave itself entirely to the idea of Pakistan
from the early 1940s; its organization, the *Jamhuriyya-
i-Islamiyya*, spread more widely throughout north India
and devoted itself to propagating the necessity of
Pakistan.[66] Indeed, the group was so committed to
Pakistan that its leader, Maulana Na'im al-din, declared
in 1946 that, regardless of what Mr Jinnah made of the
Cabinet Mission proposals, it could 'in no circumstances give up the demand for Pakistan'.[67]

The reasons why so many of the ulema from these
different schools supported the demand for Pakistan
were, no doubt, mixed. For some, the Barelvis, for

example, it was often almost a reflex action to take
a line opposed to Deoband. Not all would have been
exposed to the overwhelming hostility to the British,
which was so powerful an aspect of the Deobandi
tradition, and thus would have been open to solutions
other than the nationalist one. Personality clashes
will have played a part with some; patronage will have
influenced others. But it is hard to see why for most
of these scholars of Islam the prime motive was not
ideological. Not all who fought for Pakistan migrated
there, while those who did often did so at great cost.
Many were Sufis, and as they went to Pakistan they
severed contact with the shrines from which they and
their ancestors down the centuries had received
spiritual sustenance and from their connections with
which they frequently gained status.[68] When the ulema
came to consider the idea of Pakistan, not all, like
Maulana Maududi, who was not a UP man nor strictly an
alim, but nevertheless a religious thinker of great
influence among the ulema, were happy about the
intentions of the western-educated leadership of the
League.[69] On the other hand, Pakistan did seem the
better of two poor alternatives, and two strands
seem prominent in the thought of those prepared to
support the idea. One, which appeared to dominate
the thinking of all, was fear of Hindu domination, fear
that Muslims would not be able to survive as proper
Muslims without power. Some had been horrified by the
lengths to which Muslims had gone to win Hindu support
in the Khilafat movement.[70] It was the same for the
renegade Deobandis, the Barelvis and the Firangi
Mahalis. Maulana Inayatullah of Firangi Mahal, a
Congressman and a founder member of the Jami'yat-al-
ulama-i-Hind, summed up the position when in the late
1930s he came to the conclusion that the salvation of
Indian Muslims lay in the Muslim League and that the
means to preserve the Sharia lay in supporting the
League.[71] The sophistries of the nationalist ulema had
no appeal for these men. Muslims must have power to
protect their way of life even if the pan-Islamic
ideal of the *umma* might be compromised in the process.
But frequently this desire to defend the Sharia was
accompanied by the emotionally appealing concern to
demonstrate the superiority of Islam, to restore its
glory, which represents a second prominent strand in
the thought of the learned men. 'Our attitude',
Maulana Na'im al-din Barelvi told a conference of 5000

ulema in April 1946, 'was always governed by the
dictates of Islam. At no time did we trust non-
Muslims: now that the League took a step in the
direction of the propagation of the ordinances of
Islam, we opposed the opponents of the Muslim League
for the glory of Islam.'[72]

During the 1920s and early 1930s Muslim separatism
as a political force reached a low ebb. Western-
educated UP Muslims were scattered through several
organizations: the Khilafat Committee, the Congress,
landlord political organizations, a shrunken Muslim
League, while some dropped out of politics altogether.
It was not till they understood the consequences of
Congress power in the province after its victory in
the 1937 elections that they came together in large
numbers to support Muslim separatist politics again.
From this moment till the emergence of Pakistan they
were at the heart of the League's activities, domin-
ating many of its committees and holding many of its
top offices. Among them were: Nawabzada Liaqat Ali
Khan of Muzaffarnagar, League Secretary and in effect
Jinnah's deputy; Nawab Ismail Khan of Meerut, Chairman
of the Committee of Action; the wily Choudhry
Khaliquzzaman, a very influential member of the
Working Committee, as was the young Raja of Mahmudabad,
who gave the League the weight of his family name and
much financial support. When it came to campaigning,
students from Aligarh Muslim University played a major
role, going out in their hundreds even in their
thousands to win the support of Muslims in towns and
villages in Punjab, Sind and Bengal.[73]

Without the leadership and devotion of these
western-educated Muslims there would have been no
Pakistan. Their motives are usually summed up as
entirely self-interested. Religious ideology, we are
told, can have played no part in moving them. On the
one hand many were not practising Muslims so were
unlikely to be impelled by a desire to realize an
Islamic state, even if they knew what such a state
should be.[74] While, on the other hand, they had good
reasons to create a separate Muslim homeland. Congress
power revealed to them after 1937 what might happen to
their culture and to their jobs and to their chances of
ever being influential in an independent India, and so
they fought for Pakistan to maintain their status and
their power.[75] Much research needs to be done before
we can be convinced by such an explanation, though the

opinions of such acute, though committed, observers
as Muhammad Mujeeb and W.C. Smith demand respect.
Nevertheless, it need not be denied that an uneasi-
ness about culture, jobs and influence in a Hindu-
dominated India was an important strand in the
thinking of many UP Muslims: Choudhry Khaliquzzaman
is a good example of such men. But to see this as
explaining all is unsatisfactory. There were, for
instance, practising Muslims amongst the UP leadership. The Raja of Mahmudabad put his faith first
throughout his life; he was a member of the İslami
Jama'at, and as a believer in Pakistan as an Islamic
state disagreed with Jinnah in the 1940s.[76] Even
Liaqat Ali Khan, whose style and clothes always
seemed so westernized, is remembered by a contemporary
as a devout Muslim.[77] Then, for many of these
leaders advocacy of Pakistan seemed to involve more
sacrifice and selflessness than gain. Nawab Ismail
Khan never went to Pakistan; it took the Raja of
Mahmudabad some years to do so, while although
Liaqat Ali may have been sated by the power he
gained as Pakistan's first premier, he also lost his
large estates in west UP and died a poor man.[78] But
to discover religious conviction in a man or to point
to apparently selfless action is not all we can do
to suggest the influence of ideology. As we have
stated above, it is a commonplace of secularizing
societies that religious values still penetrate the
consciousnesses, still form part of the subjective
orientation to the world, of men who may no longer
practise their faith. Such men may well hold with
the conviction of deeply religious men secular values
derived from the culture's religious base.[79] Thus a
man may no longer pray five times a day, or look
forward to the Haj or observe the Sharia, but he may
still be moved by the sense of Muslim brotherhood, by
a belief in the superiority of Muslims and their
culture, by the feeling that Muslims live their lives
best in association with power, and by the feeling
that, although Islam and politics may be divisible,
nevertheless Muslim peoples ought to have Muslim
governments. Such considerations help explain why the
Muslim League was supported in its demand for Pakistan
by Muslim minorities in both north and south India who
could derive little benefit from it. Such considerations should also be thrown into the balance before
the UP Muslim elite can be dismissed as crude

manipulators of Islamic symbols, and their actions
robbed of any emotional authenticity.

The ideas associated with creating and sustaining 'the
best nation raised up for men' contained in the Islamic
tradition (that Muslims form part of a community; that
the laws of the community are God-given; that it is the
duty of the ruler to put them into effect; that he
must have the power to do so; that all Muslims are
brothers; and that they are distinct from and superior
to non-Muslims) have continually influenced many north
Indian Muslims towards trying to realize the ideal
religio-political community. Moreover, as a minority
in the midst of idolators, abiding concerns were both
to draw sharp distinctions between the idolators and
themselves and to ensure that Islam lived hand in hand
with power. Understandably, these were concerns which
grew in force with the decline of Mughal power and the
emergence of the modern state in non-Muslim hands.
Their action is evident amongst the ulema whose very
raison d'etre was to strive to create the Sharia
community, and for whom ideas must frequently have
operated as a motivating force. Even when the
influence of these ideas drove members of the Indian
ulema in opposite political directions in the twentieth
century, there is no doubting their separatist force.
If those of the ulema who supported the League saw the
creation of an Islamic state as the only way of protecting the Sharia when the British left, those of the
ulema who supported the Congress envisaged a Muslim
future in India which was not much less separate and
in which the sense of Muslim identity would always be
made to compete strongly with that of Indian nationality. Turning to the secular, or secularizing elite,
the influence of these ideas, though less direct and
harder to assess, is still strong. Even without
powerful religious sanction, which is not to say that
many who were not members of the ulema were not deeply
committed Muslims, they still underlaid men's assumptions about the world and helped to form what were
emotionally the most satisfying ends.
   If this understanding of the formative influence of
the ideal of the Islamic community on Muslim political
behaviour is correct, it must be seen to work more
widely than just amongst the UP Muslims, and so it
does. Take, for instance, the Moplahs of south India

who have shown for eight centuries that it is possible
to survive as a Muslim community under non-Muslim
rule. They have asserted with a practice of suicidal
jihad the distinction between the Muslim community and
the Hindus and Christians who lived around them;[80] in
recent years they have demonstrated a powerful sense of
asabiyya with Muslims elsewhere on the subcontinent;
while the essentially separatist tendencies in their
outlook are revealed in their strong preference to
act politically through an exclusively Muslim party
whose demand for the creation of a Moplah-dominated
district of Mallapuram was granted in 1969.[81] This
achievement, we are told, 'met an important psychological need';[82] within the limits of what was possible
some of the Moplahs of Kerala had at last succeeded in
combining Islam with power. We know enough about the
Moplahs to sense with some confidence the way in which
their vision of the world has been shaped by Islam,
and how this has influenced their politics. We do not
as yet know enough to assert the same of the Deccani
Muslims who support the Majlis-e-Ittehadul-Muslimeen
with its demand to establish a separate Muslim state
in Andhra Pradesh,[83] or of the Labbais of Tamil Nadu
who identified strongly with the movement for
Pakistan,[84] or of the Maharashtrian Muslims who in
recent years have joined the Muslim League in increasing numbers.[85] But it seems likely that the ideal of
the Islamic community shaped and shapes their apprehension of what is legitimate, desirable and
satisfactory political action.

   Considering Muslim minorities in Asia more generally, a similar relationship between ideas associated
with creating and sustaining the Muslim community and
political separatism is evident. In the Philipines
close connections have been drawn between the resurgence
of Islam since World War Two, with a consequent deepen-
ing of religious consciousness and the growth of more
orthodox religious practice, and the movement of Muslim
Filipinos to set up a separate Muslim state.[86] In
China, for centuries, large numbers of Muslims have
resisted absorption into the dominant culture. Muslims
have preserved their sense of superiority and distinctiveness; they have built strong communal organizations;
and throughout they have enhanced their consciousness
of the *umma* 'by cultivating in the Muslim the centrality
of Arabia, Islam, the Islamic Empire, and Islamic
traditions and values'.[87] Not surprisingly, they have

not been able to identify with the unitarian Confucian and Communist states, and have followed a politically separate path as far as possible. 'China is not the fatherland of the Hui nationality', they declared during the Hundred Flowers relaxation of 1956, 'Arabic is the language of the Hui people ... All the Hui people of the world belong to one family.'[88]

If the Islamic ideal of the religio-political community has such influence amongst Muslin minorities, it would appear also to have influence in states where the population is largely or entirely Muslim. Indeed, there is hardly a Muslim state in the world which does not have a party whose professed aim is to impose its vision of the Islamic ideal on contemporary politics and society. And whatever the motives of the leaders and followers of the Muslim Brotherhood of Egypt, the Jama'at-i-Islami of Pakistan, or the Fadayan-i Islam of Iran, there can be no doubt that their vision is formed, and limited, by the Islamic tradition. Nowhere has this process been more minutely observed in recent years than in Kessler's study of the rise of the Pan-Malaysian Islamic party to power in the Kelantan province of eastern Malaysia. Here an anthropologist with an historian's perspective shows how in the 1950s and 1960s Islamic social theory continuously impinged upon and shaped political developments.[89] The experience of Muslim-majority societies confirms our understanding of the pervasive influence of the Islamic ideal, the one difference being that whereas in minority communities a primary problem is uniting power to Islam, in majority communities it is uniting Islam to power.

The fundamental connection between Islam and political separatism suggests further modifications to Brass's theory of nation-formation. To those factors that are already agreed to be significant:[90] the ability of UP Muslims to draw on cultural and historical symbols with an appeal to a large part of the community; the existence of powerful elites willing to promote a communal identity; the fact that objective differences between Hindus and Muslims were not great enough of themselves to fuel a separatist movement; the determination of Muslims to defend Muslim interests; the importance of competition from an increasingly assertive Hindu revivalism and the significance of the imperial system of political control, we must add the religio-political ideas of Islam, in particular those

106

that stress the importance of the existence of a Muslim
community. We see these ideas not only limiting the
range of legitimate actions for the elite, which is the
process implied in (though not specifically expanded in)
Brass's article for this volume, but also forming their
own apprehensions of what was possible and of what they
ought to be trying to achieve. Brass had made a bold
attempt to delineate the realm in which the laws of
competition for power are absolute. But the example of
Muslim separatism would suggest that the area in which
we can see politics as autonomous must be cut down yet
further than he has been prepared to admit.

This conclusion has broader theoretical implications.
Brass hints at its significance for political science
in the discussion at the beginning of his article when
he points to the fundamental conceptual differences
that exist among scholars over the processes by which
nations are formed. Some, the 'primordialists', argue
that every man carries with him through life attachments (to birthplace, kin, religion, language etc.)
that are the 'givens' of the human condition, that are
rooted in the non-rational foundations of the personality, and that provide the basis for an easy affinity
with other people from the same background. Others,
the 'instrumentalists', argue, as Brass seemed to do
in *Language, Religion and Politics*, that ethnicity is
to be seen 'as the pursuit of interest and advantage
for members of groups whose cultures are infinitely
malleable and manipulable by elites'.[91] These are
extreme positions; the answer, as Brass himself now
suggests, lies somewhere between the two. He veers
towards the 'instrumentalists'' position in which the
autonomy of politics is considerable. Nation formation,
he says, is 'the process by which elites and counter-
elites within ethnic groups select aspects of the
group's culture, attach new value and meaning to them,
and use them as symbols to mobilize the group, to
defend its interests, and to compete with other
groups'.[92] These elites are fancy-free and constrained only by the cultures of the groups they wish to
lead. We propose that Islamic ideas had a moulding and
on occasion a motivating role to play amongst the elites
of the UP, that they seem to have played a similar role
amongst the elites in other Muslim societies, and that
the continuing power of these ideas suggests that the
balance of the argument should shift more towards the
position of the primordialists.

Robinson, 'Islam and Muslim Separatism'

1. R.E. Miller, *Mappila Muslims of Kerala: a study in Islamic Trends*, Bombay 1976, pp.162-5.
2. G. Ram Reddy, 'Language, Religion and Political Identity: The Case of the Majlis-e-Ittehadul-Muslimeen in Andhra Pradesh', below pp.125-6.
3. P.R. Brass, *Language, Religion and Politics in North India*, London 1974, p.124.
4. F. Robinson, 'Nation Formation: The Brass Thesis and Muslim Separatism', *Journal of Commonwealth & Comparative Politics* 15, 3 (November 1977), pp.215-30.
5. P.R. Brass, 'Elite Groups, Symbol Manipulation and Ethnic Identity Among the Muslims of South Asia': above, p.54.
6. Ibid., pp.43-6.
7. Ibid., p.40.
8. Ibid., p.43.
9. Ibid., p.67.
10. Q. Skinner, 'Some Problems in the Analysis of Political Thought and Action', *Political Theory* 2, 3 (August 1974), pp.277-303. I am very grateful to my colleague, John Dinwiddy, for drawing my attention to this article. Moreover, it should be noted that Skinner's argument goes further than stated: he points out that once a political actor has accepted the need to legitimize his behaviour, and has adopted a particular set of principles, his actions to be effective must be to some extent in harmony with the sources of legitimation he has chosen. This represents a further way in which ideas influence action.
11. Robinson, 'Nation Formation', p.222.
12. This development is powerfully analysed and evoked in C. Geertz, *Islam Observed: Religious Development in Morocco and Indonesia*, Chicago 1971, pp.18, 102-7, 114-7. See also, D.E. Smith's more general assertion of the power of religious values among the populations of secularizing societies in D.E. Smith, *Religion and Political Development*, Boston 1970, pp.169-71.
13. D.E. Smith, op. cit., pp.169-200.
14. W. Montgomery Watt, *Islam and the Integration of Society*, London 1961, p.204.
15. Ibid., pp.174-5.
16. C.P. Woodcroft-Lee, 'From Morocco to Merauke:

Some Observations in the Shifting Pattern of Relation-
ships between Indonesian Muslims and the World Muslim
Community as Revealed in the Writings of Muslim
Intellectuals in Indonesia', paper delivered at the
International Conference on Asian Islam, Hebrew
University of Jerusalem, 1977.

17. P.G. Gowing, 'How Muslim are the Muslim Filipinos?', in P.G. Gowing and R.D. McAmis, eds., *The
Muslim Filipinos : Their History, Society and Contemporary Problems*, Manila 1974, pp.284-94. Riazul Islam
considers this sense of *asabiyya* to have been the most
powerful force working amongst those Muslims who
supported the Pakistan movement: Riazul Islam, 'The
Religious Factor in the Pakistan Movement: A Study in
Motivation', in *Proceedings of the First Congress on
the History and Culture of Pakistan*, Vol. III,
Islamabad 1974.

18. M.G.S. Hodgson, *The Venture of Islam: Conscience
and History in a World Civilization*, Vol. I, Chicago
1974, pp.75-8.

19. K. Cragg, *The House of Islam*, 2nd ed., Encino
and Belmont, California, 1975, pp.82-4.

20. Maulana Muhammad Ali, *The Holy Qur'an*, 6th ed.,
Lahore 1973, III, p.109.

21. Cragg, op. cit., p.76.

22. *The Holy Qur'an*, III, p.108.

23. Cragg, op. cit., p.78.

24. *The Holy Qur'an*, LXIII, p.8.

25. P. Hardy, 'Islam and Muslims in South Asia',
unpublished paper, p.12; Hodgson, *Venture of Islam*,
Vol.III, pp.59-73.

26. Hardy, op. cit., p.13.

27. A. Ahmad, *Studies in Islamic Culture in the
Indian Environment*, Oxford 1964, p.208.

28. Full descriptions of this extraordinary jihad
may be found in G.D. Bhatnagar, *Awadh Under Wajid 'Ali
Shah*, Benares 1968, pp.117-40, and in a diary of the
jihad, Mirza Jan, *Hadikat us-Shuhada*, 1856.

29. Ahmad, op. cit., pp.60-1; F. Robinson, *Separatism
Among Indian Muslims : The Politics of the United
Provinces' Muslims 1860-1923*, London 1974, pp.112-3.

30. See for instance the supra-communal emphasis of
Sayyid Ahmad's political activities in the 1860s,
Robinson, *Separatism*, pp.84-98; and the wording of a
circular written by Sayyid Ahmad around 1872 which
talks of the Muslims forming 'an important section of
the community', 'Circular from The Mahammedan Anglo-

Oriental College Fund Committee' Tract 969, India
Office Library.
    31. A. Ahmad, *Islamic Modernism in India and
Pakistan 1857-1964*, London 1967, pp.33-4.
    32. Altaf Husain Hali, *Hayat-i-Jawid*, quoted in
J.M.S. Baljon Jr., *The Reforms and Religious Ideas
of Sir Sayyid Ahmad Khan*, Leiden 1949, p.86.
    33. Ahmad, *Islamic Modernism*, p.32.
    34. C.W. Troll, *Sayyid Ahmad Khan: a Reinterpre-
tation of Muslim Theology*, New Delhi 1978, p.223.
    35. M. Siraj al-Din, ed., *Lectures ka Majmu'a*,
p.210, quoted in Baljon, op. cit., p.87.
    36. Ibid., p.12 n.38.
    37. Ibid., p.88.
    38. M. Sadiq, *A History of Urdu Literature*,
London 1964, p.264.
    39. Ibid., pp.279-80.
    40. S.M. Ikram, *Modern Muslim India and the Birth
of Pakistan (1858-1951)*, 2nd ed., Lahore 1965, p.120.
    41. Muhsin al-Mulk was most powerfully opposed to
Sayyid Ahmad's attempts to reformulate Islam, and
emerges from his writings as a man for whom matters of
faith were of the first importance, which was perhaps
not surprising for a convert from Shiism. Baljon,
op. cit., p.74 and especially n.24.
    42. Ahmad, *Modernism*, p.71.
    43. Ikram, op. cit., p.140.
    44. Robinson, *Separatism*, p.276.
    45. Ibid., p.286.
    46. Ibid., pp.289-337.
    47. Ibid., pp.328-30.
    48. Fortnightly Report (Bihar) for the second
fortnight of September 1924, Home Poll. 25 of 1924,
National Archives of India.
    49. *Jadu* (Jaunpur), 21 May 1918, United Provinces
Native Newspaper Reports, 1918.
    50. Ahmad, *Modernism*, pp.123-4.
    51. Robinson, *Separatism*, pp.289-325 and especially
p.325.
    52. P. Hardy, *Partners in Freedom - and True Muslims:
the Political Thought of some Muslim Scholars in British
India 1912-1947*, Lund. 1971, p.22.
    53. A. Iqbal, ed., *My Life: a Fragment: An Autobio-
graphical Sketch of Maulana Mohamed Ali*, Lahore 1942,
p.35; the English novelist, E.M. Forster, witnessed this
moment in Muhammad Ali's life, P.N. Furbank, *E.M.
Forster: A Life*, Vol. I, London 1977, pp.228-9.

54. A. Iqbal, *Life and Times of Mohamed Ali : An Analysis of the Hopes, Fears and Aspirations of Muslim India from 1778 to 1931*, Lahore 1974, p.313.
55. Hardy, *Partners*, p.32.
56. Ibid., p.41.
57. Ibid., pp.37-8.
58. Ibid., p.35.
59. Ibid., pp.40-1.
60. I.H. Qureshi, *Ulema in Politics : A Study Relating to the Political Activities of the Ulema in the South-Asian Subcontinent from 1556 to 1947*, Karachi 1972, p.360.
61. Ibid., p.357.
62. Ibid., pp.362-3.
63. Ibid., pp.360-2.
64. Ibid., p.362.
65. Ibid., pp.358-9; Z. Faruqi, *The Deoband School and the Demand for Pakistan*, Bombay 1963, p.102 n.4.
66. Qureshi, op. cit., pp.365-6.
67. Ibid., p.366.
68. For instance, those Firangi Mahalis who migrated to Pakistan, for the greater part, severed connections with the Qadiri shrine of Shah Abd al-Razzaq of Bansa which for 200 years had both supplied them with spiritual resources and, by giving them great prominence at the Urs, added status. They also lost contact with another important spiritual resource which was derived from Bagh Maulana Anwar in Lucknow where most of their ancestors, some of whom were saints, were buried. Together with these spiritual losses, deeply felt, they cut themselves off from a family tradition built up over 250 years, and sacrificed the benefits derived from an eminent position founded on spiritual and intellectual leadership over that period.
69. L. Binder, *Religion and Politics in Pakistan*, Berkeley 1963, pp.94-5.
70. Qureshi, op. cit., pp.358-9.
71. Sibghat Allah Shahid Ansari, *Sadr al-Mudarrisin*, Lucknow 1941, p.73.
72. Qureshi, op. cit., p.366.
73. K.B. Sayeed, *Pakistan: the Formative Phase 1857-1948*, 2nd ed., London 1968, p.200; I.A. Talbot, 'The 1946 Punjab Provincial Elections', paper delivered at Royal Holloway College, University of London, June 1978.
74. M. Mujeeb, 'The Partition of India in Retrospect', in C.H. Philips and M.D. Wainwright, eds., *The Partition of India : Policies and Perspectives 1935-1947*, London

1970, p.408.

75. Ibid., p.410 and W.C. Smith, *Modern Islam in India*, London 1946, especially pp.246-92.

76. The Raja of Mahmudabad, 'Some Memories', in Philips and Wainwright, op. cit., pp.388-9.

77. I.H. Qureshi, 'Liaquat - The Ideal Muslim', in Z. Ahmad, ed., *Liaquat Ali Khan: Leader and Statesman*, Karachi 1970, pp.80-3.

78. Ibid., p.82.

79. D.E. Smith, op. cit., pp.169-200.

80. S.F. Dale, 'The Islamic Frontier in Southwest India: The Shahid as a Cultural Ideal among the Mappillas of Malabar', *Modern Asian Studies* 11, 1, pp.41-56.

81. Miller, op. cit., pp.176-83.

82. Ibid., p.183.

83. Ram Reddy, op. cit.

84. M. Mines, 'Labbai', in R.V. Weekes, ed., *Muslim Peoples: A World Ethnographic Survey*, Connecticut 1978, pp.227-31.

85. M. Shakir and U.B. Bhoite, 'Maharashtrians', ibid., pp.246-50.

86. C.L. Reimer, 'Maranao', ibid., pp.267-72 and P.G. Gowing, 'The Muslim Filipinos', in Gowing and McAmis, op. cit., pp.288-90.

87. R. Israeli, 'Muslims in China: The Incompatibility between Islam and the Chinese Order', paper delivered at the International Conference on Asian Islam, Hebrew University of Jerusalem, 1977, pp.25-6.

88. Ibid., p.29.

89. C.S. Kessler, *Islam and Politics in a Malay State: Kelantan 1838-1969*, Ithaca 1978, especially pp.208-34.

90. I must reiterate that I cannot accept the significance Brass gives to social mobilization, Robinson, 'Nation Formation', op. cit., pp.218-21, and this position has recently been emphasized by the detailed research of Ian Talbot on the Muslim League's rise to power in the Punjab in the 1940s: Talbot, op. cit.

91. Brass, above, p.39.

92. Above, p.41.

LANGUAGE, RELIGION AND POLITICAL IDENTITY - THE CASE OF THE MAJLIS-E-ITTEHADUL-MUSLIMEEN IN ANDHRA PRADESH

G. Ram Reddy

The process of nation-building in the third world countries which became independent in the 1940s and 50s has been a bewildering task to the leadership in these countries. It has been made even more difficult because most such countries are plural societies with many social divisions creating their own particularisms. Edward Shils, for example, has written:

> The constituent societies on which the new states rest are, taken separately, not civil societies, and, taken together, they certainly do not form a single civil society .... They lack the affirmative attitude toward rules, persons, and actions that is necessary for consensus. They are constellations of kinship groups, castes, tribes, feudalities - even smaller territorial societies - but they are not civil societies. The sense of identity is rudimentary, even where it exists.[1]

The existence of a high incidence of group conflict generated by segmental social divisions which are related to competing demands made on the national political authority on the basis of ethnic, religious, and linguistic loyalties has made commentators doubt the capabilities of these political systems to achieve political development.[2] For these particularistic loyalties are often treated as anti-national, and it is felt that their destructive impact may drive the drama of development towards a tragic end. Political authority may be weakened by social conflict.

Democratic methods and measures are likely to provide a fertile ground for these sub-national loyalties. It could be argued, therefore, that the democratic system is inconsistent with national integration and orderly political development.[3] Thus, the problem which has to be faced is whether sub-national loyalties are necessarily inconsistent with national loyalties. Das Gupta argues that social divisions are not automatically translated into political cleavages. Even when some of them are politically translated, there may be wide variation in their direction, momentum and consequence. Not all cleavages are translated into open conflicts, and when they are, such conflicts may promote integration rather than disintegration. The extent to which political groups and group conflicts may be channelled into integrative behaviour will depend on, among other things, the nature of the general decision system in which they are made to operate. If the political system in which they operate is based on a pluralist decision system rather than an authoritarian one, the probability of political integration will be higher. The integrative consequences of group conflicts are likely to be greater in a political system where the distribution of cleavages is cross-cutting and mutually offsetting, and where plural divisions are likely to be accommodated in aggregative social and political organizations. Certain positive factors of cohesion may achieve an overarching dimension so that the scale of damaging conflict does not substantially disturb the foundations of the national community.[4]

Dilemmas of Muslims in Independent India

The experience of independent India shows that the group conflicts generated by factors such as ethnicity, religion, language, and region have been managed by a pluralist decision-making system.[5] Although there was a tremendous temptation for the ruling elite of the country when it became independent to resort to an authoritarian political system, they opted for a democratic system. However, they have built into the democratic system several safeguards which would not only assure order but also accommodate group conflicts in competitive and participatory politics. As Rajni Kothari writes:

> the model of democratization based on incremental political involvement of social strata provides us with a picture of the social dynamics of state and nation building in India. The general thrust of national integration in India is toward structuring a unity out of the common involvement of diverse elements in which competition and opposition become the vehicles of a consensus. This is matched at the level of societal interactions by a similar process: by giving free scope to inter-group conflicts and opposition and then ordered by accepting a new model of reaching agreements and making decisions.[6]

Nevertheless, the one cruel dilemma that has faced the political leadership in the country immediately after independence in view of the partition, a partition based on religion, has been the problem of religious particularism. While the leadership emphasizes secular politics, the background of partition makes many think in terms of religious politics, even though the political structures have been so devised as to provide for free play and participation in secular competitive politics.[7]

The role of minorities has attracted considerable attention from the political elite of independent India. While all the minorities, Sikhs, Christians, and Harijans, have been seeking political identity by various means within the framework of the democratic polity, the problem of Muslims in India has remained a difficult one.[8] This is mainly because of the effects of partition which gave legitimacy to the two-nation theory based on religion. Writers on Muslim problems contend that the partition of the country created peculiar problems for both Muslims and Hindus. In the words of Moin Shakir, 'The creation of Pakistan rocked the secular outlook of the Hindus who began to nurse a sense of permanent "injury". What the Muslim community got out of independence and partition was a sense of insecurity, frustration and uncertainty.'[9] The after effects of partition are still visible in the thinking of the Muslims in India. It is argued that as a result of partition the Muslims paid a heavy price in terms of culture and political status.[10] The Hindu community on the whole remained intact while the Muslim community was truncated and split into three groups - in Pakistan, Bangladesh, and India. It is pointed out, therefore, that the Muslims of independent India emerged as a new community and their position is no longer similar to what it was prior to independence. The result is continuing mistrust between the two major communities of the country. Since the two-nation theory is no longer valid, the Muslims in India are faced with the dilemma of their new role in the country - their political identity is still to be firmly established.[11]

It is often stressed by commentators on Muslim politics that Muslims in India have yet to identify themselves fully with the mainstream of national life. This is principally because of a feeling among them that they have become second-class citizens since

partition.[12] It is pointed out that the privileges of
the community have been snatched away: reservation in
the services has been abolished, adult franchise and
joint election have replaced separate and limited
electorates; the zamindari system which benefited a
number of Muslims has been done away with. There is
large-scale unemployment among the Muslims. In some
states recruitment of Muslims to the police was stopped
under ministerial orders on the plea that they had been
over-represented in the past. The evacuee property law
was used to deprive Muslims of their property on a wide
scale. The result has been, writes Moin Shakir:

> Demoralized by events of partition, Muslims, have a
> tendency to live in the past, the habit of clinging
> to memories of the past power and the glory and the
> isolationists conservatism constituted a serious
> handicap to a readjustment required of them in
> independent India.[13]

The elite among the Muslims play upon this psychology of the Muslim masses and have furthered their own
interests at the expense of the national by making an
issue of the neglect of the Muslims. The Muslim elite
in independent India has become 'a great hindrance'
for the community in its identification with the
national mainstream, i.e. the process of nation-building
on democratic and socialist lines. It is believed that
the elite can afford to be communal 'without losing anything' and without losing its effectiveness. 'Being
the leader of the community the elite operate only with
a traditional idiom.'[14] Thus, one sees the phenomenon
of a mass sense of insecurity being exploited by the
elite, to whom religion has become a symbol to rally
the general masses.

Against this background there has been a crisis of
identity for Muslims in independent India. One can
discern two approaches to the role of the Muslims in the
country. Some like Maulana Azad pleaded for national
integration. Azad was in favour of Muslims sharing the
common political destiny of the country.[15] Others have
advocated an isolationist approach - the approach of
the communal leaders. The several Muslim organizations
which have started functioning in independent India
'nursed the fears of the most Muslims', and advised
them not to participate in democratic elections 'for
their own safety and in their own interest.'[16] They
advocated separate electorates and the right to impart

religious instruction to Muslim boys and girls in
educational institutions. Their objective was that
'Muslims should form themselves into strong pockets....
This should be done even with the best cooperation in
the world with the Hindus. It is politically desirable as well as necessary for survival and also
culturally desirable.'[17]

Caught up in this fierce controversy, the Muslims
are divided among themselves - a small secular-minded
elite pleading for full integration into the national
stream; others arguing for maintaining their separate
identity.[18]

Minority politics in the state of Andhra Pradesh, in
particular in Hyderabad city, should be viewed in this
all-India perspective. While Muslims remained aloof
from politics for some time after 1948, they started
taking part in the late 1950s. There are several
Muslim organizations which claim to represent the
Muslims in the state, but the most important of them is
the Majlis-e-Ittehadul-Muslimeen, which has been playing
a significant role as the champion of Muslim interests.
Majlis (its popular name) as an association is a case
of a minority party articulating the interests of the
community and promoting the exclusive character of this
community, leading its followers to believe that by
joining the mainstream they would lose their identity
and their interests would suffer.

The Majlis has had its ups and downs in its political history of nearly half a century, including a period
of about nine years when it was dormant. It had its
birth in the old Hyderabad state in 1929 with the object
of bringing the different sects of Muslims together in
a state where the majority of the people were Hindus
and the ruler was a Muslim. There have been four
distinct phases in the life of the Majlis.[19]

1) 1929 to 1938: During this period its main aim was to
   unite the various sects of Muslims in Hyderabad
   state; in other words, its accent was on religion.

2) 1938 to 1944: This is the period during which it
   became a predominantly political organization.

3) 1944 to 1948: This was a period when the Majlis
   developed a para-military wing called the Razakars.
   The role of the Majlis ended with the Police Action,
   as a result of which the state of Hyderabad was
   merged with the Indian dominion. Majlis ceased to
   exist for about nine years.

4) 1957 to the present: Majlis was revived and continues to play an active political role.

The beginning of the Majlis in Hyderabad where,
though the Hindus were in a majority, the Muslims were
the ruling elite, can be traced to religious intentions.
Majlis was formed as a 'defence mechanism' to unite the
fragmented Muslims of the different hostile sects in
Hyderabad.[20] A few 'pious Muslims' gathered together
and considered steps to promote unity among the Muslims.
The declared objectives of the Majlis at that time were
three:

1) to unite and help the various Islamic sects in the
   solution of their common problems within the principles of Islam;

2) to protect the economic, social and educational
   interests of the Muslims;

3) to express loyalty to the land and to the ruler, and
   to respect the prevailing laws of the realm. Though
   occasionally it made representations to the government, it remained largely a quasi-religious body.

There was no need for the Majlis to be politically
active at that time because of the privileges which
were enjoyed by the upper and middle strata of the
Muslims. A political party was

> considered not only anti-social and uncultured but
> also below the dignity of the elite who visualised
> it as being contrary to their basic values of life,
> in which association for political or economic
> demands was recognised as being a big come down from
> the high pedestal of noble 'individualised' living.[21]

The proverbial hypocrisy of the feudal environment was
such, writes Rasheeduddin Khan, that even the large
'have-not' section of the Muslims imagined that they
also by the fact of being Muslims were part of the
ruling elite, and that indeed 'they' in their totality
were the real rulers of Hyderabad![22]

The second phase of the Majlis starts with the
eruption of communal riots in 1938 in the city in which
two Muslims closely related to the organization were
killed. The communal tension that prevailed not only
in the city but also in certain districts made the
Majlis impress upon the Muslims the need for an organization of their own. It was felt that the interests

of the Muslims should be defended in an organized manner. This is the period which saw the rise of Nawab Bahadur Yar Jung, who became the undisputed and distinguished leader of the Majlis. It was he who made the Majlis effective in the eyes of the general Muslim community. He 'soon became a hero and continued to have the mandate of his community until he breathed his last.'[23] Bahadur Yar Jung was a charismatic personality, a deeply religious and widely read man. He was one of the finest speakers of the Urdu language. Though an aristocrat by birth, he was able to command the loyalty of the Muslim masses. It was largely due to his dedication and untiring efforts that the Majlis became a very popular organization among the Muslims. Several branches were established in the various districts of the state. During his time, it was asserted in the constitution of the Majlis that

> The ruler and throne are the symbols of the political and cultural rights of the Muslim community in the State. This status of Muslims must continue for ever. It is, therefore, for this, that the maintenance of the prestige of the ruler must attain first importance whenever a change in the constitution has to be effected.[24]

According to him the Nizam was the symbol of Muslim sovereignty. 'We are the monarchs of Deccan. His Majesty's throne is an expression of our political and cultural sovereignty. Ala Hazrat is the soul of our monarchy and we are the organism of his monarchy. If he does not remain we also do not and if we vanish he simultaneously does.'[25]

This was the period of the second world war and towards its end the intentions of the British became visible. The Majlis felt that with the lapse of British paramountcy Hyderabad should become an independent state.[26] They asserted the right of Muslims to remain dominant and powerful in the state; Hyderabad was a permanent empire, Hyderabad had a Muslim monarchy, and it should remain so; Hyderabad is a part of the Islamic organism that spreads over north and south, east and west. This was the time when the Majlis was seeking an independent status for Hyderabad from Britain and also from the Indian dominion which was likely to emerge. As Bahadur Yar Jung said, 'what Majlis wants is complete independence which while releasing Hyderabad from one would not subordinate her to yet another

119

power.'[27]

The Majlis was afraid of the likely emergence of Hindu-dominated India and it struggled hard to retain Muslim dominance in Hyderabad. However, Bahadur Yar Jung accepted the futility of such an attempt because Hyderabad was surrounded by the Indian dominion; retaining the existing character of Hyderabad was only a dream. Since the Hyderabad problem could not be tackled in isolation, contacts with the Muslim League were established at the all-India level. In a way, the Majlis functioned as a unit of the League in Hyderabad and promoted the cause of Pakistan among the Muslims of the state. The Majlis vigorously championed the cause of Muslims in the state and emerged as their most important representative body.

The sudden death of Bahadur Yar Jung in 1944 was a serious set-back to the Majlis, for it had been nurtured by Jung and he had become indispensable to the organization. It is one of those instances where the organization is fully shaped by a distinguished individual and becomes entirely dependent on that individual. Jung became a father figure for the Muslims and on his death the Majlis was orphaned. There was a crisis of leadership in the Majlis; two individuals, Abul Hasan Syed Ali and Maulana Mazhar Ali Kamil, became presidents one after the other for a brief period, but neither was able to manage the organization. Then came the turn of Kasim Razvi. He was a lawyer by profession. Though highly controversial and fanatical, he was a dedicated worker of the Majlis. Thus the vacuum created by Bahadur Yar Jung was filled by the 'little corporal', the flamboyant Kasim Razvi, who had earlier given a large portion of his private property to the Majlis, thereby earning the title of Siddiq-i-Deccan (the generous of the Deccan). Razvi was a fluent rabble-rouser with histrionic talents.[28] During the period of his presidency the Majlis became a strong, militant organization and strengthened its para-military wing, the Razakars (literally volunteers, people's militia). The organization became very popular among the Muslim masses and youth, but it also became a symbol of oppression in the state.[29]

This was the time when momentous changes were taking place in the subcontinent. With the withdrawal of the British, the states were given the option of joining either of the two dominions - India or Pakistan. Though the location of Hyderabad was such that it could

120

not avoid being part of the Indian dominion, the Nizam
decided against being part of either India or Pakistan.
However, in view of the logic of its location, it was
necessary for the state to have a close understanding
with the surrounding country, for which purpose negotiations were started between Hyderabad and India.
These negotiations did not lead to any fruitful results
because the atmosphere was surcharged with suspicion
on both sides. The Nizam refused to accede or accept
the paramountcy of the Indian government, and the
latter refused to accept Hyderabad as an independent
state. It could not tolerate 'a cancer in the belly'
or a 'Pakistani Island within India'. But with a view
to strengthening his position, the Nizam began to
depend on Razvi and the Razakars for support. Though
he posed as a helpless state ruler, he was in fact
aiming at more and more concessions. This made Razvi
even more powerful and he thought in terms of making
Hyderabad not only independent but also very strong.
He was at the peak of his power and able to influence
state politics; the hold of the Majlis over the military and police was total. The Majlis raised the
slogan of independent Hyderabad, and not being content
with it even thought of a 'march to Delhi'. One would
think that it was madness on the part of the Majlis to
entertain such an idea, but their calculation was that,
since India was preoccupied with other problems like
Kashmir, Baroda, and Bikaner, it would not like to
purchase trouble in the south. But when the Indian
forces finally attacked, the Hyderabad army, supported
by the Razakars, could last only five days. They were
eventually crushed and the Nizam surrendered. The
inevitable followed: the Razakars were disbanded and
Razvi was imprisoned. With this ended the third,
authoritarian phase of the Majlis. The vain dream of
sustaining a Muslim sultanate in Hyderabad, based on an
authoritarian dynastic rule and with the support of the
eleven to fifteen per cent Muslim population, was
shattered by the Police Action of the Indian army.[30]

After 1948 there was practically a vacuum in Muslim
communal politics. Hyderabad became a part of the
Indian Union; its politics now had to be in tune with
the rest of India. The Majlis was formally dissolved
in 1949 admitting the mistakes committed in the past
and finding fault with the fusion of religion and
politics. There was no Muslim political party in the
state between 1948 and 1957. The only important forum

was the Jamiat-ul-Ulema which articulated the depressed economic conditions of the Muslims following the merger with the Indian Union. During this period one witnesses an anti-Congress trend among the Muslims: some joined the Socialist or the Communist parties.

The Police Action and the merger of the state with the Indian Union not only hurt the pride of the Muslims because it led to the fall of the Nizam, who was believed to be their symbol, it also led for some time to violence and harassment of Muslims. The abolition of the Jagirdari system, though welcomed from a progressive angle, resulted in the unemployment of those Muslims dependent on Jagirs. In some places there was unauthorized encroachment on Muslim property. In view of the fact that their percentage in the services was high, there was retrenchment and forcible retirement of Muslim personnel. These grievances of the Muslims in the post-independence period drove them into the arms of the leftist political parties immediately after 1948. This was reflected in their electoral behaviour in 1952 and 1957 which indicates that the Muslim voters mainly supported the left parties and were anti-Congress during this period.

Revival of the Majlis

The Majlis was revived in 1957 when Razvi was released from jail. Since he was migrating to Pakistan, he nominated Abdul Wahid Owaisi, a lawyer, as the president. Owaisi built up the Majlis patiently into a strong organization, basing its structure entirely on the exclusive character of Muslims.

The wounds of the partition of the country and the Police Action in the state being still fresh in the minds of the people, the general reaction to the revival of the Majlis was adverse. The secular political parties and even a few newspapers criticized its revival and felt that it was not in the interest of the Muslims. No less a person than Maulana Abul Kalam Azad was critical. 'Majlis had caused great disaster for Hyderabadi Muslims. Revival attempts would lead to dangerous consequences. Hope that this threat would be nipped in the bud', said the Maulana.[31]

These reactions did not deter Mr Owaisi from building up the Majlis. Though the build-up was quiet and unostentatious, eventually the Majlis became quite popular. A new constitution was framed in 1958, according to which the objectives of the Majlis were:

122

1) To prompt Indian Muslims to intelligently read the Quran, to propagate its teachings, and to persuade them to act on them;

2) To obligate the Muslims in general and members of the Majlis in particular to follow Shariat and avoid non-Shariat action especially in customs relating to gaiety and sorrow;

3) To try for the application of Islamic laws on Muslims through the parliament and the assembly and to urge the government to make religious instruction compulsory in public educational institutions;

4) To organize the collection of Zakat (religious tax) and the establishment of Baitul Mall (religious treasury) and through these and the Waqf (religious endowment) property to satisfy rightful Muslim demands under the Waqf laws;

5) To improve the moral standard of non-Muslim compatriots in order to help them become good citizens of India;

6) To protect and perpetuate under the Constitution of India all the interests which accrue to the Muslims either by inheritance or by fact and in the fulfilment of this object to procure subsidy from the Government;

7) To eradicate economic backwardness and unemployment among the Muslims and to procure for them jobs from the Government in consonance with the Muslim proportion in the population and in keeping with their talents and merits and find ways and means of getting other employment for them and to protect their rights;

8) To help the needy non-Muslims out of the savings of the Zakat;

9) To procure and protect, with loyalty to the Government of India, those rights which are given to Muslims of India by the Constitution;

10) To attempt that the Muslims of India, while observing Islamic tenets should maintain friendly relations with non-Muslims;

11) To participate in elections and nominations to the Parliament, the assemblies, the municipalities etc., to set up Majlis candidates, irrespective of

their caste or creed; and

12) To try to unite the Muslims religiously, socially,
    economically and for matters of common concern,
    irrespective of their sectional and denominational
    beliefs in keeping with the principles of general
    peace and morality.[32]

While the constitution points out the religious,
economic and political objectives of the Majlis, it is
emphatic on electoral participation. 'The political
aims are given a dominant position over the religious
and economic aims. Thus, even at the theoretical level
Majlis designs to survive through electoral politics
are obvious.'[33] The Majlis, therefore, no longer hid
its political intentions; it wanted to be a powerful
political organization championing the Muslim cause.
The days of being apologetic for mixing religion with
politics were over.

Role of the Majlis

During the last two decades the Majlis has emerged as
a strong, representative organization of the Muslims
in the state, especially in the city of Hyderabad. The
Majlis thrives not on any grandiose ideology but purely
on certain social, economic, religious and political
issues. No literature has been put out by the Majlis
to highlight its policies except its constitution and
the presidential addresses of Mr Owaisi. In these
speeches he has tried to invite the attention of the
Muslims to certain problems confronting them. In
every election the Congress party has obtained an
absolute majority in the state and has formed the
government since the first election. As Congress has
been in power, the Majlis has made it the main point
of attack and a whipping boy. The Majlis blames the
Congress for all the ills of the country and of the
Muslims. It portrays the Congress as a power-hungry and
self-seeking party. It blames the Congress for unemployment and vested interests. The Majlis, therefore, asks
for the creation of a special fund for economic rehabilitation of Muslims and reservation in the services
for them. It charges the Congress with promoting a
wrong type of Muslim leadership in the country. It
believes in exerting pressure on the political system
to promote the cause of its followers.

The Majlis is opposed to any amendment in Muslim
personal law. It asks for religious instruction in

state schools and universities. It is opposed to the
anti-religious characteristics of the present-day
education system. The Majlis vigorously champions the
cause of Urdu which it visualizes as the official link
language and also the second national language, so as
to solve the linguistic crisis. It asks for the recognition of Urdu as the second language in states like
Uttar Pradesh, Rajasthan, Bihar, and Andhra Pradesh;
inclusion of Urdu in the three-language formula, the
appointment of teachers who know Urdu; acceptance of
representations in Urdu in courts of law and government offices, and the establishment of two Urdu universities - Osmania in the south and Aligarh in the north.
It calls on the Muslims to preserve Islam and to work
for its ultimate domination in favourable conditions
like the Indian situation. According to the Majlis,
Islam is the only ideology which promotes the welfare
of the whole of mankind. Therefore, tremendous efforts
and sacrifices are needed to achieve these goals. All
these are very sensitive issues and the Majlis is very
skilful in exploiting them. It has no long-term
definite ideology. Barring a few general and wider
issues the entire attention of the Majlis is on local
matters.

To strengthen its claims and also to impress the
Muslim masses as their champion, the Majlis has been
demanding the appointment of a commission to look into
the grievances of the minorities. As far back as 1965
it adopted a resolution at its annual conference appealing to the government to appoint a commission of
enquiry to enquire into discrimination against Muslims.
This demand has been repeated several times. A little
later the Majlis asked for the creation of ministries
both at the state and central levels to implement
decisions taken about the Muslims.

Pointing out that the Muslim population in India is
very large and impressive, and greater in number than
in some of the sovereign Muslim countries, the Majlis
made a preposterous demand for a separate state for
the Muslims. This should be carved out on the eastern
sea board between Vishakhapatnam and Madras, where all
Muslims living in different parts of the country could
be rehabilitated and left to govern themselves within
the framework of the Indian union. The party president,
Mr Owaisi, made this formal proposal in a memorandum to
the President of India, the Union Home Minister and
others, and it was formally endorsed at the annual

conference of the party in 1968. They pointed out that
there was nothing wrong or anti-national in this
demand because the Government of India had agreed to
give a separate state to the Sikhs who were not as
large in number as the Muslims. This demand of the
Majlis evoked a furore in Parliament and invited
criticism from several quarters. The main criticism
was that the Majlis was adopting the old policy of the
Muslim League which had ultimately led to the partition
of the country. In view of this criticism the Majlis
modified its demand and asked for proportional representation for Muslims in Parliament, state legislatures,
and the services. In 1972 it demanded that Muslims be
appointed both at the centre and in the states to one
of the posts in each of the following categories:

1) President, Prime Minister, or Deputy Prime Minister.

2) Home Minister, Defence Minister, or Foreign
   Minister.

3) Defence Minister, Planning Minister, or Industries
   Minister.

4) State Governor or Chief Minister.

5) State Chief Minister or Finance Minister.

6) State Planning Minister or Industries Minister.

The resolution also desired that Muslims should be
given equal representation in high-ranking positions
in the administration, judiciary and legislature. As
an alternative to this proposal, it suggested the
formation of a Muslim sub-state in every state with a
sizable Muslim population as a solution to the communal
tangle in the body politic. This demand, however, has
not been stressed in subsequent conferences.

The Majlis advocated the need for self-defence among
Muslims at the annual conference in 1968. A resolution
was adopted approving the formation of a Muslim defence
organization and authorizing the leadership to hold
parleys with other Muslim parties and organizations.
Its president urged that the government should constitute a para-military organization of Muslims and impart
training in the use of modern weapons, and pointed out
that such a para-military force would not only counteract Hindu communal elements but would also be of immense
use in times of external aggression. A little later
the Majlis demanded that the government permit Muslims

to carry weapons of self-defence as in the case of
Sikhs. It is evident from these claims that the
Majlis harps on the psychological fear of the Muslims
that their lives are not safe in a Hindu-dominated
country. The fear of insecurity is the factor that
is always stressed by the Majlis.

Consistent with its exclusivist view of the Muslims,
the Majlis sought to mobilize Muslim opinion over the
issue of amendment to the Aligarh Muslim University
Act. It formed an All-Party Action Committee in 1972
and involved all Muslim political and cultural organizations. It pointed out that the character of Aligarh Muslim University should not be changed and that
it should remain a Muslim educational institution. In
doing this the Majlis tried to project itself as the
premier Muslim political organization in the region.
The Majlis also tried to enlist the cooperation of the
all-India Muslim bodies.

When the state was rocked by the agitation for a
separate state of Telengana, the stand of the Majlis
was that separation was an issue which did not very
much concern the Muslims. In other words, it was
indifferent on the issue and even gave a hint that in
a separate state the Muslims would be worse off. The
party announced that it would give political support
to those who were prepared to accept its fourteen-point
charter; this demands the appointment of a committee
to enquire into Muslim backwardness, an assurance that
no changes will be effected in the Sharia, recognition
of Urdu as the second regional language, representation
of Muslims in services in proportion to their population, allotment of houses constructed by the State
Housing Board on the basis of Muslim population, etc.
With a view to diverting the attention of the Muslims
from the issue of separation, it put forward the demand
that the twin cities (Hyderabad and Secunderabad)
should be constituted into centrally administered areas
if bifurcation of the state was decided. This was
indeed a very intelligent move which appeals to the
Muslims because it gives prominence to Hyderabad city
which is their stronghold. The party wants to highlight
the problems of the Muslim minority and also to maintain its separatist character in the body politic.

Electoral Performance

With a view to fighting for these causes, the Majlis
feels that it should make full use of the political

127

system of the country - it should not run away from
politics. The political weapon has to be used to
redress the grievances of the Muslims. It believes in
exerting pressure on the political system to promote
the cause of its followers. Therefore, the Majlis
thinks that it should enter local bodies, the legislature, and Parliament. To do this it must contest
elections. The Majlis contested municipal by-elections
for the first time in 1959 and came out successful by
securing 50% of the votes in one constituency and 65%
in another. Then in 1960 the Majlis entered the electoral contest with full self-confidence. It put up
30 candidates and secured 19 seats, a staggering
victory for the Majlis and a major defeat for the
Congress and other political parties. In the 1964
municipal elections it contested 33 seats but could
win only 8. This time it could not be as successful
as on the earlier occasion because of defections and
internal bickerings.

In the Assembly elections the Majlis has taken an
active part. It entered the Assembly for the first
time in 1962 when it contested three seats and won
one: Sultan Salahuddin Owaisi (son of Abdul Wahid
Owaisi) defeated Mausuma Begum, a Muslim cabinet
minister. In the 1967 general elections, the party
contested six seats from the city and won three of
them. This time the party also defeated Nawab Mir Ahmed
Ali Khan, the then Home Minister in the state government.
In the 1972 elections the party captured three seats in
the twin cities. This time, however, there was no
Congress minister to defeat. In the 1978 Assembly
elections, the Majlis contested five seats and won
three from its stronghold constituencies - Charminar,
Yakutpura, and Chandrayangutta. In the other two constituencies it secured a sizable percentage of votes.

It contested the Lok Sabha elections in 1971. These
were held against the background of separatist agitation
in the state. The Majlis was in favour of an integrated
Andhra Pradesh, arguing that integration was in the
interest of the Muslims, and not separation. It supported Badruddin Tayyabji who was a non-party candidate
for Parliament. He lost, however, to a candidate put
up by the Telengana Praja Samithi. This is a case of
regionalism winning against religious politics. In
the 1978 Parliamentary elections the Majlis president
Sultan Salahuddin Owaisi contested but lost to the
Congress candidate.

The electoral results clearly prove that the Majlis has now become in the eyes of the Muslims their main representative organization. Ever since its revival in the 1950s, writes Rasheeduddin Khan, 'the Majlis has become the focal point of Muslim communal polarisation, because it is the only exclusive Muslim political party in the city of Hyderabad.... it remains a sort of political fixation for the angry Muslim voters who having become cynical of improvement, tired of Congress hypocrisy and unimpressed by 'left' and 'right' ideology, use elections for their vicarious pleasure of mud-slinging at the authorities that be.'[34]

Despite its claim to be an all-India party the Majlis is basically a local party. Its influence confined mainly to the city of Hyderabad and a few urban centres in the state. The demographic setting of Hyderabad city is highly favourable to the Majlis. The city can be broadly divided into northern and southern zones. In the north there are different communities which intermingle with each other and no one has a majority. Southern Hyderabad is the area where most of the Muslims live and it is also economically backward. In the state the percentage of Muslims is about nine, but in Hyderabad district 26.45% are Muslims of whom 88% live in Hyderabad city. This 88% constitute about 43% of the total population, spread over 23 municipal wards, and is large enough to compose 18 Muslim-majority wards, which in turn provide for Muslim-majority constituencies. Viewed against this demographic picture, the electoral performance of the Majlis is a faithful reflection of the Muslim percentage in the electoral population. The Majlis claim that it represents the Muslims is vindicated by the electoral results.

Leadership and Organization

As a party the Majlis has been a closed or pocket organization of the Owaisi family, for since its revival in 1957 no other person than the father and the son has become president. According to the constitution the president is assisted by a general secretary, executive committee, organizing committee, and election board. There are also district organizations of the Majlis. Unlike the well-established parties, the Majlis has no youth, women's, or labour wings. The Majlis as an organization seems to become active at the time of annual conferences. The style of functioning of the Majlis is characterized by personalized leadership. 'In fact the history of the revived organization during the last 18 years has been coeval with the political life and designs of the Owaisi family and it is not for nothing that people refer to it as a two-men show.'[35] In view of the fact that the senior Owaisi is the person responsible for reviving the Majlis, a close personal relationship between this family and the Muslim community has emerged. The latter appreciate that it was he who revived the Majlis when everybody criticized it. What is more, he has the distinction of having been nominated by Kasim Razvi. At the annual party conferences people generally profess their loyalty to Owaisi.

There has, however, been criticism of the personalized and patriarchal nature of the leadership and its involvement in patronage politics. It is also believed that the junior Owaisi who now leads the party maintains the right type of relations with persons in power and does not allow them to go unexploited.

The party has been shaped in such a manner that the father and after him the son became president. It does not encourage defections from other parties and always prefers a paternal attitude towards its followers. Thus there has never been any competition for the number two position in the Majlis. The executive which consists of people who are not very well educated and have not been abroad is no threat to the president. 'From the very outset the dynastic leanings became visible when the father on his arrest in mid-March, 1958, nominated his son to the Presidentship.'[36]

Dissatisfied with the working of the Majlis, a section of the leadership led by the general secretary revolted; this led to a split in the organization. Those who left the Majlis formed a rival body but could not become a serious threat to it.[37] The main charges against Abdul Wahid Owaisi and his son were that they were playing passion politics and had adopted a pro-government stance over the Bangla Desh issue. But the rival organization could not cut into the support base of the Majlis and lost very badly in the 1972 assembly elections. This attempt to challenge the leadership of Abdul Wahid Owaisi failed miserably and it proved to be emotionally humiliating to them.[38] The earlier attempts of some of the members to shift the policy of the party over the issue of a separate

Telengana had also failed and these people had had to
resign from the party. It is clear, therefore, that
the hold of the Owaisi family on the Majlis is total
and unshakeable. It is not likely that it will produce
any new leader because it has carefully kept competent
people outside the organization. The son who has
been groomed for leadership has now emerged as a
seasoned politician and has developed a charisma
his own among the Muslim masses. His reputation as the
giant killer in elections has further strengthened his
leadership role. The rhetoric employed by the younger
Owaisi appeals to the masses. Their tactics also have
paid dividends because they have been able to get a
few concessions from government e.g., Darus Salam, the
headquarters of the Majlis, has been given back to them.
Similarly, their stand on an integrated state has been
vindicated by subsequent events. The government also
hesitates to do anything which will affect Muslim
personal law. Further, they have been able to secure
some status for Urdu in the state. These and other
gains appeal to the Muslim masses and for quite some
time to come there does not seem to be any threat to
the Majlis leadership.

Conclusion

The revival of the Majlis and its popularity among the
Muslims of the old city of Hyderabad are not isolated
phenomena, they are symbolic of minority politics all
over the country. Muslim organizations were in dis-
repute and suffered a set-back immediately after independence; the creation of a state on the basis of
religion affected the image of the Muslims in India,
for they were looked upon as people who have extra-
territorial loyalties. Most of the Muslims themselves
did not feel comfortable and their identity with the
nation was in doubt. Unlike other minorities such as
the Christians and Parsis whose nationalism was never
in doubt, in the case of the Muslims their identity
with the nation was uncertain.[39] However, with the slow
assertion of the democratic polity and stabilization of
political conditions in the country, several Muslim
organizations appeared on the scene and have taken
advantage of the opportunities that exist in the democratic set-up. By appealing to the exclusivist or
fear psychology of the Muslims, several organizations
became their spokesmen. These organizations seem to
flourish better in areas where Muslims are concentrated

in large numbers and their economic conditions are woe-
ful. Therefore, in addition to appealing to Muslims'
minority character, such organizations also derive help
from their demographic and economic conditions.

The dilemma faced by the leadership in the country,
which has a secular commitment, is how to appeal to
the masses who are steeped in tradition and religious
modes of thought and can become an easy prey to passion
politics led by a segmental leadership. This is a
phenomenon witnessed in most of the third world
countries where, with increasing mass participation in
politics, the secular elite is at loggerheads with the
communal elite, the latter's base being an appeal to
particularistic loyalties. Religion, 'that traditional
legitimizer' of socio-economic and political structures,
is presenting itself 'as a qualified candidate for the
job.'[40] Religious interest groups, religious political
parties and religious communal groups are becoming
prominent actors in the new mass activity known as
politics. Religious leaders and clerical groups
utilize sacred symbols to mobilize the masses in
elections or even in riots aimed at other religious
groups. In liberal democratic systems religious consciousness is playing an important role. However,
Donald Smith is of the opinion that while the prospects
for such religious consciousness are significant in
transitional politics, their future seems to be dim.
'Politics has its own goals and its own "laws" and
generates its own motivations. While religion, a mass
phenomenon in traditional societies, can play a useful
role in transitional societies in making politics
meaningful to the apolitical masses, the general forces
of secularization of culture and society will, in the
long run, erode its political effectiveness also.'[41]
For in the long run particularistic ideologies give
ground before universalistic ideologies such as
socialism. Smith asserts that secularization in its
many forms both subtly erodes and frontally attacks
these phenomena, but they are not going to disappear
tomorrow.[42]

The conflicts generated by segmental social divisions
in India are not inherently anti-national because social
divisions are not automatically being translated into
political cleavages. The political system, being
pluralistic, is able to absorb them. By and large,
writes Rajni Kothari, 'political involvement, wherever
it has taken place, has reduced the sense of isolation-

ism and particularism of Muslims ....'[43]

The experience of six general elections and the
performance of the political system clearly reveals
that while passion politics based on communal loyalties
play a very significant role, the secular political
parties are able to absorb these loyalties.[44] It is
true that there are pockets of communalism which are
confronted with secular forces, but the secular parties
by appealing to religion and language and by providing
opportunities in decision-making processes are, by and
large, able to weaken the communal forces at the
national level. However, these forces thrive in a
regional and local atmosphere. The case of the Majlis-
e-Ittehadul-Muslimeen proves this point clearly; the
Majlis is able to command Muslim loyalties in areas
where Muslims are in a majority and are poor. The
Muslims, writes Rasheeduddin Khan, have their best
friend in the Majlis.

> By playing passion politics, by repeating the theme
> tune: 'hum ne bhi ke hai hukamrani in mumalik par'
> (we have also ruled over these dominions); by trans-
> forming election into an end in itself, and by using
> the frustrated mood of the Muslim masses for the
> satisfaction of keeping up their own leadership
> position, the Majlis is perpetuating myth, with-
> drawal and hate and thereby postponing the creative
> and positive role of the Muslims in the functioning
> of participatory democracy in India.[45]

The Majlis has not been able to emerge at the state or
national level. It has some appeal at the state level,
but its role is insignificant and it has to give way to
the national secular parties. The political base of
the Majlis is very narrow and is confined to the municipal level.

TABLE I

Muslim Population Figures

	Andhra Pradesh	Hyderabad District	Hyderabad City
Total population	43,394,951	2,787,693	1,356,760
Urban percentage	19.35	65.99	100
Muslim population	3,955,545	737,344	579,755
Percentage of Muslim population	9.0	26.45	42.7

Source: Census, 1971.

TABLE II

Performance of parties in municipal elections in Hyderabad 1960, 1964

Party	No. of Candidates		Seats Won		Percentage of votes	
	1960	1964	1960	1964	1960	1964
Congress	66	66	33	44	38.5	49.1
Majlis	30	30	19	8	17.7	15.4
Others	127	110	14	14	43.8	35.5

Calculated from election results.

Ram Reddy, 'Language, Religion and Political
Identity - The Case of the Majlis-e-Ittehadul-
Muslimeen in Andhra Pradesh'

1. Edward Shils, 'On the Comparative Study of New
States', in Clifford Geertz, ed., *Old Societies and
New States*, New York 1963, p.22.
2. See Jyotirindra Das Gupta, *Language Conflict and
National Development*, Berkeley 1970, p.1.
3. Ibid., p.2.
4. Ibid., pp.2-3.
5. Rajni Kothari, 'Nation-building and Political
Development', in S.C. Dube, ed., *India since Independence : Social Report on India 1947-72*, New Delhi 1977,
pp.510-31.
6. Ibid., pp.519-20.
7. See Myron Weiner, *The Politics of Scarcity*,
Chicago 1962, pp.3-5.
8. Rafiq Zakaria, 'Are Our Minorities Second-Class
Citizens', *Illustrated Weekly of India*, 7-13 May 1978.
9. Moin Shakir, *Muslims in Free India*, New Delhi
1972, p.1.
10. Ibid.
11. 'Although the divisions of religious community
have been less obstructive since independence than
before, they have not been wholly absent. The real
mood of the substantial body of Indian Muslims is
perhaps one of the mysteries of Indian life. Dazed
and subdued by partition and the disappearance of their
main leaders, the community seemed to accept as
inevitable loss of political identity': W.H. Morris-
Jones, *The Government and Politics of India*, London
1964, p.104.
12. See S. Harman, *Plight of Muslims in India*,
London 1977, pp.1-23; also Rafiq Zakaria, 'Are Our
Minorities Second-Class Citizens'.
13. Moin Shakir, *Muslim Attitudes*, Aurangabad 1974,
p.3; see also V. Gautam, 'Minorities', in S.C. Dube,
ed., op. cit., pp.130-52.
14. Ibid.
15. Moin Shakir, *Muslims in Free India*, pp.5-6.
16. Ibid., p.6.
17. Ibid.
18. Ibid; also Rafiq Zakaria, 'What have Muslims

done for Indian Secularism?', *Illustrated Weekly of India*, 29 December 1974.

19. Rasheeduddin Khan, 'Muslim Leadership and Electoral Politics in Hyderabad - A Pattern of Minority Articulation-I', *Economic and Political Weekly* 6, 15 (10 April 1971), p.786.

20. Muneer Ahmed Khan, 'Majlis-E-Ittehadul Muslimeen (A Case Study in Muslim Politics)', M. Litt. Thesis, Osmania University 1975, pp.7-29.

21. Rasheeduddin Khan, op. cit., p.787.

22. Ibid.

23. Muneer Ahmed Khan, op. cit., p.12.

24. Quoted, ibid., p.16.

25. Bahadur Yar Jung, quoted, ibid.

26. Ibid.

27. See ibid., p.19.

28. Rasheeduddin Khan, op. cit., pp.787-8.

29. Ibid., p.788: 'The Razakar terror was the death-rattle of a decadent regime, supported by degenerate adventurists who exploiting the Muslim community, in the name of God, religion and historical myths, indulged in reckless political gamble, which brought misery and turmoil to the people of Hyderabad including the Muslims.'

30. Ibid.; see also Muneer Ahmed Khan, op. cit., p.46.

31. Quoted in Muneer Ahmed Khan, op. cit., p.50; for other reactions see pp.48-50.

32. Rasheeduddin Khan, 'Charminar: A Profile in Communal Politics - A Case Study of Electoral Strategy and Behaviour in the Fourth General Elections in India, 1967, in a Traditional Urban Setting', unpublished paper, Department of Political Science, Osmania University,1969, pp.44-5.

33. Muneer Ahmed Khan, op. cit., p.54.

34. Rasheeduddin Khan, 'Charminar: A Profile in Communal Politics', p.48.

35. Muneer Ahmed Khan, op. cit., p.123.

36. Ibid., p.124.

37. Rasheeduddin Khan, 'Charminar: A Profile in Communal Politics', p.46.

38. Muneer Ahmed Khan, op. cit., pp.125-6.

39. Rafiq Zakaria, 'Are Our Minorities Second-Class Citizens'.

40. Donald E. Smith, *Religion, Politics and Social Change in the Third World - A Source Book*, New York 1971, p.3.

41. Ibid., p.4.
42. Ibid., p.6.
43. Rajni Kothari, *India,* Boston 1970, p.246.
44. Ibid.
45. Rasheeduddin Khan, 'Charminar: A Profile in Communal Politics', p.48.

REGION AND NATION: THE TELENGANA MOVEMENT'S DUAL IDENTITY

Dagmar Bernstorff

For the last three decades nationalism and nation-building in the third world have preoccupied the minds of politicians and political scientists alike. Yet, so far, there are few stable nations in Asia and Africa and nationalism as a political force has largely failed to integrate segmented societies. In southern Asia, nationalism based on religion could not hold together Pakistan; Sri Lanka has not evolved a national identity binding on Sinhalese and Tamils as well; and the Indian Union survives more for practical and structural reasons than because of nationalism. Far from inspiring socio-economic development, nationalism has served as a cover for the repression of regional, ethnic and religious groups, for example the Tamil minority in Sri Lanka, the Bengalis of former Pakistan, tribal populations and regional cultures in India. Nationalism was even used as an excuse to destroy the democratic structure, to suppress all criticism and to establish an authoritarian personal rule during the nineteen months of Emergency in India.

All over the world two trends can be observed: one towards political integration into large units; the other towards decentralization to small units. India - which can compare in size and complexity with the European Community - has not yet found the small political units which could effectively replace the plural community structure with its loyalties and ties. In a way linguistic sub-nationalisms have been more successful in India than nationalism itself. The states of the Union largely coincide with linguistic groups. But this principle - borrowed from European experience - increasingly shows its defects. Not only does it make these linguistic states rather inward-looking and, with education based on regional languages, cut off from other states, but regional tensions have developed within these states - many of which are as large as or even larger in population than European nations like Britain, France or Italy. However, to political decision-makers at the centre, regionalism has been and still is anathema. In the eyes of Indira Gandhi it was as poisonous as casteism or communism: 'a very serious threat to the development, progress, and unity of the country'.[1] The Janata government favours decentraliz-ation and Home Minister Charan Singh even prepared a discussion paper on the creation of smaller states in November 1977. But Prime Minister Morarji Desai seems to share the apprehensions of his predecessor about the internal upheavals a second reorganization of the states might create.

Ironically, it is the first linguistic state ever to be formed in India, Andhra Pradesh, where regional identities persist especially strongly. The existence of these regional identities led to a movement for the partition of that state and the formation of a state of Telengana, comprising the nine Telugu-speaking dis-tricts of the erstwhile state of Hyderabad, which had been merged with Andhra in 1956.

It is unnecessary to do more than summarize the main features of the Telengana Movement.[2] It lasted from 1969 until 1971 and its most obvious cause was the non-implementation of the safeguards for Telengana (the 'Gentlemen's Agreement' of 1956) by the Government of Andhra Pradesh, which has been dominated by politi-cians from Andhra, the more advanced region of the state. The movement started in January 1969 as a students' agitation which was joined by a civic associ-ation and later taken over by professional politicians, who effectively combined agitational methods with negotiations at the central level. After a peak of violence and counter-violence at the end of June 1969 the leaders were arrested and the agitation petered out. The Telengana Praja Samithi (TPS) then decided to work within the parliamentary framework and to endeavour to capture sufficient seats, both in the Assembly and in Parliament, to press their demand for a separate state. They succeeded in by-elections as well as in the Lok Sabha elections of 1971, when the TPS won 10 out of 14 seats in Telengana. For reasons which I shall explain below, a compromise was agreed upon and the TPS rejoined the Congress in September 1971.

The Telengana Movement can be studied under many aspects, for example what sparked it off, how it was organized, what methods it used, what was the role of the judiciary and how it affected the interplay of parties, factions, castes and communities. In this paper I am concerned only with one aspect: political identity. The Telengana Movement did more than reveal

the existence of a regional identity; it was a battle
between three identities: those of Telengana, Vishalandhra and India. And there was not just one perception of India's national identity, but two conflicting
ones: the perception of the central leadership and the
perception of the leadership of the Telengana Movement.

Telenganans see themselves as distinctly different
from fellow-Telugus of Andhra. The 'Telengana personality' - according to protagonists of the movement -
is based on refinement, cultural synthesis and what
they call 'cosmopolitanism'. Indeed, graceful manners,
tact and generous hospitality are striking characteristics of the inhabitants of Telengana, not only of
the elite, but of peasants as well. In their hierarchy
of values human relations seem to rank higher than
worldly success. Telenganans are generally unambitious
and unmercantile. I heard the view: 'We know the art
of leisure and are thus ahead of modern industrial
society'! Andhrans, in the perception of Telenganans,
are crude, their style of living primitive: 'They
drink tea out of saucers, they sleep on the floor, sit
on the floor, they walk without chappals, they spit
all around'.[3] A major criticism of the Andhrans is:
they are *nouveaux riches* and throw their money about.
Of course, only wealthy Andhrans can be seen spending
their money in Hyderabad. Hyderabadis don't even
speak of money!

Next to their refined style of living, the Telenganans are proud of their cultural synthesis between
north and south Indian, between Hindu and Muslim
culture. It is a result of history, the Telengana
having been ruled by northern Muslim dynasties since
the fall of the Kakatiya Empire in 1323. Andhra was
under Muslim rule too, but for a comparatively shorter
period, as part of Golconda and later Hyderabad and
was ceded to the East India Company in 1766. Andhra
was exposed to British influence earlier and more
thoroughly than the Telengana, and Madras was the city
Andhra looked to. Hence the two Telugu-speaking
regions developed along different lines. Andhra is
firmly a part of south India, Telengana combines
characteristics of north and south India.

There are differences also in material culture:
Telenganans, both Hindus and Muslims, mostly wear *kurta*
and *pajama*, Andhras prefer the *dhoti*, with a coloured
border. Construction of houses, bullock carts, even
rickshaws are different. Food in the Telengana is

north Indian, only hotter.

North Indian and Karnatak music coexist in Hyderabad, and Kavali performances draw large audiences of
Hindus. Andhrans and Telenganans speak the same language, but not the same Telugu. Apart from differences
in intonations, Telengana Telugu has drawn many words
from Urdu, like *derwasamu* (door) or *qalamu* (pen).
Andhra Telugu has borrowed words from Tamil and from
English, like *kappu* (cup). Both regions claim to
speak 'pure' Telugu. More important than the difference in spoken Telugu is the fact that the elites of
the two regions do not share the same literature.
Telengana has hardly produced Telugu writers, but it
has produced Urdu poets. Urdu was not only the language of the Muslim rulers, it was and is the *lingua
franca* in urban centres and the language of the Hindu
rural elite. This custom was strengthened by the fact
that until 1952 the medium of instruction at Osmania
University, Hyderabad, was Urdu, not English. Hence
members of the Hindu elite often know only spoken
Telugu, and read and write the more sophisticated
literary Telugu with difficulty. Their world of
symbols is drawn from Urdu literature.

From this cultural synthesis Telenganans derive that
element of their self-interpretation which is most dear
to their hearts: cosmopolitanism. Their meaning of the
term is: belonging to a centre where different cultures
meet, tolerance towards the many communities which have
moved into Hyderabad from all over India. It is argued
that different languages were no barrier to understanding: 'No one felt that one language was inferior and
the other was superior, the complexes we see today were
totally absent then.'[4] Asked to explain the term 'cosmopolitanism', Dr Chenna Reddy wrote: '...literally
the meaning is that in Telengana, because of the influence of Urdu and also the Marathi and Karnataka languages in the old Hyderabad State, they had given a
broadbased outlook and tolerance of different languages
and cultures. It transformed the nativity, narrowness
and, if I may say so, the crudeness of an isolated
[society]....'[5] Telenganans claim that Hindus and
Muslims lived very happily together in old Hyderabad
and point out that all religious festivals were
celebrated by everybody. This is somewhat euphemistic.
It is true that Hindus take part in the Moharram
processions and can even be seen performing *pujas* in
mosques, but religious peace in old Hyderabad was

141

guaranteed by very strict security measures, such as
confining Hindu processions to temple grounds or for-
bidding them to play music. And the years when Dasehra
and Moharram - rejoicing for Hindus and mourning for
Shia Muslims - coincided were a nightmare for the
Hyderabad police.[6] Intermarriages between Hindus and
Muslims took place only amongst the aristocracy.

In contrast the Telenganans see the Andhrans as
narrow-minded, provincial and particularly caste-
conscious. The future state of Telengana, so Madan
Mohan promised, 'will be an ideal place to live in,
where there will be no barriers of language, caste,
belief or sect.'[7]

How do the Telenganans see the relationship between
their regional and their national identity? It is
quite clear that the Telengana Movement never aimed at
secession from the Indian Union. On the contrary, they
see the Telengana with its 'tolerance and cosmopolitanism' as a model for the rest of India: '[Telengana] has
been a miniature India synthesizing the heterogenous
cultures of India. We shall ever preserve its cosmopolitan nature as an example for a whole nation that
peoples belonging to heterogenous languages, cultural
or ethnic groups could live together in harmony and
absolute fraternity. This will be a living example for
the whole of India to emulate.'[8] Needless to say, this
perception of Indian national identity - not entirely
inadequate - did not find acceptance at the centre,
even though at the time of the states' reorganization
Jawaharlal Nehru did see this advantage of Hyderabad
and tried to prevent the dismemberment of the princely
state. During the Telengana agitation it was suggested
that the Hyderabad state might be revived under the
name Deccan Pradesh, but this idea remained without
response.[9]

Telengana identity, obviously, is not based on either
language or religion; it is based on history. In the
course of history cultural characteristics and social
structures have grown in Telengana, characteristics and
structures different from those in the rest of the
Telugu country. If one wants to look for influences of
language and religion: it has been the language and
religion of the rulers - Urdu and Islam - which have
had their influence, but not as strong an impact as
they have had on the north of India. The refinement
of manners is part of a court culture at the centre of
the Telengana districts. The general attitude towards

life is pre-industrial and pre-colonial, and it is
tempting to speculate: was the whole of India like this
before colonial rule?

The seclusion of Telengana was helped by geographical factors. The Deccan Plateau is distinctly different from coastal Andhra beyond the eastern hills. With
Hyderabad at the centre of a (totally inadequate) road
system, there was little social communication with
Andhra before independence. As also the caste systems
of the two regions are somewhat different, marriages
across Andhra and Telengana remained rare even in the
1960s.

The cultural and historical identity of the Telengana posed a difficult problem for the leadership of
the movement for a separate state. The identity
largely derives from Muslim rule, but the predominantly Hindu leadership cannot admit this circumstance.
The Hindu leaders cannot possibly identify with the
feudal rule of the Nizams of Hyderabad, who treated
Hindus as second class citizens. Hence the stress on
'cosmopolitanism', which includes also immigrants from
other regions of India, like Marwaris or Tamils. Still,
Telengana is short of historical symbols, like heroes,
wars, glorious periods of the past, and this is a
weakness of the movement.

Political identity is, of course, not sufficient
in itself to start a movement for a separate state, but
without it, popular support cannot be mobilized.
Identity is an emotional group feeling which needs
other factors to translate it into political action,
namely: first, the experience of inequality - here *vis-
à-vis* Andhra, which started at a higher level of
development and continued to develop faster at the
expense of the Telengana, in spite of the Telengana
safeguards; second, an event to serve as a spark - in
this case the expiry of the Telengana Safeguards in
1969 and the world-wide students' movements; third, a
leadership which channels a latent feeling into action
and gives it organizational structure. Political
identity also has to be perceived, both by a large
number of inhabitants of the region and by the opponents of the manifestation of such an identity.

Before I deal with the problem of perception it is
relevant to analyse briefly the opposing political
identity, that of Vishalandhra, or Greater Andhra.[10]
The Andhrans too share a common group feeling, which
perceives the Telenganans as different. In the eyes of

143

the Andhrans, the people of Telengana are lazy, plea-
sure-loving, 'feudal', inefficient. They see themselves as active, modern, progressive. In fact,
Andhrans tend to have a superiority complex towards
Telengana and do not hesitate to show it. Having
fought for their own linguistic state, carved out of
Madras, they have some experience in drawing symbols
for Vishalandhra from history and culture. They
appeal to the memory of 3,000 years of 'common history',
starting from the Satavahana empire in the third century
B.C. Strictly speaking, only the Kakatiya Kingdom
(1081-1323) comprised approximately the area of present-
day Andhra Pradesh, but the argument runs: '... despite
various vicissitudes in political history, the Telugu
people have preserved their cultural unity uninterruptedly. Nannaya, the great pioneer hailing from Rajah-
mundry; Tikkana, who wrote his epic at Nellore; Pothana,
who was worshipped as the Doyen of poets from Telengana
- all three are equally enshrined in the hearts of the
Telugu speaking people, transcending all barriers of
time and history.'[11] The slogan 'The people are one,
but rulers have divided us' dominated the political
meetings of the integrationists. Andhrans would
probably be less interested in Telengana, if they had
an urban centre like Hyderabad in the Godavari delta.

As decisions on the creation of new states have to
be taken at the centre, it is relevant to ask how the
central leadership reacted to the two different identities articulated in Andhra Pradesh.

The central leadership perceived the movement for a
partition of Andhra Pradesh as a threat to the federal
structure and to economic development. There was a
fear that if Telengana was conceded, other movements
for the division of linguistic states would follow, for
example in Vidarbha, the old Mysore, in eastern Uttar
Pradesh (UP) and many other places. Indeed it would
have been difficult for the central government to find
a new principle to substitute for the language principle as a basis for the creation of new states.
Telengana's case was, however, fairly strong, as the
States Reorganisation Commission had in 1955 recommended
a trial period of 5 years for the merger of Andhra and
Telengana.

Neither the leadership at the state level, nor that
at the central level understood the political identity
underlying the Telengana Movement. While Brahmananda
Reddy treated it as a law and order question, Mrs

Gandhi and her Cabinet perceived the movement as an economic problem, which had to be dealt with at the economic and administrative levels. The creation of a new state was categorically ruled out: 'The states were reorganized after careful deliberations and if we are to achieve accelerated progress of the country as a whole, and specially to solve the problems of more backward areas and sections of people, we have to move now towards unity of purpose and national integration .... The dismemberment of a state is no solution to such problems: in fact it may well handicap economic progress. Any talk of separate statehood for Telengana is fraught with great consequences and needs to be discouraged with all the emphasis at our command.'[12]

The hypothesis underlying this statement, that economic progress can best be achieved in large states, has never been proven; on the contrary, Indian experience shows the opposite: the larger states like UP and Bihar are economically the most backward, whereas small states like Haryana, Punjab, Tamil Nadu are more advanced, albeit for more reasons than that of size.

Studying the reactions of central leaders to the Telengana Movement it struck me that their analysis was severely limited by firm assumptions about how Indian politics work: any trouble at state level was automatically attributed to factional conflicts. In the case of Telengana, another explanation - first advanced by the Communist parties - dominated the analysis of politicians and journalists alike: the Telengana Movement was termed a 'feudal movement'. Both notions are wrong. The movement started as a students' agitation and was then taken over by a group of lawyers, teachers and journalists without party affiliations. The main social base was provided by the Non-Gazetted Officers, who were hit by the integration of the two administrations. The first Congress politicians to defy party discipline and back the movement were all members of Chief Minister Brahmananda Reddy's own group: Konda Lakshman Bapuji, T. Anjiah, M.M. Hashim, Manik Rao. And these politicians do not belong to the politically dominant rural gentry. Hashim is an urban Muslim, the others belong to Backward Classes. So do Madan Mohan, the first president of the Telengana Praja Samithi, and Mallikarjun, the main student leader. Other student leaders come from families with small or medium-sized landholdings; most of them were in the first generation to receive university education. The insecurity of this

145

social group made them politically active. Factional
conflict entered into the movement later, after the
professional politicians joined it.

Madan Mohan, himself a Munnur Kappu, saw the movement for the separate state of Telengana also as a
movement to overcome caste barriers. Asked why they
had then made Dr Chenna Reddy chairman of the TPS, he
said they needed a Reddy to lead them for the time
being, 'but we have no patience with this caste business any longer'. But this integrative potential of the
Telengana Movement was not perceived by the central
leadership; the 'miniature India' was not conceded.

It is relevant here to ask how the Muslim minority
in the Telengana reacted to the movement for a separate
state. Out of the 3.5 million Muslims in Andhra Pradesh 2.5 million live in the Telengana, 500,000 of them
in Hyderabad itself, the rest mostly in small towns.
The Muslim population is largely an urban population,
but with the exception of the scattered remnants of
the former Muslim elite (many of whom moved to Pakistan) - a poor urban population. Politically, they
are mainly represented by the Majlis-e-Ittehadul-
Muslimeen, which won all the three seats in the old
city of Hyderabad at the assembly elections of 1967,
1972 and 1978. The leadership of the Majlis declared
itself neutral in the Telengana issue. In practice
the leaders stood behind the Chief Minister Brahmananda
Reddy, who had skillfully placated them by looking into
some of their grievances. A personal antipathy existing between the leader of the Majlis, Sultan Salahuddin
Owaisi and Dr Chenna Reddy seems to have influenced the
relationship of the two parties. (The estrangement
goes back to the early 1950s, when Dr Chenna Reddy had
to deal with the retrenchments of Muslims in the service
of the Nizam). Sultan Salahuddin Owaisi's personal
opinion was that Muslims have been neglected not for
twelve, but for the last twenty years (since the collapse of the Nizam's rule). He tends to think that
Telengana Hindus are 'worse' (i.e. more anti-Muslim)
than the Andhra Hindus - mutual prejudices have not
been overcome.

However, the reformist organization Tameer-i-Millat
supported the Telengana Movement. Their leaders
thought that Muslims would indeed be better off in a
separate Telengana State. As Taheer Ali Khan, the
Secretary-General, pointed out to me: 'I can't talk to
a minister from Andhra, he does not speak our language

146

(Urdu)'. The TPS promised that in Telengana Urdu would be restored as the second official language.[13] It was thought that the younger Muslims were more in favour of a Telengana State than was the older generation. A Congress Muslim, M.M. Hashim, the MP for Secunderabad, expressed the view: 'Muslims as a minority did not take part in the Independence Struggle. We must not repeat the mistake of staying aloof, but fight for Telengana.'[14] Obviously memories of the history of the Telengana region differ and the 'Telengana cosmopolitanism' is not perceived in the same manner by all inhabitants!

Curiously, it was another regional movement in the subcontinent which contributed to bringing the Telengana Movement to a halt: the movement for East Bengal's autonomy which led to the creation of Bangladesh. It is beyond the scope of this essay to examine the interaction of regional, national and international factors and their effect on Telengana. In short, during the surprise Lok Sabha elections of 1971 the TPS took part as a political party and won 10 out of 14 seats in the Telengana with 47% of the votes. This success was even more remarkable, as the Congress won a landslide victory nearly everywhere else in India, having mobilized the support of Harijans, Muslims and women with the 'Garibi Hatao' slogan. But with the balance of power in parliament so much in favour of Mrs Gandhi and her Government, the ten TPS members had less leverage than they had hoped for. The central cabinet was as adamantly against the creation of Telengana as before. The TPS leadership now had a choice between continuing the struggle, uncertain whether the electoral success of 1971 could be repeated in the Assembly elections due in 1972, or of negotiating a compromise. Dr Chenna Reddy chose the latter alternative and agreed on a six-point formula with Mrs Gandhi intended to remedy the economic, legal and political grievances of the Telengana, but within the framework of the continued existence of an undivided state of Andhra Pradesh.[15] Dr Reddy was much criticized for this decision, particularly as no written assurances were given by the centre and differences arose later as to the interpretation of the six-point formula. The TPS leader surely based his decisions on down to earth calculations. At the same time the crisis in East Pakistan built up, with India involved in it. One of the reasons Dr Chenna Reddy

advanced for having entered a compromise was: 'Inter-
nationally we can't give the impression the country
does not stand unitedly behind the Prime Minister!'[16]

Since that agreement was concluded, the Andhrans
have made some serious efforts to carry their Telugu
culture into the Telengana. The medium of instruction
at the university level is English and even young
Muslims do not learn Urdu properly any longer. However, the developmental gap between Andhra and Telengana has not been closed at all.

The Janata government is committed to decentraliz-
ation but has not so far taken any practical steps in
this direction. In Andhra Pradesh itself the power
constellation has been thoroughly changed as a result
of the Assembly elections in 1978. The Congress
(Conventionist) under the leadership of Dr Chenna Reddy
(who, having failed to be accommodated by the Janata
party, became reconciled with Mrs Gandhi) won a hand-
some victory in the Legislative Assembly elections in
1978 and the very leader of the Telengana Movement is
now the Chief Minister of Andhra Pradesh! The victory
can be only partly explained by the support Mrs Gandhi
still enjoys among Harijan and Backward Classes in
Andhra Pradesh (where the cruder policies of the
Emergency were not implemented). It is also due to Dr
Chenna Reddy having forged a coalition of enemies of
both Brahmananda Reddy (then Congress President) and
the (then) Chief Minister Vengal Rao. Last but not
least Dr Chenna Reddy is a dynamic and skilful organ-
izer of election campaigns (as he demonstrated in 1971
as leader of the TPS). If Dr Chenna Reddy was intent
on splitting the state of Andhra Pradesh, Mrs Gandhi
could not stop him now. Would he want it, being
Chief Minister of 'Vishalandhra'? The final decision
on Telengana has not been taken yet.

Bernstorff, 'Region and Nation: The Telengana
Movement's Dual Identity'

1. *Selected Speeches of Indira Gandhi. January 1966
- August 1969*, New Delhi 1971, p.85.
2. For detailed accounts see: Hugh Gray, 'The Demand
for a Separate Telengana State in India', *Asian Survey*
11, 5 (1971); Eckehard Kulke, 'Telengana - Eine neue
Variante des Regionalismus', *Internationales Asienforum*
1, 2 (1970); Dagmar Bernstorff, ed., *Wahlkampf in
Indien*, Dusseldorf 1971, chapter 6, and 'Telengana
Regionalism - Structure and Method of a Mass Movement'.
Papers presented to the 5th European Conference on
Modern South Asian Studies, Leiden, July 1976; K.V.
Narayana Rao, *Telengana. A study in the Regional
Committees in India*, Calcutta 1972, chapter 8.
3. A Telengana contractor, 11 October 1970.
4. A. Madan Mohan: 'What Telengana stands for', *The
Jai Telengana*, 10 July 1970. Madan Mohan, a young
lawyer, was the first chairman of the Telengana Praja
Samithi, He later resigned in favour of Dr M. Chenna
Reddy, a former minister in the Union cabinet and one
of the major political leaders of the Telengana. On
Dr Chenna Reddy see Dagmar Bernstorff, 'Political
Leadership in Andhra Pradesh', in B.N. Pandey, ed.,
Leadership in South Asia, Delhi 1977.
5. Dr M. Chenna Reddy in a letter to the author of
6 March 1975.
6. S.M. Ahsan, *Hindus in Hyderabad. Some facts and
figures*, Secunderabad ?1938, p.19.
7. A. Madan Mohan, 'What Telengana stands for', loc.
cit.
8. Dr M. Chenna Reddy: *Presidential Address. First
Annual Conference, Telengana Praja Samithi, 10-11
January 1970*, p.7.
9. *Indian Express* (Vijayawada edition), 28 June 1969.
10. The most substantial work on the creation of
Andhra is K.V. Narayan Rao, *The Emergence of Andhra
Pradesh*, Bombay, 1973.
11. Government of Andhra Pradesh, *United we stand*,
Delhi 1969, pp.1-2.
12. Indira Gandhi in a statement, *Indian Express*,
26 March 1969.
13. Interview with Taheer Ali Khan, 11 December 1970.
14. Interview with M.M. Hashim, 24 October 1970.

15. The six points were: 1. A separate budget and separate accounts for Telengana. 2. The continuation of the 'Mulki rules'. 3. Statutory powers to the Andhra Pradesh Regional Committee. 4. A separate State Congress Committee (PCC) for Telengana. 5. Review of the issue after three years. 6. The resignation of Brahmananda Reddy in favour of a Chief Minister from Telengana.

16. Interview with Dr M. Chenna Reddy, 23 November 1971.

CONFLICTING ROLES OF LANGUAGE AND REGIONALISM IN AN INDIAN STATE: A CASE STUDY OF ANDHRA PRADESH

R.V.R. Chandrasekhara Rao

When the relationship of language and religion to the concept of political identity is discussed the term political identity is usually used as a substitute for the term nation. And nation in its turn is understood to form the basis for a legitimate claim to the status of a sovereign state.

However, the Indian situation in this respect is entirely different. Indian nationalism actively discouraged the claims of religion to constitute a base for nationalism as also the idea of a language being a sufficient condition for separate national identity. Thus the factors, religion and language, which serve as mobilizers of political identity in most areas in recent times are regarded as detractors from Indian national identity.

But if the concept of political identity is understood in a wider and more flexible sense one finds that interaction between language and political identity is quite conspicuous in the Indian context. The division of India into linguistic provinces illustrates this point well. Though the ethos of Indian nationalism rejected the claims of linguistic identities to independent political status, it clearly recognized the fact that cohesive linguistic groups do aspire to some kind of political union and that the best way to satisfy these aspirations is to give them autonomous existence in a federal system. Yet a basic ambivalence about the effect of linguistic states on the higher all-Indian political identity remains in Indian political thinking. At one level of perception there is the strong conviction that the goal of Indian nationalism is to facilitate the development of cultural and linguistic diversity and that in consolidating the Indian linguistic sub-national identities lies the strength of the Indian nation.. On the other hand there is a lurking suspicion that identities based on language are likely to generate forces potentially harmful to the unity of India.

The point, however, is that the formation of linguistic states does constitute a deliberate policy

151

of recognizing the claims of language to separate political identity, though in a limited way. Subsequent Indian experience, especially in the case of the Telugu-speaking state of Andhra Pradesh, discloses some significant limitations to the role of language as a mobilizer. This paper seeks to highlight the experience of Andhra Pradesh.

A few background facts about the problems of the merger of the different Telugu-speaking areas of Andhra Pradesh should first be mentioned.

Broadly speaking, the present state comprises three distinct regions: (1) the coastal districts extending from the Tamil Nadu border to the Orissa border, called the Circar districts, (2) Rayalseema, consisting of four districts, and (3) the Telengana area with nine districts.

The Circar districts were acquired by the East India Company during the eighteenth and nineteenth centuries. The Rayalseema districts were ceded by the Nizam to the East India Company a little later; and the Telengana districts remained a part of the Nizam's dominions till 1949. Thus the first two areas formed part of the erstwhile Madras Presidency while Telengana remained till post-independent times distinctly separate.

The different historical settings in which the coastal and Rayalseema areas (Andhra) on the one hand and the Telengana area on the other evolved produced two distinct regional identities among the Telugu-speaking peoples. As parts of British India the Circar districts and Rayalseema registered a higher level of development, especially in terms of education. The use of English as the official language further helped the process of modernization in these areas. The Telengana areas were at a disadvantage. There was very little growth even in secondary education in Telengana under the Nizam's rule; in fact the Telengana districts fared even worse than the Kannada-speaking and Marathi-speaking districts of Hyderabad state. Economically too, little was done to improve agriculture in Telengana, which was prone to regular droughts.

The result was that the Telengana and Andhra areas drifted apart, each acquiring a separate identity associated as they were with two distinct political connections.

To this trend was added the different evolution of the Telugu language itself. Mostly because of the

domination of the Urdu language in Telengana, Telugu
experienced an arrest in development. Telugu as
spoken in Telengana was considered hybrid and impure
by the people in Andhra areas. This factor led to an
unhealthy manifestation of feelings of superiority
among the Andhrans which the Telengana people came
increasingly to resent.

The above facts are meant to explain how the Telugu-
speaking people became divided into two broad groupings
with different levels of development and even two
different levels of linguistic growth. And yet it is
in this century that the movement for Telugu unity
developed and reached fruition.

We shall now briefly trace the development of the
movement for a Telugu-speaking state and examine how
the forces of separate identity affected the role of
language.

The Movement for a Telugu-speaking Andhra State

The movement originated with the coastal Andhra people
asking for a separate Andhra province as a reaction
against the domination of the Tamils in the then
mammoth Madras Presidency. Diverse factors aided the
emergence of Andhra consciousness. The nationalist
movement lent a helping hand in recalling regional
linguistic and historical traditions. Simultaneously
in Telengana also the Telugu movement found its echo.
After all it should not be forgotten that Telugu-
speaking people constituted the bulk of the population
of the Nizam's kingdom. By the 1930s the movement for
what is called 'Vishalandhra' (Greater Andhra comprising
all the Telugu-speaking areas) came into prominence.
It is doubtful to what extent people then visualized
Vishalandhra as a practical proposition. Even the
prospect of separating the Andhra districts from Madras
was vetoed by the British. However, there is no doubt
that Telugu-speaking people started thinking for the
first time about a separate political identity
within the larger national framework. After independence the Andhra agitation for a separate province
assumed greater importance, fortified by the long-
standing commitment of the Indian National Congress to
reorganize India on linguistic lines. Even though the
central leadership vacillated for some time, the death
of Potti Sriramulu, after a fast in protest against the
centre's reluctance to form an Andhra province,
precipitated the birth of the state. The Telugu-

speaking districts were separated from Madras and the
new Andhra state was inaugurated in 1953.

This gave a spur to the aspiration for Greater
Andhra, that is, for the addition of the Telugu-speaking areas of Hyderabad state to the new Andhra state.
The appointment of the States Reorganisation
Commission and the public debate about linguistic
provinces provided a very favourable background to the
aspiration for political identity by the Telugus.

While the leadership in Andhra state was unreservedly
enthusiastic about Vishalandhra, opinion among the
Telugu people of Hyderabad was divided. Generally,
those who had been active in the movement for the
revival of Telugu literature and culture in the past
positively welcomed the proposal for a merger of
Telangana with Andhra state. But another section
opposed the proposal. Their opposition to the formation of Vishalandhra was ostensibly based on the
desirability of retaining the multilingual personality
of Hyderabad. But in reality the opposition was
caused by the fear that the Telengana area would be
taken over by the more resourceful and clever people
from coastal Andhra. That this was partly inspired by
the selfish interests of the Telengana leadership
cannot be denied. First, Telengana accounted for
little more than one-third of the population of the
proposed combined Andhra state and this meant that
the Andhra region would in fact become the dominant
region. Secondly, the Reddy community, which is the
dominant caste in Telengana, feared that they would be
overshadowed by the Reddys from the Rayalseema region.
But this wrangling among the power elites for the
retention of power would not have gained respectability
without the presence of genuine misgivings about the
economic interests of the region if it merged with
Andhra. First, there was the fact of Telengana's
underdevelopment, educationally and economically.
Would the Andhrans pay special attention to these
problems? Would not a merger enable the Andhrans to
take advantage of the job opportunities in Telengana?
Secondly, Telengana is a revenue-surplus area (mainly
because it had not adopted the policy of prohibiting the
manufacture and consumption of liquor) and there were
strong apprehensions that these surpluses might be
diverted to non-Telengana use. Yet, because of the
Congress party's influence those who favoured merger won
the day in 1957. The Andhra leaders were prepared to

provide safeguards to Telengana under which the region's economic interests, financial surpluses and future employment opportunities were to be fully protected. These safeguards were contained in the Gentlemen's Agreement signed on 20 February 1956.

This agreement guaranteed that Telengana surpluses would be reserved for expenditure on Telengana develop- ment- that policies such as the prohibition of liquor, which would reduce Telengana revenues, would not be implemented without the Telengana legislators' consent; that seats in educational institutions in Telengana would be provided in order to assure employment opportunities in the Telengana area; that sales of agricultural land were to be controlled by a regional council; that in the state cabinet, if the Chief Minister was from the Andhra area, the Deputy Chief Ministership should go to Telengana; and that at least two of the important portfolios in the state cabinet should be assigned to Telengana Ministers. But the most important part of the agreement was the decision to establish a Telengana regional council to deal with the implementation of these safeguards and those relating to planning and development, irrigation, industrial development and recruitment to services in the Telengana area.

The central government, which encouraged the Andhra and Telengana leaders to iron out their differ- ences and reach the agreement, quickly gave legal sanction to its terms by creating a regional committee and by enacting the Andhra Pradesh Public Employment Act.

The Regional Committee

Acting on the powers conferred by Article 371 of the constitution the President of India constituted regional committees for Telengana and Punjab. It is important to note that the position of the Punjab region *vis-à-vis* the Punjab (including the present Haryana state) was treated as analogous to that of Telengana *vis-à-vis* Andhra Pradesh. The Telengana Regional Committee, however, was not strictly a statutory body, in the sense that it was created by executive order and not by legislative enactment. It consisted of all the members of the Andhra Pradesh Assembly representing Telengana constituencies. It was required to meet at least once in three months. The committee, as a committee of the Andhra Pradesh Assembly, was empowered

to look into all bills (except money bills) affecting
the Telengana region. In addition, the presidential
order creating the committee also provided for a
schedule of items coming under its jurisdiction.
Issues relating to planning and economic development,
education, local administration and services formed
the core of the subjects on which the committee
concentrated.

No legislation which affected Telengana could be
enacted by the Andhra Pradesh legislature without the
regional committee expressing its opinion after
detailed discussions, although the committee could not
veto proposed legislation. In case the Assembly
disagreed with the recommendations of the committee,
the Speaker was obliged to refer both the bill passed
by the Assembly and the report of the committee for the
consideration of the Governor. The Governor was
empowered either to give his consent to the bill as
passed by the Assembly or to return it to the Assembly
recommending either that it be withdrawn or that it be
passed in the form suggested by the regional committee.
Though there have been no occasions which warranted
the reference to the Governor, or rejection by the
Council or Assembly, these provisions show that the
regional committee is an essential organ in the process
of law-making as far as regional bills are concerned
and that its recommendations cannot easily be brushed
away by the Assembly.

The chairman of the regional committee, elected by
the members of the committee from among themselves, is
a powerful figure. In this context it is significant
to note that the Chief Minister and the Speaker, even
if they belong to the Telengana region, are excluded
from membership of the regional committee. Therefore,
rivalry between the offices of Chief Minister and
chairman of the regional committee is built into the
arrangement.

The second important measure taken by the central
government to implement the Gentlemen's Agreement was
the enactment of the Public Employment (Requirement as
to Residence) Act in 1957. Under this the central
government imposed residential requirements for
recruitment into the public services (including local
bodies). By this measure job opportunities in Telengana were to be reserved exclusively to Telengana
people.

It is relevant to state that, under the general

scheme of fundamental rights, discrimination in matters
of public employment within a state on grounds of
caste, sex, language and residence alone is not
allowed. But an exception was made: under special
circumstances residential qualifications could be
prescribed even within a state. This was provided for
precisely to meet situations where, because of
different historical backgrounds, a particular region
might have to be given special treatment in matters of
employment.

The provision for reserving Telengana jobs for
Telengana people is known locally as the Mulki rules.
The word 'Mulki' connotes the concept of 'son of the
soil'. Hyderabad state had similar rules for quite
some time. In fact these rules came into existence
because of local peoples' resentment at the importing
of Muslims from outside to fill high posts in the
Nizam's administration. In the course of time local
feeling crystallized into opposition to the entry of
the Andhrans into Telengana jobs and educational
institutions. Therefore the Public Employment Act
meant the continuation of the Mulki rules through
central enactment.

The spirit behind the Gentlemen's Agreement reveals
the ambivalence of the parties on the issue of a
single Telugu-speaking state. The fact that at last
the concept of Vishalandhra was realized and that the
leaders had agreed to the merger could be taken as
proof that language as a unifying factor was able to
prevail over other considerations. However, the
Gentlemen's Agreement and the bargaining that it
reflected show the limits to this conclusion. In so
far as the Andhra leaders agreed to safeguards which
put a premium on the retention of a Telengana regional
identity they were hoping that the arrangement would
lead to the gradual fading of the separatist spirit in
Telengana. Implicitly, the hope was that language
would provide the necessary incentives for integration.
A good section of the Telengana leadership also
believed likewise. However, a strong minority in
Telengana apparently believed that the economic and
cultural interests of the region could never be secured
under a united state of Andhra Pradesh.

The subsequent history of the state shows how
limited was the hold of language as a unifying factor.
More than any other instance of intra-linguistic
quarrel, Andhra Pradesh exhibited the relative failure

of language as a source of political identity. The
agitations of 1969 and 1972 clearly demonstrated this.
This is not to say that the state has not survived
and that language may not ultimately generate a more
harmonious relationship. The point is that the Andhra
experience discloses that the claims of language may
not prove stronger than those of other claims to
constitute regional identity.

What are the factors that counteract the cohesiveness of the language bond? Obviously the strength of
old historical identities and perceived injustices on
the economic front constitute major explanations. It
has been noted that at the time of the formation of
the state in 1956 the leaders of both the regions, as
also the Government of India, explicitly recognized
the importance of these two factors as warranting
special safeguards for the Telengana people. The
provision of a regional committee for Telengana to vet
all legislation concerned with the region so as to
ensure that the state legislature's actions did not
militate against the interests of the region was a
device designed not only to oversee Telengana's
economic interests in a most comprehensive way but to
continue the separate identity of the rump of the
former Hyderabad state. The regional committee was
given jurisdiction over a vast range of subjects.

However, in terms of results the general impression
is that the Andhra-Telengana accord was not faithfully
implemented by the Andhra leaders and that both the
economic interests and social sensibilities of the
Telengana peoples have been systematically ignored.
Subsequent enquiries established that development work
in Telengana was neglected even though the region had
surplus funds accumulating in the treasury. Major
irrigation projects, approved and decided upon,
remained on the drawing board. A major controversy
developed over the issue of Telengana revenue surpluses.
The regional committee also contended that most of the
surplus money remained unspent by the Andhra Pradesh
government.

In matters of the composition of the state cabinet
too, resentment grew among the Telengana leaders. It
is a fact that, for some time, Telengana ministers
were not given certain key portfolios and in particular
the practice of having a Telengana Minister as Deputy
Chief Minister when an Andhran was Chief Minister, was
also given up. These trends were in patent violation

of the terms of the Gentlemen's Agreement.

If on the economic front Telengana felt badly let down, the results of the new and massive social intercourse between the peoples of the two regions did not prove   favourable to harmonious relations either. Since Hyderabad - the premier city in Telengana - became the capital of the state of Andhra Pradesh, it was the Andhrans who trekked to Hyderabad as government servants, businessmen and in various other capacities. Apart from the misunderstandings that arise when strangers come to interact, the Andhra-Telengana interaction was destined to prove even more embarrassing because of stereotyped perceptions about each others' cultural levels. It has already been mentioned how a feeling of superiority was present among the Telugus of the Andhra area because of the so-called purity of the Telugu language they wrote and spoke. Ironically enough, it was the Telugu language which was to have been the ostensible agent of unification that was the stumbling block on the cultural plane. But, of course, it was on the issue of employment in the public services that the crisis exploded in 1969.

It has been noted how the spirit and content of the Mulki rules of the old Hyderabad state were once again put into effect through the Public Employment Act. The Telengana leadership claimed that, in spite of this measure, their job opportunities were misappropriated by non-Telengana Telugus. To understand the complaint, a brief explanation of the nature of the protection given by the Act is useful. The most pertinent point is that the Mulki formula was in the shape of a residential requirement. It declared that:

'A person is not eligible for appointment to a post within the Telengana area under the State Government of Andhra Pradesh or to a post under a local authority (other than a cantonment Board) in the said area unless

(i) he has been continuously residing within the said area for not less than fifteen years immediately preceding the prescribed date; and

(ii) he produces before the appointing authority concerned, if so required by it, a certificate of eligibility granted under these rules.'

It is by this method that the Act envisaged reservation

of public employment within the Telengana area. But
there were some major exceptions:

(1) these reservations did not apply to offices above
    the middle-range ranks.
(2) the reservations were also not applicable where
    one in every three posts was set apart for Telen-
    gana candidates.
(3) the state government could exempt in certain cases
    recruitment which was not in accordance with the
    Mulki rules. Originally the act envisaged that
    these rules would operate for ten years, from 1959-
    69.

The most bitter aspect of the Telengana complaint
related to the administration of the Act, the charges
being that the Telengana people were denied their due
share of the jobs, that certificates of domicile became
a farce as these could be bought for a consideration,
that the state government granted too many exemptions
and that, in general, Telengana residents were cheated
out of their employment opportunities. And most of the
allegations were proved to be true to some degree.
The state government's explanation, on the other
hand, was that it was only the lack of qualified
persons in Telengana, especially in the categories of
trained teachers, engineers and doctors that compelled
the government to recruit non-Mulkis.
What concerns us here is not so much a detailed
assessment of these claims and counter-claims, but an
appreciation of the extent to which perceived denial
of legitimate employment opportunities overrode the
bonds of linguistic unity. The fact is that the
economic and employment factors constituted the main
causes of the Telengana movement of 1969.
In a sense, the 'solution' that ended the agitation
confirmed this view. It was on the basis of Prime
Minister Indira Gandhi's eight-point formula that the
Telengana separatist agitation ended and the eight-
point formula was nothing else but a programme for the
more faithful implementation of the original agreements
relating to the protection of the region's financial
surpluses; the identification of new development
schemes and the speedy implementation of the existing
development projects; the increasing association of
regional bodies with decisions on economic development
of the region; and finally the securing of adequate
protection for the service opportunities of the

Telengana people. It is relevant to note that two of
the eight points related to the assessment of Telengana surpluses, three to the issue of the development
schemes, and two to the issue of safeguarding the
special provisions relating to public employment.

To attribute a political crisis that challenged the
bonds of language and religion to economic causes is a
satisfying prospect indeed. It fits in with what has
by now become the orthodoxy of Marxist interpretation.
It seems quite reasonable to hold that the loyalties
of language or religion are subject to an overriding
loyalty to the perceived economic interest of a group
of people.

The Regional Committee and the Perpetuation of Separate Identity

However, the role of the economic factor needs to be
qualified in the context of other facts. There is
the serious contention that institutions like the Telengana Regional Committee and devices like the Mulki
rules were themselves responsible for perpetuating a
feeling of separate identity and helping to magnify
perceptions of deprivations on the economic and employment fronts. The way in which the regional committee
was used as an instrument to consolidate and mobilize
this separate identity sufficiently illustrates the
point.

It is no surprise that, as a sort of mini-legis-
lature empowered to give a second opinion on legislation affecting the Telengana region, the composition of
the committee was quite comprehensive - consisting of
all the Telengana MLAs - but what is a matter of
surprise is that it was seized by the separatists from
the start, becoming as it were, a rival to the state
assembly. It is significant that the chairmen of the
regional committee have been avowed opponents of integration. For example, even when the Congress party
was in a majority on the regional committee and was
officially committed to integration it had to decide
on nominating Mr Achuta Reddy, a separatist, to the
chairmanship, instead of a well-known integrationist
who was earlier thought to be the favourite. Subsequently too, the chairmanship mostly remained in the
hands of separatists. Yet another fact is that, for
a long time, leadership of the regional committee and
leadership of the government (i.e. the cabinet)
remained two distinct groups, one serving as the focal

point of the separatist camp and the other representing the official, integrationist line. During the
first ten years of its existence only two among those
who served as the chairmen of the committee and its
sub-committees became ministers. There was thus no
scope for communication between the two wings, each
tending to stay in the comfort of their respective
convictions. A situation thus developed in which
Chief Ministers never bothered even to try to coopt
separatists into the cabinet and thereby provide an
occasion for fruitful interaction to take place. It
must be mentioned that during this time the Chief
Ministers were invariably from the Andhra area. To
this circumstance should also be added that in many
state cabinets a Telengana minister was not even
given the honour of the second rank in the cabinet.
There was thus a callous flouting of the Gentlemen's
Agreement, entered into at the time of the merger,
that a Telengana minister should be given the rank of
Deputy Chief Minister. It proved to be a great
tactical error to keep out the separatists; all the
more so because the very existence of the regional
committee provided an admirable base for them to keep
alive the flames of separatism.

And the regional committee went about its task of
overseeing the interests of Telengana in a vigorous
manner. It was a very active body in which membership
attendance was always quite high. It is also important
to note that the committee became the core of the
separatist conscience. It took up individual grievances relating to public employment and university
admissions; and the access that it gave to the two
most vociferous elements of the Telengana movement, the
teacher and student bodies of the Osmania University
and the Telengana Non-Gazetted Officers' associations,
was extraordinary. It is not suggested that but for
the existence of the Telengana regional committee there
would have been no Telengana movement. But the point
is that in terms of leadership, in mobilizing and
consolidating the constituency for separatism, and,
above all, in providing legitimacy for separatism, the
committee contributed directly to the origins of the
separatist movement.

The device of the Mulki rules also provides interesting insights into the ways in which such instruments of
social policy function. At one level of analysis one
can straight away say that these rules were meant to

guarantee limited employment opportunities to the
people of the region and that when these were not
faithfully observed the Telengana people rose in
revolt. Viewed thus one can say that the Mulki rules
provided a sort of measuring rod to detect trends
detrimental to regional interests. The immediate
causes of the 1969 agitation provide a good illustration.

First, there was a demand from Telengana that the
Mulki rules originally envisaged to last for ten
years (from 1959-69) should be extended further.
Secondly, the urgency of this demand was reinforced by
the controversy about the applicability of the rules
to certain grey areas. In fact, it was a dispute
about whether the Mulki rules applied to a public
corporation like the Electricity Board (which technically is neither a government department nor a local
body) that triggered off the agitation in 1969. The
Andhra Pradesh High Court, in a judgement in 1969,
decided that the Mulki rules did not apply to employment in such bodies as the Electricity Board. The
state government rectified the position. The point is
that the Mulki rules became a symbol of regional
identity rather than a significant instrument for the
protection of employment interests in Telengana. Many
analysts at the time of the agitation and afterwards
pointed out that, after all, the total numbers of
public posts available in the whole of the state ran to
only a few thousands and that it was meaningless to
become involved in such violent movements merely for
the sake of legal niceties about hypothetical job
vacancies.

Thus it would seem that the institutions and devices
designed to bring about a spirit of integration through
a strategy of the careful nurture of relatively deprived
regions had in the end only resulted in consolidating
regional identity.

Other Factors Aiding Separatist Sentiment

In this context it is necessary to realize that the
task of bringing together identical language groups
living in different political regions with a consequential differential in political and social-cultural
levels is not unique to Andhra Pradesh. Wherever areas
once ruled by Indian princes were integrated with areas
emerging out of British rule, this type of problem
existed in one form or the other. The case of

Marathwada joining Maharashtra, the Kannada-speaking
districts of former Hyderabad joining Karnataka, and,
even more importantly, the merger of a vast number of
tiny princely states in Orissa joining the erstwhile
Orissa province, are identical with the case of the
Telengana districts merging with the Telugu-speaking
Andhra state. Yet, the important question is why have
the Oriya, Maratha and Kannada languages apparently
proved a more enduring and firmer bond than Telugu?
Once again we come back to the point regarding the
strength of an historical, regional identity in Telengana, a factor which is not observable in other
situations.

While these factors served as background props to
the feeling of separateness there were more immediate
causes. The first among these was the central government's inclination to continue the existence of
Hyderabad as a separate unit in the Union federation.
This attitude was also endorsed by the States Reorganisation Commission which recommended in 1955 that the
Nizam's dominions should not be split up to join their
respective linguistic groups. The central government's
attitude was motivated by diverse considerations.
First, there was the feeling that retention of multilingual states might act as a countervailing factor to
the possible release of linguistic chauvinism after
the reorganization of India on linguistic lines.
Secondly, in relation to Hyderabad state, people like
Nehru were anxious to retain former identities.
Probably the desire to facilitate the continuation of
the cultural diversity of the region was very much in
Nehru's mind. One may even go to the extent of saying
that Nehru's catholicism favoured the notion that the
sentiments of the minority Muslim population of the
state of Hyderabad ought to be respected by not dismem-
bering the political identity of the region.

The latter point in particular is of some importance.
In the case of Pondicherry and Goa Nehru also decided
that distinct historical and cultural identities should
not be disturbed in favour of the linguistic identity.
That was why Tamil-speaking Pondicherry was not merged
into neighbouring Tamil Nadu, or largely Marathi-
speaking Goa into Maharashtra.

Eventually, of course, the claims of language
apparently prevailed over other considerations, but the
point is that the very fact that initially there were
hesitations about breaking up Hyderabad lent legitimacy

to those who questioned the merger.

In assessing the various components of Telengana's separate identity it is also necessary to touch upon the role of the Muslim minority. Either because of the their concentration in the twin cities of Hyderabad and Secunderabad, (according to the 1951 census Muslims constitued 45.4 per cent of the twin cities' population) or because of a general feeling that they were more secure in a separate state of Telengana, the Muslim element gave strong support to the separatist movement. In fact it is interesting to note that the symbolism and imagery in the Telengana agitation were strongly influenced by the Muslim minority. Separatist leaders addressed meetings in Urdu, slogans and placards were in Urdu, and the paraphernalia accompanying separatist processions reminded one of Muslim religious processions. This strongly suggests that in Telengana the hold of the linguistic bond was certainly weaker when compared to the other criteria of political and social identities.

It is important to note that in other mergers of linguistic groups the complex interplay of different religious minorities, strong elite cultures and other factors did not exist. Significantly enough, the cities of Hyderabad and Secunderabad themselves provided yet another basis for non-Telugu and indeed anti-Telugu identity which came into full play once the intra-Telugu rivalries came to the fore. It must be mentioned that, apart from the role of the Muslim elite in the city before the integration, in the public life of Hyderabad non-Telugus played a more influential rule. There was thus always an element of latent resentment among the non-Telugu sections. We therefore find that, even though the Nizam's dominions were split, yet the Telengana region, especially the twin cities, were still left with the essential components of their former historical identity which seriously challenged the inroads of the new linguistic identity.

It can also be asked whether but for the location of the capital in Telengana the leverage of the Telengana separatists in increasing the effectiveness of agitation would have been as great as it proved to be. In all other instances of merger between former princely areas and areas under British rule we do not find any example of the capital being located in the territories of the former princes. The capital not only helps to keep up erstwhile historical identities but gives a positive bargaining power to the separatists in getting their demands accepted. It is well known that one of the main incentives for the formation of a united Andhra Pradesh was the attraction of the twin cities.

The foregoing points highlight some of the important causes that seriously countered the role of the language factor in creating a single political identity among the Telugu-speaking people. The evidence seems to suggest that while genuine grievances regarding the implementation of the terms of the merger had considerable weight, institutions devised to supervise the implementation of these terms proved to be as responsible in actively fostering the consciousness of a separate identity.

If the 1969 agitation suggests that it was institutions like the Telengana Regional Committee and solutions like the Mulki rules that helped to perpetuate the regional identity and override the bond of language, the facts of the 1972 separatist movement largely confirmed this view. It is not my purpose to undertake a detailed analysis of the causes, progress and effects of the movement. What is necessary is to bring out the implications of the 1972 agitation for the problem of the strength of language as a sufficient condition to forge an identity.

It is well known that in 1972, it was among the coastal Andhrans that an agitation spread to sever the link with Telengana. Here again the immediate cause of the agitation was a decision of the Supreme Court of India which reversed the decision of the High Court of Andhra Pradesh holding the Mulki rules unconstitutional. In so doing the Supreme Court held that not only was the policy of reservation of jobs and places in educational institutions in the Telengana area exclusively for the residents of the area valid, but it went further. Whereas previously the Mulki rules envisaged that jobs in governmental offices in the twin cities should be allocated in the ratio of 1:2 between the Telengana and non-Telengana areas respectively, the Supreme Court judgement held that under article 16(2) of the Constitution the original Mulki rules were themselves valid. The net effect of the decision was to give the coastal Andhrans the impression that they were not eligible for any public employment, even in their capital. It was this that

triggered the agitation at the end of 1972. The
central government proceeded to mitigate the rigours
of the judgement by readjusting the Mulki rules in
such a way as to keep open to the non-Telengana
Andhrans at least two-thirds of the employment
opportunities in the capital and putting a time limit
to the operation of the Mulki rules. But these
attempts could not contain the agitation which proved
a very costly one indeed in terms of loss of public
property, human life and the closure of all educational
insitutions in the Andhra area for nearly six months.
The damage to the prospects of emotional integration
between the two wings of the state was incalculable.

It cannot be denied that political factors like
factionalism in the Congress, and economic causes like
the role of vested interests in delaying the implementation of land ceiling bills then underway, were
also responsible for the agitation. All the same the
divisive role of the Mulki rules seems much more
consequential.

The conclusion of this case study is that the
process of bringing about a fusion between two units
of a single linguistic group which have lived as two
distinct historical entities for some time is indeed a
hazardous one. Policies like the creation of regional
committees, designed to protect legitimate interests,
may end in further solidifying regional identities and
may even lead to the projection of subnational claims.

How then to harmonize the two potentially incompatible goals of: (1) safeguarding the economic interests
of the backward areas and (2) facilitating the speedy
fusion of the two elements in a single linguistic
identity?

One wonders whether the policy of identifying the
whole of a tract of territory like Telengana as a
backward area is strategically sound. Of course it is
true that more areas in Telengana remained backward
than in the rest of Andhra Pradesh. Still, superimpos-
ing the concept of economic backwardness on an already
existing regional identity would generate counter-
productive trends in terms of the goal of linguistic
integration. Some observers during the Andhra agitation of 1972 drew attention to this aspect of the
problem and suggested that areas of backwardness
should be identified at lower levels and corresponding
development strategies evolved. The solutions
adopted by the centre and state governments to pacify

167

the crises still remain indecisive and ambivalent. On
the one hand, we find the strategy of encouraging
intra-language regional identities remains. For
example, the Telengana Regional Committee's powers are
now enlarged - and instrumentalities are now added to
oversee the spending of the surplus of revenues that
the Telengana areas yield. Yet on the other hand there
are clear indications of the realization that the
longer institutions like the regional committee and
the Mulki rules are continued, the weaker will be the
role of the language factor as an agent of fusion.
This realization is reflected in the reiteration of
time limits for the operation of the Mulki rules and
partly by the creation of regional committees for non-
Telengana areas too. For instance regional committees
for the coastal districts are now established with
powers almost identical to those given to the
Telengana Regional Committee. In a sense there is now
an added premium put on regionalism. But the point is
that these incentives to regionalism are no longer
confined to the context of Telengana where
already regionalism is conspicuously intensive. The
result, it is to be hoped, would be that the criterion
of backwardness would not further endorse the
legitimacy of Telengana's separate identity.

It would be useful to make a few remarks about the
interrelationship between language and political
identity, and how this interrelationship is institu-
tionalized in near-similar cases like Andhra and Punjab.
The Government of India seemed to have equated the
problem of Telengana - Andhra integration with that of
Punjab - Haryana integration. This equation is amply
demonstrated by the fact that the institutions of
regional councils were established in both these
cases. (It is important to note that in the case of
the Vidarbha-Maharashtra controversy this device was
not adopted.) In the Punjab-Haryana case we had an
attempt to retain the shape of one single political
unit which has gradually been challenged by the
diversity of language (here I am assuming that the
diversity of the Gurumukhi script in fact makes the
Haryana-Punjab dichotomy one based on language) through
the device of the regional committee. In Andhra
Pradesh it is a case of a single identity based on
language being challenged by the force of past historical associations. But here too, the policy pursued to
retain a unity based on language is identical with the

168

Punjab device. We know that in the Punjab in the end
the regional committees failed to satisfy regional
demands and the separation of Haryana and Punjab
became a reality. Can it be said that language
prevailed over the fact of the existence of a united
Punjab? It will be interesting to see whether the
obverse of the situation will take place in the Telugu-
speaking area; will the claims of distinct historical
experiences override those of a single language?

It is interesting to note that the Andhra and
Punjab situations were compared to the Scottish
situation. During the discussions on the creation of
the regional committees Nehru himself stated that some
aspects of the arrangement prevailing in Britain
vis-à-vis Scotland were being adopted in India. There
are of course many differences in matters of detail
between the structure and powers of the regional
bodies in Andhra Pradesh and those in Scotland. In
one important sense the English-Scottish relationship
is comparable to the Andhra-Telengana relationship:
one language but different historical experiences.
But in another sense, it is doubtful whether the
Telengana identity is as intense as that of the
Scots. It is also of some importance to note that in
Britain Scottish separatism is more readily conceded
than Welsh separatism, as is evident from the devolution proposals of 1977-8. Here again we have the
striking examples of one nationalism based on
separate history and one based on language, making
claims for recognition.

Coming back to the case of Andhra Pradesh it is
quite probable that for quite some time the hold of
historical memories and cultural differentials will
continue to challenge the unifying potentialities of
language.

LANGUAGE, RELIGION AND POLITICAL IDENTITY IN KARNATAKA

James Manor

Karnataka has not experienced serious internal divisions over matters of religion and language. (Indeed, Karnataka has not experienced serious internal divisions of any sort.) This may make Karnataka seem a trifle tame to observers of Telengana, Punjab or Sri Lanka. But the very tameness of this case may still prove instructive inasmuch as it may represent something of an extreme among South Asian linguistic regions, which can place other cases in clearer perspective. This region is also significant in that its society was and is highly localized in its focus when compared, for example, with Uttar Pradesh[1] or Kerala.[2] It follows from this that political loyalties were and are highly localized in their focus. This fact inspires in this writer suspicion that other contributors to this volume may have underestimated the tendency for people on the land to have a rather narrow, localized view of things. They may thus have failed to disaggregate sufficiently in their analysis of politics generally and of political identity in particular.

The term 'Karnataka' is used here to refer to the geographical area now encompassed by the state of that name, that is, the area which was known as (greater) Mysore from States Reorganization in 1956 until 1973. Prior to 1947, this area was divided between five separate administrative agencies: the princely state of Mysore, the governments of Bombay and Madras, the princely state of Hyderabad and the administration of Coorg. The territories under the last three of these agencies were both small and politically and socially eccentric. Thus, our discussion will deal primarily with the first two territories which together form the great bulk of the post-1956 state. That ruled by the Maharaja of Mysore will be referred to as 'princely Mysore' (roughly the southern half of the state today) and that under the Government of Bombay as 'Bombay Karnataka' (most of the northern half of the state today). The term 'Kannadigas', which means people who speak Kannada - the language of nearly all who live in the state - will be used to refer to residents of

Karnataka. This glosses over the Telugu-speaking
majority in Kolar District, east of Bangalore, and the
Tamil-speaking majority in the city of Bangalore. But
this seems forgivable since, as we shall see pre-
sently, linguistic identifications have had little
importance in the politics of the region.

The purpose of this essay is to discuss the extent
to which 'political communities based upon language and
religion' are to be found in Karnataka since 1935. We
will examine the behaviour of the region's elite in
political arenas at several different levels, from
regional to local, particularly when we discuss the
more interesting problem of religion and political
identity. Special attention will be given to the need
to distinguish identifications based upon language or
religion from identifications based upon membership in
a social group. We shall find that in this region
at least the latter are far more important than the
former.

Language and Political Identity

The main staple of the Kannadiga diet is *ragi* which,
when cooked, is presented for the diner's delectation
as a large grey wad, resembling damp clay. Unkind
Tamils who are repelled by this dish will tell you that
Kannadigas 'eat mud' and that this makes their wits and
their passions sluggish. It is beyond my competence to
say whether they are right, but when it comes to the
politics of language, the Kannadigas could justly be
accused of having sluggish passions. If, as Malcolm
Yapp writes,'the focus of our study is political
communities based upon language',[3] then in Karnataka
we will find little to discuss.

There has never been anything like the Andhra movement[4] in the Kannada-speaking areas. In the first
three decades of this century, a number of associations
to promote Kannada literature and language grew up in
the region. In princely Mysore, they were of very
little significance. Their members in the pre-independence years were drawn almost entirely from a small
circle of Brahman literati in Bangalore and the mainly
Brahman university student population there. Their
main aim was the introduction of modern techniques into
Kannada literature and they pursued this by way of
sporadic publications and occasional, highly sophisticated public addresses in the manner of university
extension lectures.

In princely Mysore the campaign - if it can be called that - to develop Kannada literature was not attended by any resentment against the political status quo, since its leading patrons came from the Maharaja's household. The activities of these associations were virtually free of political content or significance. In Bombay Karnataka, such efforts were infused with a mild sense of grievance over the treatment which that small Kannada-speaking island was receiving in the vast Marathi and Gujarati sea which was the old Bombay Presidency. But this literary movement never achieved much significance there for two reasons. First, Bombay Karnataka lacked a major urban centre to serve as a focus for such activities. And second, the western-ized urban elite - the only group concerned with the race for urban advancement within the Presidency and with the revival of the language along western lines - was divided between Brahmans and Lingayats.[5]

Notwithstanding the familiar generalizations about the south Indian response to the adoption of Hindi as a national language, Kannada-speakers have never excited themselves over this either. In part, this is because their language (as spoken by the state's political elite, consisting mainly of urban Brahmans and urban or urban-orientated Lingayats and Vokka-ligas) derives a very substantial minority of its words from Sanskritic roots. As a result, Hindi has never seemed as alien to Kannadigas as it has to Malayalis or Tamils.

In addition, the tone of politics in Karnataka has never reached the heights of acrimony and contention that one associates with Tamil politics, particularly those óf the DMK. The Kannadigas' sluggish passions have less to do with a diet of *ragi* than with the comparatively small disparities between rich and poor, the comparatively low incidence of landlessness in the state and a remarkable continuity in patterns of dominance and land control over the last half-century, particularly in what was princely Mysore.[6] These factors contribute to the generally temperate tone of political debate in Karnataka, particularly on the question of language. An attempt to generate a 'Kannada-in-danger' movement based on the DMK model has failed utterly in recent years, even in the wards of Bangalore, where resentment was thought to exist against the city's Tamil majority. Raucous bands of 'Kannada Chavaligars' (Kannada agitators) rode round

the city in open trucks shrieking their outrage at the
pathetic fate of the mother tongue only to be greeted
with smirks and hoots of laughter in the Kannada neigh-
bourhoods. The easy-going approach to linguistic
issues is also apparent in the role which politicians
from the predominantly Telugu district of Kolar have
always been allowed to play in Karnataka politics. The
leading figure in the struggle for popular sovereignty
in princely Mysore and the first Chief Minister of
post-independence Mysore was K.C. Reddy, a Telugu
lawyer from Kolar. And the fair treatment given to
his successors from that district has scotched any
move among Kolar people for a merger with Andhra
Pradesh.

The only important case which might begin to
qualify as a 'political community based upon language
...' in the Kannada areas since 1935 was the Karnataka
Unification movement which developed substance in
Bombay Karnataka after the transfer of power and
achieved its aim with States Reorganization in 1956.
Congress politicians in the Kannada districts of
Bombay Presidency felt the burden of their minority
status in that huge province much more keenly after
independence than before. This was mainly the result
of their unhappy position as regards political
patronage within the provincial political arena.

Under British rule, the Kannada districts had
received much less than their fair share of the spoils
from the Bombay government. This was true even before
non-official politicians gained a significant voice in
provincial politics, because the British were keen to
minimize disenchantment in the Gujarati- and Marathi-
speaking areas from which the threat of resistance to
the Raj was greatest. By comparison, Bombay Karnataka
was small (in terms of both area and population),
remote, backward (among other things, they had no urban
areas to compete with Bombay or Ahmadabad) and politically quiescent. When elected representatives gained
significant patronage powers before and especially
after 1935, the alliances which developed between
district-level politicians in the Marathi and Gujarati
areas and their cronies at the provincial level meant
that Bombay Karnataka was short-changed again. The
transfer of power exacerbated this problem because it
greatly increased both the patronage available to
elected politicians and the tendency to favour Gujarati
and Marathi districts. To see their share of the spoils

diminishing just as the dawn of *swaraj* was supposed to open up new vistas for everyone came as a cruel irony to Bombay Karnataka politicians.

This predicament clearly heightened their sense of solidarity as members of the same linguistic group. Being Kannadigas became an important element of their political identity (though by no means the paramount one). And the solution which they found to this predicament - the appeal for the unification of Karnataka as part of the reorganization of India's provinces along linguistic lines - placed linguistic identifications in the forefront of their public descriptions of themselves. This in turn generated social pressure from constituents for these leaders to conform to these descriptions, as oft-repeated public comments eventually do, although the modest public response to the unification campaign (discussed below) meant that this pressure was far from intense.

But despite all of this, linguistic identifications appear to have shaped these politicians' perceptions of themselves to a surprisingly limited extent. This was primarily because the way out of their predicament, states reorganization, always seemed a rather likely prospect to them. The leader of the campaigners for unification, S. Nijalingappa, has said that in their view the question was not whether they would succeed but when.[7] The decision in 1920 to restructure provincial units of the Congress along linguistic lines seemed implicitly to promise them success, as did comments by national leaders at later dates. Perhaps if it had seemed a more uphill struggle, a deeper sense of uncertainty and grievance might have caused them to invest more of themselves in the notion of being suffering Kannadigas. (During the grimmest days of the freedom struggle, the daunting nature of the task at hand had had precisely this effect when it turned Nijalingappa, for a time, into a passionate Gandhian.[8]) But their confidence that they would succeed led them to count in advance the chickens they thought would hatch; it led them to think in terms of a united Karnataka long before it came into being. And since that arithmetic carried with it as a 'given' factor that nearly everyone spoke Kannada, they turned their attention to that element in their political identity which would be most important once unification occurred, the element through which they would dominate the political process of a united Karnataka - their

174

status as Lingayats.[9]

Since being a Lingayat meant, among other things, belonging to a religious sect, this carries us into the realm of religion and political identity. We shall therefore postpone further discussion of this until the next section of the essay. There is only one further point to add to these comments on language and political identity. When we look beyond the small circle of full-time politicians who led the Karnataka Unification movement to the general populace of Bombay Karnataka, we find very little identification with the linguistic group - far less than existed among the movement's leaders. In these predominantly rural districts which were rather backward in terms of education and networks of transportation and communication, there was little awareness of Presidency-wide politics, and of the deprivations which they suffered at the hands of Marathi and Gujarati speakers and which their leaders felt so keenly. There was even less awareness of the promise of political spoils which a still-hypothetical united Karnataka held out to them. As a result, the campaigners for Karnataka unification found it difficult to generate substantial demonstrations of popular enthusiasm for their cause.[10] Indeed, the only show of popular excitement over linguistic unification came from princely Mysore where Vokkaligas who saw that it would mean Lingayat predominance in state politics resisted it until it was imposed upon them by the Government of India.

Religion and Political Identity

In discussing 'political communities based upon ... religion' in any part of the world, we must attempt to sort out the tendency of people to identify with religious tenets, evocative symbols, rituals and ritually-based customs from the tendency to identify with social groups in which similar beliefs are shared but are clearly secondary in importance to group solidarity. These two tendencies are always entangled with one another, and reinforce one another. They therefore present a daunting task to those of us who seek to weigh the importance of each against the other. But having conceded that our ability to solve these problems is limited, we can still venture cautious judgements on the extent to which one tendency predominates over the other. For example, we can say without great risk that in the conflict which led to

175

the departure of Roger Williams and his supporters from
seventeenth-century Massachusetts to form the colony
of Rhode Island, identifications with religious tenets
(more than symbols or rituals) far outweighed identifications with particular social groups. And to take
a less clear-cut case, in the present conflict in
Northern Ireland identifications with social groups
appear to this writer at least to predominate.

This distinction bears upon the problem of what we
mean when we speak of 'political communities based upon
... religion'. For when we find political communities
in which identifications with social groups predominate over identifications with tenets, symbols or
rituals, communities in which the latter reinforce the
former but are clearly secondary to them, can we say
that these communities are actually 'based upon ...
religion'? I think not.

This has relevance to South Asia where, so often,
identifications with social groups (usually, though by
no means always, *jatis*) predominate over identification
with religious tenets, symbols and rituals. To put it
that baldly is to overstate the point. Social group
identifications are less predominant in areas where
different religions come face to face than where a
large majority of the population are of the same
religion. But although such cases fall outside the
scope of this paper, it is my suspicion that social
group identifications may predominate even in those
areas where Muslims and Hindus or Hindus and Sikhs
encounter one another in substantial numbers. It is no
accident that these are referred to as encounters
between *communal* groups and not *religious* groups. My
suspicion extends even to Sri Lanka where a great many
things have been taken for granted.

The case in question here, however, does not involve
an encounter between groups which follow different
religions. Muslims account for less than six per cent
of Karnataka's population. As in nearly all of peninsular India, the important political groups in this
region are exclusively Hindu. In the previous section
of this essay, our comment that nearly everyone in the
region shared a common language was a signal for an
early end to the discussion of that topic. That is not
the case here, however. Kannadigas may be overwhelm-
ingly Hindu, but groups of some importance within Hindu
society in the region are derived to some extent at
least from identification with religious tenets,

176

symbols and rituals. We now turn to two questions
about these groups. How much internal cohesion and
substance do they have? And to what extent do they
derive their substance from religious identifications?

This discussion will deal with people who fall
under only two labels, the Vokkaligas and the Lingayats who are socially and politically dominant throughout the region. We exclude others for two reasons.
First, no other group has had major importance at any
level or in any arena (excluding a few urban centres)
of Karnataka politics since 1935. Second, (and this
is both a cause and a consequence of the first) with
the exception of a few tiny Brahman and mercantile
jatis, no other group is sufficiently advanced economically or educationally to have developed strong links
between members living in various, scattered
localities. Thus, when considered in the context of
supra-local political arenas, such groups turn out to
be rather artificial entities. This makes discussion
of their supra-local political identities, whether
based on religious or other identifications, a rather
tenuous enterprise. This latter problem arises in
discussions of the Lingayats and Vokkaligas as well,
and has been dealt with at length elsewhere.[11] In the
interests of brevity, this discussion will offer only
the broad outlines of the conclusions which were
reached.

The Lingayats and the Vokkaligas are commonly
described by journalists and many scholars as Karnataka's dominant 'castes', as the most important
'communities' in the state's politics. The use of
such terms is, however, highly misleading, because the
Lingayat and Vokkaliga categories lack the internal
integration, homogeneity and coherence which such
terms imply. They can be better understood if their
component parts are examined to see which unit of
social organization, among those to be found at
different levels within the Lingayat and Vokkaliga
categories, has possessed the greatest substance at
different times since 1935. For the sake of simplicity,
we shall confine our discussion here to units of
social organization at three levels. The first are the
two overarching 'categories' (i.e., 'Lingayats' and
'Vokkaligas' themselves). The next, which we shall
call 'sections',[12] are those which had come to be
commonly accepted by 1935 among Lingayats and Vokkaligas with an awareness of events beyond the localities

as the constituent parts of the two 'categories'.
(Most sections are endogamous units.) The last and
smallest unit is the 'marriage network', that circle
of families within which matrimonial alliances are
formed. Marriage networks were much smaller than
sections (and this distinction is important).

The two categories present slightly different
problems, so we shall treat them separately. The term
'Vokkaliga' literally means 'thresher' or cultivator
of grain, but nineteenth-century census takers in
princely Mysore (there are almost no Vokkaligas in
Bombay Karnataka) attached it to a catch-all census
category which included 116 sundry groups among which
were cultivators but also cowherds, toddy-drawers,
saltmakers, dyers, extractors of iron, Tamil Vellalas,
and a Telugu group which followed a 'vagrant and
wandering life'.[13] What began as an occupational
category was badly abused and this was then compounded
from 1901 onwards by the tendency to list the category
without sub-divisions, or with a drastically reduced
number of sub-divisions. The government used only the
gross category in its dealings with its people (about
whom it knew surprisingly little), and politicians
included within the category adopted the label in the
quest for patronage because it was simpler to speak to
government in government's own language. Vokkaligas
were soon being discussed in Mysore public life as a
single 'caste'.[14]

This habit has persisted ever since, but it has little
to do with real social interaction. Despite a very
small number of inter-sectional marriages among the
highly urbanized super-elite, the Vokkaliga category
even today consists of a wide array of endogamous
groups which live in different areas of the state and
neither have nor wish to have much social intercourse
with one another. The Vokkaliga label is regarded by
its many members as an occupational classification
rather than the name of a 'caste'. In 1961 for example,
an official Vokkaliga association publication asserted
that since the ancestors of most Europeans were
tillers of the soil, both Khrushchev and Kennedy
qualified as Vokkaligas.[15] The category is sometimes
used by politicians operating in the state-level arena,
especially in the state assembly (hence the fear of
Lingayat-raj before States Reorganization). But outside that rarefied atmosphere, the category is much
more artificial than the sections which compose it.

If we consider the sections in 1935, we will see
that they were themselves highly artificial inasmuch as
they were not bound together by patterns of meaningful
social interaction.[16] If we set aside the barriers
of endogamy and even language that existed within some
of them, we still find that no effective supra-local
structures of 'caste' government existed within any
section after 1901 (and most probably before) to bind
it together as a whole entity of substance. And
although many of the sections were endogamous groups,
marriage links did not contribute to sectional
solidarity either. This is because Vokkaliga families
nearly always formed marriage alliances within a day's
journey from home, within ten to thirty miles of their
home village, and usually much closer to ten than to
thirty. The marriage networks which developed out of
repeated matrimonial arrangements among Vokkaliga
families were much smaller than the supra-local section
units. The sections were not wholly devoid of internal
structural integration because the highly localized
marriage networks overlapped with one another over a
range of, say, one hundred miles, and knitted together
an entire section. But rural folk were almost wholly
ignorant of this connection and thus, in 1935, it was
a wholly meaningless structure from the viewpoint of
almost all Vokkaligas.

The most meaningful unit of social organization to
them was the marriage network. Adrian Mayer has called
the people within the marriage network 'the kindred of
recognition'.[17] This is a most appropriate term,
for the people who lived beyond the bounds of the
marriage network were, almost without exception,
strangers. The local arena was not well-integrated
into supra-local structures, either socially, economically, or politically. For most Vokkaligas, the only
meaningful arena of social and political interaction
was the area which could be traversed in a day's walk
from home.

Much has changed since 1935. Transportation, communication and education have greatly improved in the
region. Most local arenas were integrated into supra-
local economic networks by the black market during the
second world war (a much-delayed process when compared
with most of the rest of India). Local political
arenas were integrated into the regional political
system between 1951 and 1955.[18] These processes have
been attended by changes in social patterns as well,

although only to a rather limited extent. The marriage
network has remained the most important unit of social
organization in the minds of the vast majority of
Vokkaligas. The main change has been the extension of
the marriage network beyond the local arena by the
leading Vokkaliga families in most areas. As supra-
local political and economic arenas became more important and as transport and communications improved, the
most prominent Vokkaligas formed marriage alliances
with leading families of their section beyond the
reach of the old networks. As a result, each section
has gained a certain amount of substance and it is no
longer possible to dismiss them as largely artificial.
(Only a very tiny number of marriage links have been
formed between different sections, so that the Vokkaliga category remains something of an abstraction to
most of its members.) The point which deserves
emphasis here, however, is that only a *very small*
number of Vokkaliga families have extended marriage
networks across the section, beyond the old local
arena.[19] Thus, the section unit is even now much less
real in the minds of the vast majority of Vokkaligas
than the still highly localized marriage network. I
shall discuss more fully the implications of this for
our study of political identity after I have dealt with
the Lingayats. But it is worth noting here that for
this, the dominant landed elite over more than a third
of Karnataka, their political concerns and, I believe,
their political identifications are mainly focused
within a narrowly circumscribed arena.

Religious tenets, symbols and rituals have played
almost no part in political identifications among Vokkaligas. They deserve their reputation for being very
godly people, but their piety is not deeply bound up
with religious teachings or symbols which set their
category or sections off from others. In part, this
is because they have traditionally assumed no priestly
roles and thus their supra-local 'caste' government
(if it ever had much substance, and there is no evidence
to show that it did) never claimed religious justification for its actions. And they have shown a clear
disinclination to mix religion with their social identifications. An attempt by a handful of urbanized
notables to set up a Vokkaliga *swamiji* as a religious
leader to build category-wide solidarity has evoked
little response from the great mass of Vokkaligas. The
swamiji's efforts to raise funds for a student hostel,

and indeed for the maintenance of his own small retinue have only been saved from embarrassing disaster by the small circle of urbanites who are practically his only faithful followers.[20]

With apologies for what may seem a tiresome digression into the social history of Karnataka, we now turn to a discussion of the Lingayats, where the comments above will help us to move at a faster pace. Much of what was said of Vokkaligas is also true of the Lingayats. They are dominant in the villages and towns in just over half of the state (the northern and western portions) in the same manner as the Vokkaligas in their third of Karnataka - by virtue of numbers (they form a large minority of the population) and wealth based mainly upon land control. Lingayat marriage networks, which are similar in nature and size to those of the Vokkaligas, were and are more central to the concerns of the vast majority of the Lingayats than are the larger section and category units. And most Lingayat marriage networks have not been extended beyond the traditional local arena in recent years.[21]

But there are significant differences with the Lingayat case. First and most crucially, the category and the section units of the Lingayats were and are less artificial than those of the Vokkaligas. This is not to say that these units have ever taken precedence over local concerns and identifications among most Lingayats. In my view, they have not. But they are not so ephemeral and abstract as those of the Vokkaligas. Second, religious tenets, symbols and rituals and the exertions of religious leaders have contributed much to the tendency of Lingayats to identify to a significant extent with the category and especially with the section units.

It is particularly important to note the changes in the focus of Lingayats' supra-local identifications over the last four decades. From 1935 until the mid-1950s, most Lingayats viewed themselves as members of the category first and the smaller section second. In that period, neither of these identifications would have had much political content, since it was not until after 1952 that local arenas began to be integrated to any great extent into regional politics. (This process of integration occurred more quickly in Bombay Karnataka than in former princely Mysore, so the injection of political content into the identification with the Lingayat category occurred somewhat more swiftly among

Lingayats in Bombay.) From the mid-1950s onward,
however, most Lingayats tended to shift their principal
supra-local identifications from the category to the
section units. By the late 1950s, sections had
achieved clear precedence over the larger Lingayat
category in the minds of most. This remains the case
today.[22] All of this requires explanation.

The Lingayats are a religious sect which developed
from a *bhakti* movement in the twelfth century. They
share a distinct body of religious and ethical teachings which entail the abandonment of the principal
Hindu rites of ceremonial purification. Lingayats are
vegetarian and wear the *linga* - symbolic of Siva - on
their person. They are united by a common reverence
for the founder of their movement and are served by a
separate priesthood in denial of the authority of
Brahmans.[23] The Lingayat or, more precisely, the
Virasaiva movement preached a casteless society which
drew converts from a wide range of occupations including washermen, barbers, weavers, oil-pressers, various
types of artisans.[24] They have their own priesthood
(which breaks down into at least three sections and
comprises approximately ten per cent of all Lingayats),
one mercantile section (roughly fourteen per cent) and
at least three sections of cultivators (comprising
over half of all Lingayats).[25]

Throughout the period covered by this essay, the
Lingayat category has been much less artificial than
the Vokkaliga category. This greater substance is
derived almost entirely from shared religious tenets,
rituals, and especially symbols. For it must be
emphasized that, in terms of meaningful social interaction, the Lingayat category possesses very little
substance. The anti-caste fervour of the twelfth-
century Virasaivas has long since died out and the
section groups today generally remain sealed off from
one another. Many sections refuse to interdine[26] and
barriers of endogamy separate all sections with one
insignificant exception, the occasional pairing of
girls from the mercantile section with boys from one
priestly section. A tiny, highly urbanized super-elite
(the class that sends its sons to Harvard or Johns
Hopkins) has formed marriage alliances across sectional
lines, but this is as unusual among Lingayats as among
Vokkaligas.

Identifications with the Lingayat category, then,
are based on religious elements far more than on

feelings of solidarity with a social group. But
serious difficulties arise when we attempt to treat
these as *political* identifications. There is no doubt
that people's perceptions of themselves as Lingayats
have some political implications and overtones. But
since the mid-1950s, these implications, and indeed
the very tendency to identify with the Lingayat category, have declined markedly in strength and importance.

This has occurred mainly because the Lingayat
category has proved to be too large to be relevant to
the vast majority of political disputes in Karnataka.
At the state level - within the state assembly, the
always-dominant Congress party and the upper levels
of the bureaucracy - Lingayats sometimes unite to
operate as a group. But the position of Lingayats at
that level is so strong that they seldom *need* to unite.
And because it is taken for granted that Lingayats
will get the lion's share of political spoils, conflict
usually develops over *which* Lingayats will get it.
This of course threatens Lingayat solidarity.

But the state-level arena is no longer the most
important. A more crucial element in the decline of
identifications with the category is the rising
importance of sub-regional political arenas. The most
important Lingayat sections live in adjacent but quite
distinct areas of the state. This means that within
the state assembly constituencies, only one Lingayat
section is usually found to be heavily represented.
As a result ambitious men in search of grievances
against incumbents commonly seize upon signs of less-
than-total commitment to the section's interests. This
ploy has proved consistently effective and it has
generated sectional solidarity at the expense of the
larger category. The Community Development programme,
which was ironically intended as a 'progressive' scheme,
has injected great power into even smaller political
arenas. This has intensified the trend which I call
the *re-parochialization* of the dominant peasantry.

The political logic which is generated by the imposition of these sub-regional political arenas upon the
distribution of dominant social groups across Karnataka
has forced identifications with the Lingayat category
into decline. And as the political importance of the
category has decreased, so inevitably has the political
content of identifications with it. This then would
seem to be an example of the eclipse of what was once
something of a political community based (for once,

genuinely *based*) on religion.

We now turn to the Lingayat sections which have been the beneficiaries of this eclipse. The process described above was the most important reason for the growing strength of identifications with the sections. But there is another element to consider, and this carries us into the realm of religion. In each of the more important sections, a single *matha* (monastery sometimes transliterated as 'mutt') and its *swamiji* have traditionally claimed to be the spiritual focus of the group. There has always been some substance to the claim. These focal *mathas* have networks of subordinate *mathas* which extend their influence over a wide area. And the Lingayats' extraordinary reverence for the *guru* eases the *swamijis'* task.

Before 1935, most of the *swamijis* performed what could be described as political functions. These varied with the ambition of each, and could range from merely advising followers on marriage alliances to (less often) the creation of the beginnings of an alternative government in their sub-region, with their traditional appellate role in local disputes augmented by vigorous collection of a tithe which could approximate a second revenue system.

In the period up to the late 1940s or early 1950s, however, the *swamijis* did not contribute greatly to political identifications with the section unit. Most were prevented from reaching all the members of a section by difficulties with transportation and communication. Networks of subordinate *mathas* could easily cease to be effective links to the faithful if left untended. Squabbles over control of the principal *mathas* sometimes went on for years, dividing sections in the process. The authority of these *mathas* was also seriously undermined by a number of highly revered *mathas* which also had networks of subordinate *mathas* and which drew their followers from many different Lingayat sections. (These *mathas* have generally tended to refrain from political involvement.)

But in that period, the most important reason for the weakness of identifications with the section was the low level of interaction *between* sections. In the highly localized, traditional political arenas within which nearly all Lingayats moved, only one section was usually represented in strength. *Swamijis* generally sought to develop solidarity within a section in order to counteract the influence of rivals who drew upon many sections, not to prepare their section for competition with another section in particular. It was only during the 1950s, when the new regional political arena fostered competition between sections, that firm political identifications with the section units developed.

Solidarity at this level among Lingayats was much stronger than among Vokkaligas. But to what extent are these post-1955 identifications with the sections based upon religion? Religious tenets, symbols and rituals clearly play an important part, most crucially in the use which the *swamijis* make of the *guru*'s place in Virasaivism and of rituals which they customarily perform. But these elements are outweighed by other things which fall outside the realm of religion. Most important is the development of the new regional political system discussed above. More crucial than the *swamijis*' religious role is their role in providing the sections with tenuous *organizational* foci which Vokkaliga sections never had.

The fierce rivalry between two Lingayat sections - the merchant Banajigas and the agrarian Sadars - which has produced the most clamorous and often the most important conflicts in Karnataka politics since 1956, has been almost entirely generated by economic and occupational differences. Finally, those who would view the *swamijis*' cultivation of section identifications as religiously based must be reminded that the act of fostering divisions among Lingayats is a direct contradiction of one of the central aims of Virasaivism - the creation of a casteless society.

At this point it is important to re-emphasize that the unit of social organization with which the vast majority of Kannadigas (including Lingayats) identify most strongly is the marriage network. The political arena which is most real and important to the vast majority is still the local arena, within which the marriage network is the most important social unit.

It is also true, however, that nearly all of these people have some awareness of and identification with higher levels in the Indian political system. We have dealt at length with the section and category levels and, despite quiescence on the language issue, most people have some sense of belonging to a distinctive region within the Indian Union. The nation itself has a discernible place in the political identity of most Kannadigas. One of Gandhi's great achievements was to create the perception of an ideal India, shaped by values which disparate groups had come to share by experiencing adversity together. If in the years since his death, this ideal has come to have less than ever to do with the real India which Kannadigas know, it is far more widely known than in 1948, thanks to improvements in education, communication and transportation.

But changes in the strength of identifications with various groups along this rising scale, from the marriage network to the nation, have not all flowed in one direction since 1935. There is no steady march towards increasingly cosmopolitan views. Identifications with the nation have increased in number but declined in intensity. The marriage network remains the principal preoccupation of the vast majority. But most telling are the changes at the middle levels of the scale. Identifications with the Vokkaliga and Lingayat categories intensified slightly in the years up to about 1950, before the logic of the new political system was fully understood. Since that understanding dawned, they have decreased considerably in intensity (and have lost much of their political content) as the section units - especially among Lingayats - have captured popular attention. This process of re-parochialization has occurred, ironically, as a direct result of the penetration of new electoral and parliamentary processes into local arenas, processes which were intended to promote 'nationality-formation'. This need not be seen as a threat to the nation. That could only arise from strong regional solidarity, and regional (and linguistic) identifications are weak in Karnataka because there is no social group whose interests will be served by building solidarity at that level.

Identifications with social groups have taken precedence over identifications with religious tenets, symbols and rituals - even among Lingayats. This is not because religion is waning in influence. It is not. In the case of the Vokkaligas, religion and politics have never mixed to any great extent and cannot easily be made to mix now, largely because neither the habits of mind nor the institutional structures which are necessary to link religion and politics have taken root.

Among Lingayats, the logic of the post-independence

system has given religious leaders in Lingayat
sections an opportunity to build group solidarity,
thereby enhancing both the section's ability to compete
for spoils and their own positions within the sections.
But the key to their success lies more in the peculiar
interaction of social structure and the political
system than in the evocative power of religious tenets,
symbols and rituals, some of which mark their very
success as anathema.

Manor, 'Language, Religion and Political Identity in
Karnataka'

1. Compare R.G. Fox, 'Resiliency and Change in the
Indian Caste System', *Journal of Asian Studies* 26, 4
(August 1967), pp.575-87 with J. Manor, 'The Evolution
of Political Arenas and Units of Social Organization:
The Lingayats and Vokkaligas of Mysore', in M.N.
Srinivas, ed., *Dimensions of Change in India*, New
Delhi 1976.
2. D.J. Arnold, R.B. Jeffrey and J. Manor, 'Political Mobilization and Social Change: Caste Associations
in Three Regions of South India', *Indian Economic and
Social History Review* 13, 3 (July-September 1977),
pp.353-74.
3. Above, p.1.
4. See J.G. Leonard, 'Politics and Social Change in
South Asia: A Study of the Andhra Movement', *Journal of
Commonwealth Political Studies* 5, 1 (1967), pp.60-77.
5. G.R. Swamy, *Mysuru Rajakiya Parichaya*, Bangalore
n.d., p.5; KPCC, *The Karnataka Handbook*, Bangalore
1924, pp.1, 190-6; the *Hindu*, 15 March, 19 November
1935, 28 March, 7 April, 27 August 1936, 19 July 1937;
Interview with D.V. Gundappa, Bangalore, 5 April 1971.
6. From these necessarily rather crude generalizations must be excluded the coastal districts of
Karnataka, which form a quite small portion of the
state. In the region as a whole, traditional socio-
economic patterns have undergone nothing like the
disruption described in, for example, R.B. Jeffrey,
*The Decline of Nayar Dominance: Society and Politics
in Travancore, 1847-1908*, London 1976. See by comparison J. Manor, *Political Change in an Indian State:
Mysore, 1910-1955*, Canberra and New Delhi 1977,
especially chapters two, four and nine.
7. Interview with S. Nijalingappa, Bangalore, 24
August 1972. See also the *Hindu*, late 1948 to 1955.
Also, Karnataka Unification Sabha ...., *United Karnataka or a case for Karnataka Unification*, Dharwar
1948. It is significant that they concentrated their
energies on publications in English, aiming for a
national-level audience rather than among Kannadigas
who seemed rather apathetic.
8. See the section on Nijalingappa in J. Manor,

'The Lesser Leader amid Political Transformation...',
in W.H. Morris-Jones, ed., *The Making of Politicians*,
London 1976, pp.140-55.

9. By 1945, Lingayats - the dominant landed group
in Bombay Karnataka - had ousted the numerically and
economically weak Brahmans from nearly all positions
of influence in the Congress which was the only important political force there.

10. This is clear from even a cursory reading of
the *Hindu*, 1948-1955. Also, interviews at Bangalore
with S. Nijalingappa, 24 August 1972, and J.M. Imam,
10 October 1972.

11. Manor, 'The Evolution of Political Arenas'.

12. What I call 'section', Adrian Mayer calls
'sub-caste' in *Caste and Kinship in Central India: A
Village and its Region*, London 1960, pp.4-9. I have
avoided his term because the prefix 'sub-' might be
taken to mean that that unit was of less importance
than the larger unit. In Karnataka, it was not
less important.

13. Census of India, 1891, XXV, 1, p.250; *Extracts
of a ... Survey of the Mysore Dominions ...*, 2nd
bound book, pp.312, 452 and 474, Mysore State
Archives; J.A. Dubois, *The People of India*, Madras 1862,
p.340; and B.L. Rice, *Mysore, A Gazetteer compiled for
Government*, rev. ed., London 1897, p.229; and F.
Buchanan, *A Journey from Madras through the Countries
of Mysore ...*, London 1807, I, pp.257-8 and 318 and II,
pp.27-9.

14. See for example, *Census of India*, 1911, XXI, 1,
p.175.

15. B. Shivamurthy Sastry, 'Samajadalli Vokkaligara
Sthanamanagalu' in *Vokkaligara Sangha ... Suvarna
Sanchike*, Bangalore 1961, p.99.

16. The discussion which follows is based on interviews with large numbers of Vokkaliga leaders in
different parts of the state, and on documents in the
archives of the Vokkaligara Sangha, Bangalore.

17. Mayer, op. cit., p.4.

18. See J. Manor, 'K. Hanumanthaiah in Mysore: The
Style and Strategy of Individual Leadership in the
Integration of a Region's Politics', *South Asia* 4
(1974), pp.21-38.

19. In addition to interviews with Vokkaliga
leaders, I may cite H.D. Lakshminarayana, *Analysis of
Family Patterns through a Century: Mysore State*, Poona
1968.

20. This is the Chunchanagiri *swamiji*. Interviews with H.H. Anniah Gowda, Mysore, 28 August 1972, and K. Marudeva Gowda, Bangalore, 4 June 1972.

21. In the interests of brevity, I am once again omitting most of the details of findings on this topic. These are set out fully in Manor, 'The Evolution of Political Arenas'.

22. As in the case of the Vokkaligas, these comments are based on interviews with a large number of Lingayat leaders in different parts of Karnataka. I have also used material from the archives of the Mysore Lingayat Education Fund Association in Bangalore.

23. W. McCormack, 'Lingayats as a Sect', *Journal of the Royal Anthropological Institute* 93, 1 (1963), pp. 59-71, and R.E. Enthoven, 'Lingayats', in J. Hastings, ed., *Encyclopaedia of Religion and Ethics*, Edinburgh 1915, VIII, pp.69-79.

24. L.K. Ananthakrishna Iyer, *Mysore Tribes and Castes*, Bangalore 1935, II, pp.29-31; *Census of India*, 1891, XXV, 1, pp.246-9; and E. Thurston, *Castes and Tribes of Southern India*, Madras 1909, II, p.98, IV, p.288 and VI, p.390.

25. *Report on the Mysore Census of 1881*, Bangalore 1884, pp.26-7, and *Census of India, 1891*, XXV, 2, pp.206-13 and 230-3.

26. See, for example, H.M. Sadasivaiah, *A Comparative Study of Two Virasaiva Monasteries: A Study in Sociology of Religion*, Mysore 1967, p.213.

ETHNIC GROUPS IN THE POLITICS OF SRI LANKA

Urmila Phadnis

1

Almost half of the countries in the world, those
populated with diverse ethnic groups, have experienced
or can expect inter-ethnic group conflicts in the
second half of this century.[1] Ethnic divergences, it
is maintained, have been the 'single most important
source of large-scale conflict', leading to civil war,
insurgencies and even to the disintegration of states.[2]

This phenomenon has manifested itself in the developing countries of Asia and Africa and it is not surprising that, over the past few decades, a major preoccupation of the leadership in many of these states
has been to cope with the problem of managing such
conflicts. To the social scientist, the manifestation
of these conflicts is one dimension of the problem, and
an analysis of their sequential impact is another.

To begin with, it has been assumed in many popular
as well as scholarly writings that ethnic pull is
basically a pre-modern phenomenon, implying thereby
that primordial loyalties tend to be road blocks in the
path of national integration, the maintenance of
political order, and modernization.[3] It has been
argued that it may therefore be necessary to counter
such political impulses and bring about a re-ordering
of ethnic consciousness in favour of the state. This
has been sought to be achieved through an increased
sharing of values associated with the modernization
syndrome - industrialization, urbanization, communication, higher GNP etc.[4]

Such generalizations, however, tend to be inadequate
in explaining the complex dynamics of ethnic conflicts
for three reasons. First, the persistence of ethnic
loyalties and the phenomenon of ethnic nationalist
demands on the central authority is not unique to the
developing world but is also prevalent in some urbanized modern states.[5] Second, there seems to be a
general tendency to view ethnic conglomerations as
monolithic groups. While a certain degree of distinctiveness and exclusivity has been the hallmark of ethnic
groups, they contain vertical and horizontal divisions
which are as likely to reinforce each other as to

cancel out.[6] Finally, the modernization-integration
theorists tend to underplay political factors which,
particularly in the economically backward third world
countries, assume a critical significance.

Closely related to the notion of the centrality of
politics is the factor of 'power-sharing'[7] - who
gets what, from whom and how much. In such a
competition, ethnic loyalties are mobilized and
manipulated by political parties and groups. 'Linguistic cleavage', observes Das Gupta, is 'politically generated cleavage, and the kind of conflict
and the outcome of the conflict generated by these
cleavages can be understood only in the context of
the use of language loyalty as a valuable resource by
the modernized political strata in these communities.'[8]
This will prove to be true of other attributes of
ethnicity too.

In the context of the South Asian states which are
undergoing rapid social change and are confronted with
simultaneous and cumulative challenges of participation, distribution and integration, the rise of ethnic
nationalism has brought inter-group cleavage into the
open. At the same time, it has also facilitated the
political socialization, articulation and aggregation
of group interests. In the process, not only does the
'identity horizon' of the constituents of ethnic
groups become enlarged but such a mobilization of
group identities also possesses tremendous potential
for widening the base of the modern sector of society.
Further, while group demands may be anchored to primordial ties, they avowedly aim at the economic and
political amelioration of the group itself. Moreover,
the institutional mechanism for such demands is anything but primordial. As such, the ethnic group leadership, even though asserting the political identity of
its group in particularistic terms, does have a tremendous potential to emerge as an intermediary between the
centre and the periphery. In the process, this leads
to the possibility of a meaningful pluralism as a base
for a viable democracy[9] provided the linkages of such
'intermediaries' *vis-a-vis* the centre do not become
too tenuous.

In the context of these generalizations, it is argued
in this essay that in a plural society like that of Sri
Lanka -

1. Inter-ethnic group conflicts remain submerged during

the colonial period if the politics of the time remain dominantly an elite-style politics and the 'political community' encompasses the power elites of the various ethnic groups.

2. In the democratic framework of the post-independent polity and with the advent of mass politics, the scramble for power intensifies the adoption and use of linguistic and religious motives for political mobilization and electoral contests in a society with scarce resources. These circumstances bring inter-ethnic group cleavages into the open.

3. The gap between governmental policies and performance in those socio-economic areas perceived as 'critical' for the sustenance of group autonomy and the power of the minority ethnic group leadership leads to an exacerbation of inter-ethnic group cleavages.

4. In the event of an ethnic minority being numerically large, socially mobilized and having a well-defined regional base, the possibility of its autonomist demand being transformed into a secessionist one by its leadership cannot be ruled out.

2

A striking religious and linguistic congruence has been the hallmark of group differentiation amongst the two largest ethnic groups of Sri Lanka, the Sinhalese and the Tamils.[10] Thus, more than 90% of the Sinhala-speaking majority community (70% of the population) are Buddhists. The case of the predominantly Hindu,[11] Tamil-speaking community of the Tamils (21%) is similar. As regards the Moors, the second largest minority community (7%), almost all of them are Muslims, with Tamil as the language of their hearth and home.[12] Notwithstanding such distinctiveness in linguistic and religious terms, Sinhalese/Tamil social structures do have certain areas of religio-cultural commonality. This can be seen in the similarities of their respective caste systems. In the Sinhalese-Buddhist pantheon it is the Hindu gods which hold significant positions and the Hindu goddess, Pattini, at Katargama has national recognition. These features reflect the processes of integration and assimilation underlying the two-way interaction between the Sinhalese and the

Tamils, the genesis of which can be traced back to the period preceding the advent of the western colonial powers.

During the colonial period, religio-cultural revivalist movements undoubtedly strengthened the group solidarities of the Sinhalese, the Tamils and the Muslims. However, such assertions and manifestations of group distinctiveness, though operating as parallel streams, did have a point of convergence, for the target of attack in all cases was the same - the aggressive thrust of Christian missionaries during this period. Significantly enough, though the revivalist movements were initiated by learned religious dignitaries, they were supported and financed by the English-educated, non-Christian middle class of entrepreneurs and professionals who perceived themselves as discriminated against, compared with the Christian Ceylonese, in the processes of government.[13]

It was this stratum of the Ceylonese middle class which dominated the reformist movement from the beginning of the twentieth century.[14] It was multi-communal in its composition and relatively cosmopolitan in outlook, with English forming a common bond between the leaders of various ethnic groups. The high-water mark of Sinhalese - Tamil elite cohesiveness was the election of a Tamil, Sir Ponnambalam Ramanathan, from the constituency of the 'western educated Ceylonese' in 1912. Ramanathan's brother, Sir Ponnambalam Arunachalam, was the first president of the Ceylon Reform League and subsequently of the Ceylon National Congress, which was launched in 1919 and was an amalgam of several political organizations - Sinhalese as well as Tamil.

Such Sinhalese-Tamil elite cohesion, however, seems to have come under heavy strain in the 1920s when universal adult franchise was introduced in the island. Underlining the implications of majoritarian rule, it was deemed to be detrimental to the interests of the minority group elites to whom the arithmetic of numbers was far too clear. On the other hand, the controversy concerning the grant of the electoral franchise to the 'Indian Tamils' and the statements of some of the Sinhalese leaders reflected not only Sinhalese doubts about the national loyalty of the Tamil segment of the population but was also indicative of their resentment towards the Tamils in economic terms.[15]

On the other hand, the boycott of the first State

Council elections by a major segment of the Tamils
(leaving the four northern seats unfilled), the famous
fifty-fifty demand of G.G. Ponnambalam, founder of the
Tamil Congress, and a spurt of memoranda and petitions
to the Colonial Office by the Tamil leadership manifested the gradual political mobilization of the Tamils.

However, such inter-ethnic rivalry remained limited
mainly to the domain of the political 'notables' who,
while espousing the cause of their respective ethnic
groups seemed to have a close affinity for each other
and some sort of mutual understanding due to their
similar educational background, social status and mode
of living. As such, notwithstanding such disputes,
bridges were built and coalitions formed. These seemed
to be enduring enough for a while because, notwithstanding the affirmation of their minority status through
electoral politics, the minority elite continued to
have an adequate share in the power cake along with the
political notables of the majority community due to
their eminent position in the bureaucratic and other
professional services. The continued use of English
as the official language and the convergence of their
economic interests facilitated an equilibrium which
did not allow inter-ethnic rivalry to oscillate beyond
manageable bounds. This equilibrium was also reflected
in the consitution (which continued to be in use till
1972), which was modelled on the recommendations of the
Soulbury Commission and included certain provisions to
safeguard the special interests of the minorities.

With the introduction of mass politics and the
demise of English as the official language - the twin
legacies of the 1956 elections - inter-ethnic competition moved from the phase of rivalry to that of overt
conflict, the sources of which were religio-political
but with strong economic undertones.

3

In his perceptive study of north India, Brass maintains
that the process of transforming the 'objective characteristics of a group into the subjective consciousness
of a community' entails four prerequisites; namely, the
existence of a pool of symbols, the presence of an elite
willing to select, transmit and standardize these
symbols, a socially mobilized population and the existence of one or more other groups from whom such a group
can be differentiated.[16]

Viewed in the context of Sri Lanka, the pool of symbols for the majority community included Buddhism, Sinhala, and historical traditions as enshrined mainly in the chronicles written by the Buddhist monks. The task of selecting and transmitting such symbols had been traditionally performed by the Buddhist monks. In the first few years of independence, however, certain Buddhist lay organizations as well as the monks, were deeply concerned with the onslaught of an alien religion and its values on Buddhist cultural traditions and sought the support of the ruling United National Party to rectify the situation by appointing a commission to go into the causes of the cultural erosion of Buddhism and suggest remedies. The ambivalence of the UNP did not deter them and they went about systematically collecting data to identify the factors and forces which had led to the decay of Sinhalese-Buddhist values and culture. In the process, they not only emphasized the need for a Buddhist renaissance but also provided an explanation for the socio-economic backwardness of the Buddhist masses. Such organizations found in S.W.R.D. Bandaranaike, the founder of the Sri Lanka Freedom Party (SLFP), their political leader. It was with the help of these organizations that the SLFP-led United Front achieved considerable success in the 1956 elections in the mobilizing in its favour the lower-middle strata of the Sinhalese, particularly the vernacular school teachers, the Ayurvedic physicians and the Buddhist monks who held an elite position in the Sinhalese rural areas but had felt discriminated against in terms of material benefits and status *vis-a-vis* the English-educated elite.[17]

In the religious context, the major target of the Sinhalese Buddhist revivalists was Catholicism. However, they insisted equally on giving the Sinhala language an exclusive official status. And it was in this respect that the Sinhalese and Tamil group interests clashed with each other for a variety of reasons, subjective as well as objective. Subjectively, the selectivity of historical myths and symbols tended to turn the hero of one group into the foe of another; their victories and defeats overlapped in similar fashion. Coupled with this was the factor of the similarity and close linguistic interaction of Ceylon Tamils with those of Tamil Nadu, leading to the self-perception of the Sinhalese as a linguistic minority 'in the shadow of India'.[18] Further, the (at times

highly exaggerated) preponderance of the minority
Tamil community in public services as well as in other
economic sectors gave an economic edge to the demand
of 'Sinhala only'.[19] 'The fact', argued Bandaranaike
in 1955, 'that in the towns and villages, in business
houses and in boutiques, most of the work is in the
hands of Tamil-speaking people will inevitably result
in a fear, and I do not think an unjustified fear, of
the inexorable shrinking of the Sinhalese language.'[20]
Since 1955, though Buddhism has been an important
symbol for the Sinhalese assertion of its group
differentiation, it has been around the issue of
language that Sinhalese-Tamil confrontations have
concentrated.

The grant of official status to the Sinhala language
alone, it was obvious, held the prospect of providing a
steadily increasing number of the Sinhala-educated
middle class (with its preference for white-collar
jobs), better chances for employment and promotion in
public and other governmental services. In a scarce-
resource economy like that of Sri Lanka, with the state
the largest employer, the language issue was thus not
merely emotive, but was also infused with hard,
rational politico-economic calculations. 'We have
tried to eliminate', declared Bandaranaike's widow and
political successor in 1964, 'the wide gap which
existed between the government and the governed, between
the elite and the masses. By giving the due and rightful place to the Sinhala language as the official language of the state, we have made it possible for those
voiceless millions who spoke only that language, to
play an effective part in the affairs of the country.'[21]

The extent to which considerations of popular
support and the introduction of mass politics gave this
issue centrality was evident from the reversal of the
SLFP's stand on it in 1955 and the chain of events
which followed. It is noteworthy that since 1944, when
the issue of according official status to Sinhala and
Tamil as national languages appeared on the governmental
agenda for the first time, there has been an almost
identical approach by the various political parties on
this issue.

Soon after the reversal of the SLFP's earlier stand
for parity of Sinhala and Tamil as official languages
and its espousal of Sinhala as the sole official language, the governing UNP also changed its earlier stand
under pressure from the Sinhalese Buddhist elements

within the party. Consequently, it decided to seek a fresh popular mandate on its language policy by bringing forward the election by one year.[22]

In this context it is noteworthy that in the initial phase of Sinhalese-Buddhist resurgence, culminating in the landslide victory of the SLFP-led United Front, it was the militant Sinhalese-Buddhist groups which succeeded to some extent in pressuring Bandaranaike on the language issue leading eventually to the dramatic abrogation of the Bandaranaike-Chelvanayakam Pact of 1957. Subsequently, however, it was the compulsions of oppositional politics within a democratic parliamentary framework which prompted the SLFP to oppose the regulations which were brought forward by the UNP-led coalition government in 1966 to give effect to the Reasonable Use of Tamil Act of 1958.[23]

In this move, the SLFP also had the support of the leftist Lanka Sama Samaj Party (LSSP) and the Communist party, both of whom had maintained their commitment to the parity of Sinhala and Tamil as official languages in the 1956 elections. Soon after, the LSSP leadership had admitted that it had paid a heavy price for this stand and had lost heavily among the Sinhalese. By 1960, the Communist Party had followed the footsteps of the two major parties and so did the LSSP when it joined the SLFP-led coalition in 1964. Partly, this change of policy can be explained in terms of their support base being mainly in the Sinhalese-dominated areas. Partly, it was the price which both of them had to pay as minor partners in the processes of alliance formation and coalition building with the SLFP.

Thus, by 1964 the parties of the left had fallen into line with the SLFP and the UNP in ascribing official status to only one language - the language of the majority group. As regards the status of Tamil, while all of them subscribed to the formula of its 'reasonable use', the extent to which that formula was to be implemented seemed to be a matter of dispute, as was evident in 1966. In the intervening period, the majority-minority confrontation on the language issue had taken heavy tolls in 1956 and 1958 and had reached a near-explosive point in 1961.

Reference was made above to the gradual emergence of Sinhala over Buddhism as the core symbol of intergroup conflict. However, Donald Smith's explanation of such a 'decline' of Buddhism as a dialectical process, with a stage of 'secular elite politics' leading to 'mass religious politics' and acquiring its 'synthesis in the secular mass politics', a system which implies the 'decline in political saliency and influence of religious leaders, religious interest groups, religious political parties and religious issues' and also connotes the 'weakening of the religious identity and ideology of actors as a consequence of participation in the political process',[24] appears to me to be an over-simplified interpretation of a highly complex phenomenon.

To begin with, there is no doubt that Buddhism does not evoke the same emotive response today as it did during the mid-fifties. This has been because of the fulfilment of several of the Sinhalese Buddhists' demands by the state and because of the reduced efficacy of the Buddhist monks, a product of their partisan attitude. However, the neutralization of their political efficacy (due to the competitive nature of the party system in Sri Lanka) has almost simultaneously and ironically maintained them as factors of political relevance whose influence cannot be ignored.

Elsewhere, I have described the party system in Sri Lanka since 1956 as a two major party system under which the SLFP and the UNP, along with their allies, have succeeded in maintaining a more or less evenly balanced support base; and with the minor parties - whether rightist, leftist or regional - allying with one of the two major parties or remaining in the political wilderness.[25] In such an electoral context, both the SLFP and the UNP needed to pursue calculated moves which necessitated, amongst other things, competition with each other in manipulating similar symbols to appeal to the mobilized and mobilizing segments of the Sinhalese-Buddhist community. Thus there were many occasions when both the parties vied with each other to appear more Buddhist than the other. For example, during the 1965 elections both had the declaration of the Poya day (the Buddhist equivalent of the Sabbath) as the weekly holiday in place of Sunday as an electoral promise. Further, the opposition UNP's endorsement of the clause in the 1972 consitution which gave Buddhism the 'foremost' status seems also to fit into this pattern.[26]

The extent to which such political calculations concerning the mobilization of the Bhikkhus - the professional religious elites of Buddhism - have been

prominent, is evident from the correspondence of the
UNP premier Dudley Senanayake with the president of a
Buddhist organization in 1966. In his letter to the
premier, the president, making a general plea to keep
the Bhikkhus out of politics, sought the UNP's cooperation in the matter.[27] In his reply, the UNP leader
maintained that, while his party was willing to endorse
such an objective at the policy level, the desired
result could not be achieved without enlisting the
support of other parties for, 'if the UNP alone is to
take an independent position so as not to seek the
services of Bhikkhus in politics, such a decision may
cause an irrevocable loss to the party itself.' The
organization, continued Mr Senanayake, should therefore
make 'an earnest appeal to secure the support of other
parties to achieve the desired result.'[28] Needless to
add, the other parties did not heed the request.

Thus, though increasing partisanship and the gradual
polarization of the political monks had neutralized
their political weight to a considerable extent as
compared to their influence during the mid-fifties,
they continued to persist as pressure groups which had
to be cultivated in order to counterpoise those on the
other side.

Finally, the dominantly Sinhalese-Buddhist ideology
and character of the 1971 insurgency[29] seems to dis-
prove further the 'Secular Mass Politics' syndrome.
Nor is it possible to agree with Smith that the 'gravi-
tation of politics towards economic issues, means the
emergence of secular mass politics in Sri Lanka.'[30]
For, as has been discussed already, even in the case of
the Sinhalese-Buddhist community, the era of religious
mass politics had deeply embedded economic undertones.
In a society like Sri Lanka, where economic modernization and development has yet to go a long way to match
the aspirations and expectations of its people,[31] the
increasingly important economic issues need to take
account of the non-secular, primordial elements and
attributes almost as often as the primordial elements
were obliged to heed economic imperatives in the past.

Thus, it is not the transition from communalism to
secularism but the nature and context of their juxta-
position that needs to be emphasized in the context of
contemporary social, economic and political changes
in Sri Lanka. Such changes have led to the widening
of the avenues for social mobility and an intensifi-
cation of economic activity and political awareness.

The absence of sufficient economic growth in the new state resulted in an imbalance between socially induced aspirations and the capacity of its competitive political system to fulfil them. This led to a situation in which traditional cleavages and idioms became operative in the competition for political spoils as well as for economic goods and services. The position was not so much that traditional wars were being waged in the twentieth century but that modern battles were 'being waged for modern trophies but with traditional slogans and revivalist dogmas', as and when necessary.[32]

4

The device of employing traditional symbols to make political and economic gains was put to effective use to kindle ethnic nationalism both by the leadership of the Sinhalese-Buddhist community and by that of the Ceylon Tamils. As regards the leadership of the minority community, this found its political niche in the Federal Party (FP). Emerging in 1949 as a breakaway party from the Tamil Congress in protest against its acquiescence in a unitary constitution and the citizenship legislation of 1948-49, (which had affected the political status of the Indian Tamils adversely) the FP claimed to be the 'Federal-Freedom Party of the Tamil-speaking people of Ceylon', and had as its major objective 'the establishment of an autonomous Tamil linguistic state within the framework of a Federal Union of Ceylon.'[33] However, its major support base lay, initially, amongst the Ceylon Tamils of the Northern and the Eastern Provinces. By 1956, the language controversy had won for the FP the sympathy and support of the Ceylon Tamil civil servants and other professionals living outside these areas too.[34]

As for the Sinhalese, so also for the Ceylon Tamil elite, the language issue had an emotive as well as a material dimension. Many Tamils, enjoying the benefits of good educational training provided by the missionary schools in Jaffna, had moved from their arid homeland and towards the south and occupied positions in government services and other professions which, at the time of the transfer of power, had surpassed numerically that proportion which they would have held if such jobs had been distributed according to population numbers.

As long as English continued to be the official language, the privileges of the Ceylon Tamil elite

seemed to be secure. However, the introduction of
'Sinhala only' as the official language was viewed as
a serious threat to the position of the Tamil elite
adversely affecting not only its economic future but
also its cultural distinctiveness. The denial of equal
status to the Tamil language in official transactions
was thus perceived as a demotion of the Tamil language
with its long literary traditions. It was maintained
that, apart from such a demotion of the language of the
minority community, the promulgation of the Sinhala-
only formula would also lead to forced bilingualism
for the Tamil elite when it sought entry to the government services. It was also felt that because the
medium of instruction in the schools was the mother
tongue - Tamil or Sinhala - the vernacular-trained
Tamils might find entry to the public service fairly
difficult if not totally impossible. Finally, with
partisan and communal considerations becoming sharper
those Tamils already in the services did not rule out
the hypothetical possibility of their promotion
chances being adversely affected and those Tamils
preparing themselves for entry were uncertain whether,
having similar qualifications, a Sinhalese might not
be preferred to a Tamil.

That such misgivings of the Tamil community were
effectively mobilized and channelled by the FP was
evident from its choice of symbols to assert the political identity of the minority community. While it under-
lined the distinctiveness of the Tamil 'nation', through
a set of historical, territorial, linguistic and
religious symbols,[35] the religious symbol was under-
played in view of the multi-religious confluence of the
Tamils, and language was accorded centrality, facilitating, in the process, the congruence of other symbols
with the central one.

By the 1950s, the political dominance of the FP over
the Ceylon Tamils was unchallenged. It was the FP
leadership which had spearheaded the language agitation
as the spokesman of the Tamils in 1956, 1958, and 1961
through parliamentary as well as extra-parliamentary
means and had succeeded in obtaining some of its demands
in its position as a partner in the UNP-led coalition,
during 1965-68. Finally, in electoral terms, it had
surpassed the rest of the Tamil parties since 1956 in
the Northern and the Eastern Provinces.[36] It is noteworthy that in both these provinces the Sinhalese are in
a minority, with the Tamils accounting for 85% of the

total population in the Northern Province and 42% in the Eastern Province, with the Moors coming next with 34% of the population.[37]

The FP could not, however, make inroads amongst the Tamil-speaking Moors of the Eastern Province who were being continuously and consistently wooed by the SLFP as well as by the UNP, partly as a counterpoise to the FP in the Eastern Province. In view of their demo-graphic dispersion and their economic interests all over the island, the Moors had found alliance with one of the two major parties to be much more beneficial and rewarding in social, political and economic terms than collaboration with the FP.[38]

As regards the Indian Tamils, who were resident mainly on plantations in areas which were dominantly Sinhalese, they had viewed the arrival of the FP in the '50s and '60s with certain misgivings, because of their geographical location. It was also felt that the high-caste leadership of the FP viewed the Indian Tamils with disdain; at best it was interested in making political capital out of them and was not really serious about their problems concerning citizenship and consequent employment difficulties. The slow pace of the imple-mentation of the Sirimavo-Shastri agreement of 1964 and the increased employment of Sinhalese on the estates had further restricted employment avenues for many Tamils. Besides, to their eyes, even the acquisi-tion of Ceylonese citizenship did not seem to improve their employment prospects, particularly when they found themselves pitted against the Kandyan Sinhalese.

In this situation, it was perhaps a tactical move on the part of the leadership of the Ceylon Workers' Congress (the largest political organization of the Indian Tamils) to join the FP when the latter decided to launch a Tamil United Front (TUF) in 1972 after it had protested against the 'discriminatory' clauses per-taining to minority religions and the Tamil language, and had ultimately walked out of the Constituent Assembly during the debate on the Tamil provisions. Initially, the Tamil Congress was divided on the issue but ultimately it too decided to lend its support to the FP and joined the TUF.

For the first time in the history of post-independent Sri Lanka, the leadership of virtually all the Tamil parties and groups were united. And though constitu-tional provisions pertaining to language and religion had clinched this unity, the major impulse to it was the

rising fear of young Tamils of finding no place under
the majoritarian rule from Colombo. Such an apprehension did have some basis. In the 1973 Administrative
Service Examination, out of 100 successful candidates,
only 4 were Tamils. In the services, it was reported
that the percentage of the Tamils had come down from
30% in 1948 to 6% in 1975.[39] Besides, the standardization and regionalization formula which was introduced
in 1974 for university entry (which introduced a
district-wise quota based on population and added
certain weightage to the economically backward areas),
considerably affected the future prospects of Tamils
in medicine, engineering, agriculture etc.[40] In a
memorandum to the International Commission of Jurists
the president of the Ceylon Institute of National and
Tamil Affairs had argued that the chances of a Tamil
securing government employment were negligible if he
was not Sinhala-educated. And in government-sponsored
corporations, where the recruitment was at the dis-
cretion of the minister and not by open competition,
the occasions when a Tamil secured employment were
'very rare'.[41]

Finally, as regards the Reasonable Use of Tamil Act
of 1958, although the enabling legislation for its
implementation was promulgated in 1966, its validity
was questioned by the SLFP and its allies, then in
opposition. After their electoral victory in 1970, the
legislation remained on paper. Moreover, though the
enactment of 1973 provided for the use of Tamil in the
courts in the Northern and Eastern Provinces, adequate
facilities for its implementation, it was argued by the
Tamils, were not provided by the government.

Such assumptions were at times exaggerated, for both
psychological and political reasons. Unlike the '50s
and the '60s, when there were times when the FP was in
a position to bargain with the SLFP/UNP because the
elections had given one of them a mere plurality or a
small majority, the 1970 elections had not provided
such an opportunity for the FP as the SLFP-led United
Front (UF) had gained a massive majority.

During the first half of the '70s, the chasm between
the UF and FP elites deepened due to the pattern of
patronage politics as well as the constitutional and
educational measures mentioned already. However, while
political interaction between the two was at a low ebb,
there was an increase in economic transactions between
the north and the south, following the new-found

prosperity of Jaffna in the agricultural sphere. But in the existing mood of the minority community leadership, the economic prosperity of Jaffna was viewed merely as another positive dimension to the economic viability of a unit which could find its salvation only in a separate state, comprising the Tamil-dominated Northern and Eastern Provinces.

To what extent such a demand emanated from the youth wing of the FP is difficult to determine but there is no doubt that the two-decade old political ethos in the island had alienated many of them from Colombo. This sense of youth alienation (particularly in the context of the overall spectre of unemployment) was mobilized and channeled by the FP in espousing the cause of Tamil nationalism. The doubts of the Tamil youth concerning the good faith of the government in Colombo had already found violent expression during 1974-75 and had had deep reverberations in the TUF too, as was obvious from the deliberations of the first convention of the Front in 1976, when it changed its name to Tamil United Liberation Front (TULF) and turned its earlier movement for regional autonomy and due recognition of Tamil into a movement for secession.

5

Over the decades, an acute competition for political resources and scarce economic opportunities has been the major cause of the exacerbation of inter-ethnic group conflicts in the politics of Sri Lanka. In such a competition, the political leadership of both the Sinhalese and the Ceylon Tamils manipulated ethnic symbols to underline the political identity of the respective groups and thereby mobilize community consciousness.

Alongside the evocation of ethnic symbols, the perception of the existence of unevenness in development between the majority community and others and the effective mobilization of such a sense of relative deprivation by the SLFP led to the kindling of Sinhalese-Buddhist nationalism, which was also facilitated to a considerable extent by the nature of mass politics in the island. The ethnic nationalism of the Sinhalese had its resonance amongst the Ceylon Tamils, whose minority complex was aggravated by the circumstance of their being a socially mobilized community with a distinct regional and linguistic identity. For historical reasons, the substitution of Sinhala for English as the official language was perceived as inimical to the community interests and projected as such by the political leadership of the minority community.

Language thus assumed centrality in Sinhalese-Tamil politics presumably because it was as effective a symbol of tradition for assertion of group-distinctiveness as it was a harbinger for socio-economic benefits in modern times. The use of language as a core symbol of political identity had much potential as a factor integrating the community but it had its own limits, particularly in situations where there was non-congruence of language symbols with others such as religion. This is evident from the pattern of political interaction between the Tamil-speaking, but religiously different groups of Tamils and Moors. Besides, even amongst those groups which had religio-linguistic congruence, horizontal and vertical cleavages based on caste and class minimized its effectiveness. This is borne out by the intermittent character of the alliance pattern between the leadership of the Ceylon Tamils and the Indian Tamils. The basic referent for such alliances when they did take place was not the religio-linguistic affinity but the common politico-economic grievances of both in relation to the majority-group dominated Colombo government. That such alliances were for a limited purpose only was also evident from the non-endorsement of the secessionist demand by the Indian Tamil leadership[42] which, owing to its close and intertwined demographic and economic linkages with the majority community, could not afford to subscribe to the Tamil nationalism which envisaged the partition of the country.

As regards the majority community, there is no doubt that both the UNP and the SLFP did try to outdo each other in manipulating ethnic symbols and competed in claims to be more Sinhalese-Buddhist than the other. However, there were occasions when the political dynamics of ballot box politics forced both of them to seek coalition with the regional Tamil parties. As such, though the processes of negotiations and bargaining between the predominantly Sinhalese and the Tamil parties did tend to be too tenuous at times, the relationship did not totally fall apart.

Alongside the compulsions and constraints of a democratic parliamentary framework, another explanation for this continued habit of seeking cooperation could lie in the fact that notwithstanding the four-decade old experience of an universal adult franchise, the leadership of virtually all political parties belonged to a narrow social range, with a similar social and educational background.[43]

The major challenge to this elite Sinhalese leadership came from the 'emerging' elites - the educated unemployed Sinhalese-Buddhist youth - who, in 1971, questioned the legitimacy of such a narrow-based leadership. As for the Ceylon Tamil leadership, with an oppositional role and a declining ability to bargain with the UF, it seemed to be willing enough to give way to the militancy of the Tamil youth which had already been fairly volatile and active in its organizational activities and agitational politics.

And yet the secessionist demand of the Ceylon Tamil leadership did seem to be, at best, a tactical move to mobilize and contain the rising resentment of the Tamil youth as well as a weapon to wrest concessions from Colombo. As such, while treating the 1977 elections as a mandate for a separate Tamil state, the Ceylon Tamil leadership found in the accommodative gestures of the new government (for example, the introduction of the three-language formula at the school level, the abolition of the standardization formula for entry to university, the publication of electoral registers in Tamil as well as in Sinhala etc.) an opportunity to turn its confrontationist politics into a collaborative-responsive one. In the process it seems to have lost credibility with the militant youth wing of the party. Caught in the vortex of its own demands, the Ceylon Tamil leadership seems to have no option except silently to watch the violent activities of the militant youth (the 'Liberation Tigers' for instance) and build bridges with the ruling regime for its own survival.

If the rising tide of Tamil ethnic nationalism was symbolic of the wants and expectations of Tamil youth in 1978, so was the insurgency of 1971, the paternity of which could be ascribed to the Sinhalese-Buddhist nationalism of 1956. The highly competitive political ethos of the island has thus had its own momentum in ethnic terms, in the shaping of which the political parties and leadership have played a significant role. However, if the competition for scarce resources has tended to be the major source of ethnic conflicts in

the island, the exigencies of politics have also
produced situations where the leadership of both
communities have built bridges and formed coalitions.

Phadnis, 'Ethnic Groups in the Politics of Sri Lanka'

1. Ethnic group refers broadly to any group of individuals who have some objective characteristics in common, for example, language, religion, culture, diet, dress, etc: Paul R. Brass, *Language, Religion and Politics in North India*, London 1974, p.8.

2. Martin O. Heisler, 'Ethnic Conflict in the World Today: An Introduction', *Annals of the American Academy of Political and Social Science* 433 (September 1977), p.1.

3. Literature on systems analysis and political development is replete with such assumptions. See for instance, Talcott Parsons, 'Some Theoretical Considerations on the Nature and Trends of Change of Ethnicity', in Nathan Glazer and Daniel P. Moynihan, eds., *Ethnicity: Theory and Experience*, Cambridge, Mass., 1975, pp.56-71, and Clifford Geertz, 'The Integrative Revolution: Primordial Sentiments and Civil Politics in the New States', in Clifford Geertz, ed., *Old Societies and New States*, New York 1963, p.111.

4. Karl Deutsch, *Nationalism and Social Communication*, Cambridge, Mass., 1953. See also for a similar exposition, D.G. Morrison and H.M. Stevenson, 'Cultural Pluralism, Modernization and Conflict: An Empirical Analysis of Sources of Political Instability in African Nations', *Canadian Journal of Political Science* 5, 1 (March 1972), p.90.

5. For articles on Canada, Belgium, Ireland and Soviet Union see *Annals*, (n.2 above).

6. P.C. Mathur, 'Loyalty-Pyramid of the Indian State: A Diagnosis of the Political Implications of Multiplicity of Social Identities', *Plural Societies* 6, 4 (Winter 1975), pp.25-36.

7. Asaf Hussain, 'The Politics of Ethnic Nationalism in Pakistan', paper presented to the 5th European Conference of Modern South Asian Studies, Leiden, July 1976.

8. Jyotirindra Das Gupta, *Language Conflict and National Development*, Berkeley 1970, p.265. This point has also been well emphasized by Brass, op.cit.

9. Ibid. See also Robert L. Hardgrave, *The Dravidian Movement*, Bombay 1965, p.80, and Iqbal Narain, 'Cultural Pluralism, National Integration and Democracy in India', *Asian Survey* 16, 10 (October 1976), pp.903-17.

10. It is noteworthy that the term 'ethnic group' was used for the first time in the census of 1971 in place of the term 'racial group', which had been in vogue since 1911 when it was substituted for the previously employed term 'nationality'.

11. Along with the Burghers, a small percentage of the Sinhalese and the Tamils are Christians of varying denominations, the largest group among them being the Catholics. The Tamils are subdivided into 'Ceylon Tamils', i.e. those who came to the island in several migratory waves from south India over several centuries; and 'Indian Tamils', i.e. those who migrated from south India during British colonial rule to work on plantations. It is the latter category whose political status has been in dispute since 1948.

12. Mohamed Mauroof, 'Aspects of Religion, Economy and Society Among the Muslims of Ceylon', *Contributions to Indian Sociology* N.S.6 (1972), p.68.

13. Visakha Kumari Jayawardena, *The Rise of the Labour Movement in Ceylon*, Durham, N.C., 1972, pp.39-64.

14. Ibid., pp.73-76.

15. E.g. as early as 1940-1 S.W.R.D. Bandaranaike had referred to the complete political and economic extermination of the Ceylonese, primarily the Sinhalese, should Indians, in large numbers, continue and multiply in Ceylon. Ceylon State Council, *Indo-Ceylon Relations Exploratory Conference, December 1940*, Sessional Paper 8 of 1941, Colombo 1941, pp.8-9.

16. Brass, op.cit., p.44.

17. For an elaborate discussion of these points see W.H. Wriggins, *Ceylon: Dilemmas of a New Nation*, Princeton 1960; I.D.S. Weerawardana, *Ceylon General Election 1956*, Colombo 1960; Robert N. Kearney, *Communalism and Language in the Politics of Ceylon*, Durham, N.C., 1967; and Urmila Phadnis, *Religion and Politics in Sri Lanka*, Delhi 1976.

18. Wriggins, op.cit., p.252.

19. Ibid., p.236. According to Tambiah's analysis of the civil list, i.e. those who had entered the government services through public examination, about 20% were Ceylon Tamils in 1946. S.J. Tambiah, 'Ethnic Representation in Ceylon Higher Administrative Services, 1870-1946', *University of Ceylon Review* 13, 2 and 3 (April-July 1955), p.133.

20. Ceylon, Department of Information, *Towards a New Era: Selected Speeches of S.W.R.D. Bandaranaike Made in the Legislature of Ceylon - 1931-1959*, Colombo 1961,

p.395.

21. *Ceylon News*, 9 July 1964.

22. For details of the language policy of various parties during 1944-55, see the works listed under n.17 above.

23. Kearney, op.cit., pp.130-36.

24. Donald E. Smith, 'The Dialectic of Religion and Politics in Sri Lanka', *Ceylon Journal of Historical and Social Studies* N.S.4, 1 and 2 (1974), p.117.

25. Phadnis, op.cit., pp.115-18.

26. Ceylon, *The Constitution of Sri Lanka*, Colombo, 1972. It is noteworthy that during the discussion stage on the Basic Resolutions (which provided the framework for the final draft of the constitution), Buddhism was accorded the 'rightful place'. Subsequently, the word 'foremost' was substituted in place of 'rightful'.

27. *Ceylon Daily Mirror*, 5 October 1966.

28. *Ceylon Daily News*, 20 December 1966.

29. Gananath Obeyesekere, 'Some Comments on the Social Background of the April 1971 Insurgency in Sri Lanka (Ceylon)', *Journal of Asian Studies* 33, 3 (May 1974), pp.367-84; see also by the same author, 'Sinhala Nationalism and Culture in Relation to April 1971 Insurgency in Sri Lanka', Mimeo.

30. Smith, op.cit., p.117.

31. For a lucid exposition of the nature of Sri Lanka's colonial economy, along with the dichotomies of its social welfarism and economic growth, see Marga Institute, *Participatory Development and Dependence - The Case of Sri Lanka*, Colombo 1977, mimeo.

32. S.J. Tambiah, 'The Politics of Language in India and Ceylon', *Modern Asian Studies* 3, 1(1967), p.216.

33. The Ilankai-Tamil Arasu Kadachi, *The Case for a Federal Constitution for Ceylon as Embodied in the Resolutions passed at the First National Convention held on the 13th, 14th, 15th April 1951 at Trincomalee*, Colombo n.d.

34. A. Jeyaratnam Wilson, 'The Tamil Federal Party in Ceylon Politics', *Journal of Commonwealth and Political Studies* 4, 2 (July 1966), p.131.

35. In its first convention held in 1951 the FP maintained that the Tamils were a separate 'nation' distinct from the Sinhalese, first because of a 'separate historical past' as glorious and ancient as that of the Sinhalese; secondly, because of their distinct linguistic identity with long literary traditions and heritage; and

thirdly because of their 'territorial habitation' of definite areas constituting about one third of the island: The Ilankai-Tamil Arasu Kadchi, op.cit.

36. For a constituency-wise break-up of the performance of the FP till 1965 see Kearney, op.cit., pp.91-3. In the 1970 elections the FP won 13 (as against 14 which it had won in 1965) out of a total of 24 seats in both the provinces. For details, see A. Jeyaratnam Wilson, *Electoral Politics in an Emergent State: The Ceylon General Election of May 1970*, London 1975, p.165. In the 1977 elections, a redrawing of the constituency boundaries by the third Delimitation Commission in 1976 had increased the number of seats in these two provinces from 24 to 26. Out of these, the TULF (of which the FP was the major partner) won 18. Sri Lanka, *Report of the General Election to the Second National State Assembly of Sri Lanka (Eighth Parliamentary General Election), 21st July 1977*, Colombo 1978, pp.87 and 89, mimeo.

37. Percentages drawn from Ceylon, *Census of Population 1971, Preliminary Release No. 1*, Colombo 1972, mimeo. Of the total Moor population of about 800,000, approximately 30% resided in the Eastern Province.

38. For an account of the Moor community's political behaviour and the causes underlying its opposition to the TULF's demand for a separate state see Urmila Phadnis, 'Political Profile of the Muslim Minority in Sri Lanka', *International Studies* (forthcoming).

39. Walter Schwarz, *The Tamils of Sri Lanka*, London n.d., pp.13-14.

40. In his study C.R. de Silva concluded that the major blow of such a formula fell on the Ceylon Tamils. The Tamils' share of engineering admissions, for instance, fell from 24.4% in 1973 (standardization only) to 16.3% in 1974, and is likely to fall to 13.2% if the direct quota system is applied without modification. The parallel figures for medicine would be 36.9% in 1973, 25.9% in 1974 and 20% (estimated) in 1975. The percentage losses in dental surgery and agriculture are even greater. C.R. de Silva, 'Weightage in University Admissions: Standardisation and District Quotas in Sri Lanka, 1970-1975', *Modern Ceylon Studies* 5, 2 (July 1974), p.165.

41. Schwarz, op.cit., p.13.

42. *Ceylon Daily News*, 22 May 1976, and *Ceylon Observer*, 26 May 1976.

43. James Jupp, 'Political Leadership in Sri Lanka
- The Parliamentary Parties', in B.N. Pandey, ed.,
Leadership in South Asia, Delhi 1977, pp.483-95.

LANGUAGE, RELIGION AND POLITICAL ECONOMY: THE CASE OF BANGLADESH

T.V. Sathyamurthy

1

Much of the discussion of the role of language and religious conflicts in the politics of underdeveloped countries - at least until recent years - has focused upon the question of nationalism. In the context of South Asia, most of the writing of Western scholars, at any rate until the mid-sixties, tended to concentrate on linguistic and communal (i.e., religious) problems as though they were *in themselves* fundamental to the survival of the polity as a nation, and to regard them as *ipso facto* centrifugal in their impact and running counter to the ideals of secularism, constitutional (parliamentary) democratic norms and whatever watered-down version of socialism that individual authors might have happened to believe to be good for poor countries.[1]

During the last ten years, however, a widening gulf has tended to separate this kind of writing from a more sophisticated approach. Language and religion are no longer linked in an abstract framework or scheme with nationhood, but consciously related to the concrete conditions under which they emerge as potent factors in politics. Questions are posed in such a manner that one is compelled to consult evidence. For example:

1. Though there might be an undercurrent of linguistic or religious dissatisfaction with the centre, it is only at certain times that specific groups emerge as champions of a particular line or policy affecting large numbers of people and elevate their struggle to the political plane.[2]

2. By the same token, a particular official linguistic policy is successful and popular at a specific conjuncture; yet the very same policy acquires universal odium and is abandoned by its progenitors in favour of its diametric opposite within a short period of time.[3]

3. Similarly, religious tensions have always provided a political opportunity for representatives of

aggrieved communities to mount political agitation highlighting, say, the economic and material disadvantages of belonging to a minority religion or community. These alignments do shift from time to time, and, within a generation or so, dramatic changes can take place in the political relationship between religious communities.[4]

This more sophisticated treatment characteristic of some of the better works on this complex of subjects relating to underdevelopment is the result of scholars undertaking, to an increasing degree, research of an empirical nature relating to specific areas of policy, interest formation, movements of a political character, etc., involving an interplay of language and/or religion and social, economic and political as well as administrative aspects of a given phase of development of a specific region or country. Where such empirical concern is given historical depth by probing the antecedents of specific groups involved in conflicts and attempting some kind of coherent explanation of what weight should be attached to which movement in a longer time perspective, the result can be even more gratifying.

Unfortunately, however, the mould into which the molten alloy of empirical and historical material is cast leaves - in terms of explanatory qualities required to enable one to reach a satisfactory characterization of the relationship between politics, economics and language/religion - much to be desired. To cite only one example, Jyotirindra Das Gupta's work *Language, Conflict and National Development*[5] is the result of a very good empirical examination of the role of language in Indian politics coupled with several excellent insights into the historical aspects of linguistic conflicts. Yet the entire superstructure of this book simply serves to rob its base of its explanatory richness and potential. Das Gupta is a captive of the modernization school which twists and turns from 'the model of the modern' to 'political order' and ranges from prescription to prescription in the garb of objectivity. He makes a superficial and general equation between the success of India's language policy and its political integration rather than interpreting his excellent material in terms of the development of the Indian state. The conflicts and contradictions involved in the shaping of the Indian state, the formation of classes and the interperetration

of class-consciousness with other levels of cultural,
political, and economic consciousness, and above all,
the role of the state in the articulation and control
of potentially explosive issues that bring to the fore
over time the irreconcilable ends of those who
control state power and those who constitute the bulk
of the mass base of society, have been completely
ignored. To be sure, these larger questions cannot be
answered wholly satisfactorily on the basis of a
single study; but, for whatever reason, the opportunity
for a conscious and informed attempt to bring out the
links between the various factors affecting the whole
relationship between the base and the superstructure
has been missed.[6]

In this paper, an attempt is made to analyse the
political role of language and religion in the shaping
of the political economy of what now constitutes Bangladesh. The approach is, broadly speaking, historical,
and the material (except that relating to political
economy) has been drawn not from the author's own
research but from the research of other scholars.
Attention will be focused on the period during which
Bangladesh constituted the eastern wing of Pakistan.
However, sufficient understanding of the role of
religion and language in the political and economic
relations between the two wings of Pakistan cannot be
gained without some attempt to locate it in the wider
context of the origins of Hindu-Muslim politics in the
subcontinent. First, a brief interpretation of the
dynamic forces underlying the political phenomenon of
Pakistan; second, an account of the significance of
Bengal politics for the formation of Pakistan; third,
a discussion of how language, religion and material
factors interacted within Pakistan as a whole and
specifically within the context of east-west relations
within Pakistan; finally, a few tentative conclusions.

2

While the first main threat to their status, culture
and interests was felt by the Muslims in north India
during the period in which the Hindi movement sought
to replace the established administrative language
of Urdu with a standardized form of Hindi, even during
the period 1856-80 they witnessed the gradual rise to
prominence of a new administrative elite consisting of
Hindu notables in areas of north India (e.g., the

North-Western Provinces (NWP) and Oudh, later to become
the United Provinces) which had for centuries been the
exclusive preserve of a Muslim administrative hierarchy
employing variants of the Persian language as the
language of law and administration. It was natural,
therefore, that in the eyes of Muslim administrators,
members of the Muslim elite, and the Muslim members of
the landlord class, the vigorous propagation of Hindi
served to promote the interests of a rising group of
Hindu intellectuals as well as the economically powerful Hindu families making inroads into the colonial
administrative hierarchy at various levels, and constituted a threat to their own established position. The
fact that the Muslims in general lagged behind the
Hindus in acquiring English-language skills only served
to exacerbate their predicament.[7]

The response of the Muslim community as a whole to
what its elite considered to be the colonial policy of
favouring Hindus at the expense of Muslims was interestingly complex. A section of the Muslim elite led by
Sir Sayyid Ahmad Khan reacted to the emergence of a
Hindu administrative elite by propagating the view
that Muslims should form organizations through which
they would acquire the tool which had become indispensable for maintaining their position within the changed
circumstances of colonial administration - i.e.,
English-language education.[8] Sayyid Ahmad Khan staged
a series of efforts in this direction by promoting a
number of Muslim elite organizations centred in Aligarh (e.g., 1893 - the Mohammedan Anglo-Oriental
Defence Association). The main point to note about the
Aligarh movement is that it emphasized Muslim interests
not in terms of the interests of the Muslim community
as a whole, a majority of which was impoverished and
neglected in the rural hinterland of northern and
eastern India, but in terms of the interests of the
Muslim elite. The accent was primarily on Anglicization, secularization and acquiring a modern outlook,
and only secondarily on Islamic particularity. To this
extent the movement represented a powerful interest
group with a widening base to include the bulk of educated Muslims who would claim lower positions within
the hierarchy in due course, and not the Muslim
community as a whole, even though its political
rhetoric made it appear at times as the champions of
the entire Muslim community.

The Aligarh movement relied upon the financial,

political and moral support of the landowning class which, as Das Gupta has noted, was the only group which had begun to articulate Muslim interests even prior to the emergence of Sir Sayyid Ahmad Khan as a Muslim leader of north India. It is well known that Sir Sayyid Ahmad Khan became, during the course of his political career, an ardent champion of Muslim separatism. Even as early as 1886 he advised the Muslims to keep aloof from the Congress agitation 'as the success of its efforts must result in the Muslims being reduced to an ineffectual minority'.[9] In order to appreciate the all-India significance of Sir Sayyid Ahmad Khan's advocacy of Muslim separatism, it is necessary to place the problem posed by the Hindi-Urdu conflict in perspective. In NWP the language controversy was no doubt acute during the second half of the nineteenth century.[10] But in the eastern and other parts of India, large numbers of Muslims did not speak Urdu, and to them the Hindi-Urdu controversy could not have been of any immediate moment. The Bengali Muslims, for example, who constituted a substantial proportion of the total population of the presidency, had a strong interest in Bengali culture and language. Yet the Bengal-based Central National Mohammedan Association (which represented the elite and landlord Muslims of Bengal) echoed the separatist demands of the Aligarh movement.

The Aligarh movement then, centred as it was in the heartland of north India, championed Muslim separatism on the basis of the view strongly held by its leaders that religion, language and culture together constituted the cement that bound a people into a national polity. When this was generalized to apply to the rest of India where Urdu was not the bone of contention (as in Bengal, where Urdu did not play any political role), Islam became the overriding criterion of separate nationhood for Muslims. In economic terms, the aspirations of the vast mass of illiterate rural Muslims (as well as those moving to urban areas to become unskilled workers), upon whom enormous burdens had been imposed with the advent of colonial rule and the gradual introduction of new systems of law and production affecting agriculture, did not form part of the overall concerns of the Aligarh movement. It was purely a pressure group which aimed at providing for the Muslim elite the best possible means of retaining its influence, and, if possible, augmenting it by

218

becoming trusty collaborators of the Raj. In emphasizing that the Aligarh movement was not mainly a
linguistic but a politico-religious separatist movement led essentially by Anglicized men such as Sir
Sayyid Ahmad Khan, Das Gupta at no point draws
attention to what that movement, in politico-economic
terms, did *not* represent. In fact, the main distinction between the Deoband movement and the Aligarh
movement lay in the fact that the former came to
acquire a wider base and attracted a greater degree of
grass-roots following than the latter by virtue of the
populist character of its ideology. Here, again, its
forte was not economic but cultural.

The Deoband school was led by a traditional elite of
the Muslim community which viewed with suspicion the
new ways introduced by the colonial power, and
distrusted the political motives of Sir Sayyid Ahmad
Khan. It was clearly nationalist in the sense of being
anti-colonialist;[11] it was traditionalist in the sense
that it was opposed to the brand of secular oppor-
tunism which, in its view, the Aligarh movement's
religio-linguistic separatism in fact represented. The
crucial difference between the Aligarh movement and the
Deoband movement lay in their attitudes to the majority
community. Unlike the former, the Deoband movement,
while stressing the cultural uniqueness of Islam,
favoured cooperation with the Hindus as long as it did
not lead to a violation of any basic principle of
Islam. This meant that the Deoband school, which
through the popularity it enjoyed among the Muslim
community as a whole commanded a greater appeal at the
grass-roots, eventually drew closer to the Indian
national movement. Thus, while the bulk of the Muslim
elite gave its support to the Aligarh movement, the
nationalist Muslims tended to favour the Deoband
movement. It is interesting that the Deoband school,
despite its strong commitment to unite with the Hindus
'on all worldly matters' (which in no way required
compromising the principle of Islam), was nevertheless
determined to retain the separate identity of Urdu.
During the early years of this century, the declining
fortunes of the Urdu movement were revived with the
establishment, under the direction of a Deoband leader
who subsequently joined the national movement, of the
Anjuman Taraqqi-i-Urdu.[12]

The ideological divergence between the Aligarh
movement and the Deoband movement was temporarily

bridged by the events affecting the Islamic world as a whole in 1919 when the Khilafat movement was launched.[13] The mass agitation provoked by the concern for the traditional Caliphate brought the leaders of both movements together for a time. While the Islamic dimension of Khilafat brought (or rather forced) leaders of the two movements (Aligarh and Deoband) to a common political platform, its anti-colonial (and anti-British) stance drew Hindus and Muslims together into the new phase of the Indian national movement launched by Gandhi.[14] During the 1920s, however, with the dissipation of the exogenously induced cohesion between the two movements, the relationship between politics and language assumed a new orientation. The main conflict on the national scene emanated from the differences between the Indian National Congress and the Muslim League, both of which competed for the mass support of the Muslim community. The main political conflict *within* the Muslim community, however, was between those who held the view that the identity of Urdu could and should be safeguarded without separatism[15] (this group received Gandhi's blessings and was given active support by and within the Congress) and those who believed that the Urdu movement was part and parcel of the movement for separatism.[16]

It is not appropriate here to dwell on the political developments of the last twenty-five years of colonial rule during which the Muslim League attained formidable strength as a separatist movement which finally succeeded in attaining its political objective. What has been attempted above is a bare outline of the main thrust of the Urdu agitation and a description of the dominant role that it played in the whole movement in favour of separatism. At this point it is sufficient to note that the Muslim League itself rode the crest of popularity among large segments of the Muslim masses with very few concrete organizational links established at various levels of Muslim society. This was amply reflected in the structure of the League and the background of its top leadership. The distance between the Muslim masses and the Muslim League leadership (in economic and social terms) was effectively masked by the political urgency with which the latter was able to invest the question of separatism.[17] For our purposes, it would be appropriate at this stage to turn to the significance of Bengal politics for the overall question of separatism and the eventual formation of Pakistan.

3

Prior to the Turco-Afghan invasion of Bengal, the
Bengali masses (belonging to low castes) had been
subjected to harsh conditions during several centuries
of Brahmanical hegemony. With the removal of Hindu
Brahman influence and the capture of state power by
Islamic rulers, nearly half the Bengali low-caste
population,[18] a vast mass of people, underwent conversion to Islam.[19] Unfortunately, however, large-scale
conversion to a professedly egalitarian religion did
little to alter their material condition. The practice
followed by the Turco-Afghan ruling groups of distinguishing themselves (as the noble-born *ashraf*) from
the low-caste converts of Bengal (the ignoble *ajlaf*)
served as a thread of continuity with the past experience of repression of a majority of the people under
Brahman hegemony.[20]

At the time of its conquest by the East India
Company, Bengali society was characterized by a complex
organization of castes and communities linked together
by a variegated pattern of ties reflecting numerous
cleavages and differences. But the basic division ran
along the simple but profoundly significant economic
line that separated the vast mass of peasants and
artisans from the Bengali ruling elite and their
collaborators who lived off the surplus produced by the
former ('in the form of state taxes, feudal exactions
and commercial profits').[21] The relationship between
the poorer Hindus and the poorer Muslims in rural
Bengal was such as to permit intimate contact between
the two communities within a framework of common social
and cultural forms.[22] The initial impact of colonialism
adversely affected the fortunes of the Muslim elite of
Bengal. The East India Company's policy of successfully detaching Bengali Hindu and Baniya collaborators
from their Muslim masters resulted in the isolation
and subsequent reduction to noble penury of the erstwhile ruling class. During the years following the
Battle of Plassey,[23] the colonial power made strenuous
efforts to bring Bengal within the sphere of capitalist
production. In the process, it succeeded in invert-
ing[24] the hierarchy of the propertied classes of Bengali
society while radically transforming the relations
between the cultivator and the peasant on the one hand

221

and those classes living off their surplus on the
other. The stimulus given to the formation of a new
rentier strand of the exploiting class served to
magnify further the severity of oppression to which
the Bengali peasant masses had been traditionally
subject. During the nineteenth century, the traditional landed Hindu families were given the opportunity
to consolidate their hold throughout Bengal, while in
Calcutta the *bhadralok* stimulated a wide variety of
cultural and literary movements which together
constituted the Bengal Renaissance. Essentially, however, their economic role consisted of 'receiving
rents in a predominantly agrarian economy of insecure
tenants, sharecroppers and casual labourers', and
'becoming landlords in a predominantly Muslim population'.[25] Of the major peasant struggles of the
nineteenth century,[26] the Fara'izi movement began as
a Bengali variant of the Wahhabi movement with the
ostensible purpose of purifying the religious orientation of Bengali Muslims. Its effect was to undermine the 'syncretic cultural fabric which tied Hindu
and Muslim cultivators in a common social life'.[27]
The main thrust of the movement was directed against
the Hindu landlord class which had supplanted the
declining Muslim aristocracy. In due course, the
Fara'izi movement broadened along class lines.[28] The
suppression of Bengali peasant movements was, however,
accompanied by changes in the agrarian structure
(e.g., the Tenancy Act of 1885).[29]

By the end of the nineteenth century, a section of
the *bhadralok* leadership initiated a militant revival
of buried nationalist aspirations; the main form that
this revival took in its initial stages was agitation
for civil liberties for which the leaders (pre-eminently a dismissed ICS officer, Surendranath Banerjea)
sought peasant support. The development of the nineteenth century cultural renaissance into early twentieth
century political agitation led by middle-class Hindu
leaders evoked an ingenious response from the colonial
authorities culminating in the Partition of Bengal.[30]
The underlying logic of the colonial power was to
weaken the predominantly Hindu leadership of the
national resurgence that arose in the presidency by
creating a new centre of power in Dacca, the centre of
Muslim Bengal, where Muslim political influence could
be fostered as an effective countervailing force to the
newly emergent nationalism of the whole of Bengal.

Even though the initial response of key Muslim leaders
was one of staunch opposition to Partition   by their
inability to attract the support of the Muslim masses[31]
the Hindu leaders played into the hands of the colonial
authorities whose aim had all along been to undermine
the nationalist movement by employing the Partition
strategy. It is not surprising, therefore, that one
of the founding leaders of the Muslim League (1906)
was the decadent Nawab of Dacca. The reunification of
Bengal (1911) was forced upon the colonial authorities
by developments of an all-India character, while it did
little to repair the damage that had already been
wrought upon Bengal's nationalist politics by the Muslim backlash of 1905-11. The net result of these
developments in Bengal during the first decade of this
century, so far as the *bhadralok* leadership of Bengal
was concerned, lay in the exposure of its isolation,
its inner contradictions and the essentially opportun-
istic character of its politics. During the last three
decades of colonial rule, the old-style *bhadralok*
leadership was largely dislodged and the dominant
strand of nationalist politics in Bengal was woven
into the fabric of the Indian national struggle for
independence. At the same time, terrorism, communalism
and popular militancy came to stay as integral parts
of the political manifestation of the vast mass of
Bengali populace.

The impact of Gandhi's emergence as India's foremost
national leader, and, in particular, the temporary
effect of the Khilafat campaign on the developing
communal situation in India has already been briefly
noted. The objective significance of Gandhi's overall
strategy was to protect the class character of
Congress[32] in an atmosphere of rising Hindu-Muslim
harmony, a harmony which, he hoped, could be sustained
by a combination of Hindu and Muslim revivalism. While
he left the existing economic relationship between the
zamindars and the peasants intact, he failed to preserve 'the inter-communal character'[33] of prevailing
class relations in India. For Bengal this failure
was to have profound consequences.[34] In assessing the
role of the Indian national movement in the struggle
for independence, account must be taken of the profound differences between town and country, the
domination of the capitalist mode of production in
the former and the persistence of pre-capitalist modes
in the latter, the penetration of powerful market

forces into the countryside,[35] and the impact of these
far-reaching economic developments on communal and
caste interrelationships. The growing rift between the
Hindus and Muslims becomes more comprehensible when
the nationalist movement is studied in the context of
the wide gulf between its concern for central power
and its understanding of the local situation, or, more
accurately, the situation in the entire country
affecting basic economic relations between the classes.

Gandhi's refusal to support peasant movements (in,
among other areas, parts of Bengal) which attempted
to graduate from refusal to pay taxes to refusal to
pay rents, and his fierce opposition to any interference in the property relations obtaining in the
countryside alienated considerable sections of Muslim
peasantry in Bengal.[36] During the 1920s and 1930s,
the survival of the Congress as a political force in
Bengal depended on the militant leadership given by
Subhas Chandra Bose. But, tinged as his leadership
was by communal particularism, it was unable to reach
the vast mass of Muslim people.[37] By and large the
limited influence of Congress in Bengal can be accounted for by the alienation to the point of collective
inertia of the Muslim peasant masses on the one hand,
and on the other to the influence that communism came
to exercise among the Bengali masses during the
thirties and forties.[38] On the eve of independence,
the Communist Party was in a position to pose a
political challenge to the Congress party. In East
Bengal, it led the Tebhaga peasant uprising in 1946.[39]

Despite these ramifications of anti-colonial
politics, the main division which had been given its
original political shape by the colonial power at the
time of Partition remained throughout the final phase
of the nationalist struggle. As the differences
between the Congress party and the Muslim League
became irreconcilable, the Bengali Muslims, despite
cultural, social and linguistic differences which
separated them from the Muslims of northern India, were
brought into the mainstream of vivisectional politics
under the banner of one religion and one language -
Islam and Urdu. The fact that Urdu had no place in
the social life of Bengali Muslims whose devotion to
the Bengali language ran deep did not seem to matter
during the 1940s. Nor indeed was it of any relevance
to the immediate situation that the Muslim League
leadership of Bengal, with a few exceptions, had no

enduring link with the vast mass of people in the
countryside. While religion provided the cementing
factor between East and West Pakistan, and language
was deemed (implicitly) to be coextensive with religion,
the Muslim League came to power in East Pakistan (East
Bengal) without any appreciation of the sort of
economic and political links between the two wings
that would ensure a minimum safeguarding of the basic
interests of the majority of the people.

4

Even before the economic disparities between the
eastern and the western wings of Pakistan thrust themselves to the forefront of political relations, the
linguistic question loomed on the horizon as the single
most important point of conflict. Like the Congress
in Madras, the Muslim League in East Bengal became
tainted as the central government's local agent for
the imposition of Urdu. Viewed against the background
of the emergence of the language factor in Pakistan as
a whole (both East and West) as an undermining influence on the religious cohesion of the country, it was
rather strange that Jinnah should declare in 1948 in
East Bengal that anyone who opposed Urdu as the 'state
language of Pakistan' was 'really the enemy of Pakistan'.[40] During the brief interval between 1947 and
1951 an enormous head of steam was generated in East
Bengal against Urdu. During this period, too, the
broad outlines of the relationship between East and
West Pakistan envisaged by the West Pakistani Muslim
League leadership, in the important economic, political and administrative spheres, were becoming clear.
By the beginning of February 1952, large-scale popular
agitation was mounted throughout East Pakistan demanding that not Urdu alone but Urdu and Bengali should
both be co-equal official languages. We shall here
consider the political developments that led to the
swift erosion of the unifying force that had been
symbolically attributed to Urdu during the period
immediately prior to the emergence of Pakistan.

Even before partition, the Bengal Muslim League
witnessed the development of inner party struggle
between the older, conservative leadership (e.g.,
Khwaja Nazimuddin) on the one hand and, on the other,
the progressive forces under the leadership of H.S.
Suhrawardy and Abdul Hashim. In the 1945 election to

the Bengal Muslim League Parliamentary Board, the
Nazimuddin group was defeated by the Suhrawardy group.
During the period immediately preceding partition,
Suhrawardy served as the Prime Minister of undivided
Bengal for over a year (March 1946 - August 1947)
during which period he - along with Sarat Bose and
Abdul Hashim - mooted a proposal aimed at creating a
sovereign state of United Bengal separate from both
India and Pakistan. The failure of this proposal was
exploited, after the creation of Pakistan, by the
Nazimuddin faction to discredit Suhrawardy and his
followers as anti-Pakistan elements. Nazimuddin's
base of support was too narrow to include any elements
other than the landlord class, the decadent Muslim
aristocracy, a section of the mullahs and non-Bengali
speaking Muslim businessmen based in Calcutta. The
central Muslim League, however, gave full support to
the Nazimuddin group despite its unrepresentative
character and the widespread unrest to which its
emergence as a political force gave rise among
large sections of the Muslim electorate and their
representatives within the League.

The preponderance of non-Bengalis in the new
administrative set-up which resulted from the central
government's conscious policy of favouring West
Pakistanis (especially Punjabis) at the expense of
Bengalis was deeply resented by nationalistically
minded East Pakistanis.[41] Even as early as 1948, an
East Pakistani member of the Pakistan Constituent
Assembly[42] was moved to complain that East Bengal was
being treated as a 'colony' of West Pakistan. The
language policy offered itself as a tailor-made issue
calculated to incite the aroused East Pakistanis. By
June 1949, the initial upsurge against Urdu domination
had led to the formation of the East Bengal Awami
League (EBAL) under the presidentship of Maulana
Bhashani. Its convener, Suhrawardy, revived the Lahore
resolution of the All-India Muslim League (1940) which
demanded that provinces in which Muslims were numerically a majority (i.e., Bengal and the north-western
zone) should be grouped to constitute independent
states in which the constituent units 'shall be
autonomous and sovereign'. The 42-point manifesto of
the Awami League contained a number of far-reaching
political, economic, educational, and other demands
including the demand for the recognition of Bengali as
a state language of Pakistan.

226

When in January 1952 Nazimuddin, who had by then
become Pakistan's Prime Minister, revived the language
question by reiterating Jinnah's Urdu policy, the
whole of East Pakistan was electrified into agitational
action led by the EBAL.[44] Representatives of the Youth
League (affiliated to the East Pakistan Communist
Party) and the Students League along with representatives of the Awami League constituted an Action
Committee which launched a protest against the Bengali
Prime Minister's Urdu policy. The police opened fire
on marching protesters on 21 February 1952. The
martyrdom of the students who fell victim to police
bullets spurred further and continued agitation in
which wide segments of East Pakistani society took an
active part under the joint leadership of Suhrawardy,
Bhashani, Sheikh Mujibur Rahman and others. In the
East Bengal-wide mass agitation led by the Awami
League and Students League, linking the Bengali
language issue with the wider political issue of autonomy, the Krishak Shramik Party (led by the veteran
octogenarian, A.K. Fazlul Huq)[45] joined forces to form
a United Front which administered a major defeat to the
Muslim League in the State Assembly elections of
1954.[46]

The 1954-56 period, during which Suhrawardy was
drawn into the central arena (becoming Prime Minister
in 1956), witnessed a temporary but noticeable cooling
down of Bengali nationalist ardour, with the language
question having been settled to the satisfaction of
those who had spearheaded the 1952-54 agitation.[47]
Before proceeding further with the East Pakistani
developments, it would be appropriate at this juncture
to draw together a few threads relating to the political situation in the whole of Pakistan and the precise
manner in which developments in the East had impinged
upon the centre. The Constituent Assembly in Karachi
registered the main fear of West Pakistani politicians
in general, and the Punjabi politicians in particular,
in relation to the developments in East Pakistan: that
East Pakistan would inevitably come to occupy the
dominant position in central politics within the framework of a representative democracy and constitutional
government, given the population figures and the
political determination of the Awami League (which had
already supplanted the Muslim League as the main force
in East Pakistan politics and staked its claims as a
national political party) to reap for the bourgeoisie

227

and the petit-bourgeoisie of the eastern part a fair
(if not yet a strictly proportionate) share of
Pakistan's national economy. To some extent, the
political troubles within West Pakistan itself, at
this stage mainly centring upon the deep division
between the religious leaders of the more traditional
segment of the region and the Muslim League leadership,[48]
in which the tension between the claims of Islam and
the claims of day-to-day politicians came to a bitter
clash, only served to exaggerate the tensions between
East Pakistan (i.e., the AL) and West Pakistan (i.e.,
the ML).

It was during Ayub Khan's military dictatorship
(1958-69)[49] that the political tensions affecting the
relationship between East and West Pakistan reached
the point at which the drive for independence in East
Bengal became irreversible. Ayub Khan's systematic
policy of bleeding the East Pakistan economy in order
to develop capitalism in West Pakistan, his political
formula of Basic Democracy intended to silence mass
opposition, and his belated and half-hearted attempt
to create an economic class of East Bengali collaborators during the 'Decade of Development and Progress' (1958-68)[50] were aimed at discrediting the East
Bengal national movement. This had been gathering
m mentum under the leadership on the one hand of the
Awami League which had itself over the years undergone
a transformation into a solid petit-bourgeois party
with widespread support not only in the towns but also
in the countryside,[51] and on the other the East Pakistan National Awami Party (EPNAP) with its roots mainly
in the countryside.[52]

By 1964, however, after four years of sustained
opposition to the Ayub Khan regime mounted by the two
main student organizations of East Pakistan,[53] the AL
re-emerged as a political force under the populist
leader Mujibur Rahman. The failure of Fatima Jinnah to
emerge as a national leader in the place of Ayub Khan
(in what was in effect a mockery of a presidential
election held in January 1965) was convincing proof, if
convincing proof were needed, that the electoral path
would for a long time be a non-starter for the AL.
The India-Pakistan War (September 1965) provided an
appropriate context for the acceleration of the mass
movement, for it was on the question of India in the
general area of foreign policy that the AL (and in
particular Mujibur Rahman) and the central government

differed sharply.[54]

After the conclusion of the war, Mujibur Rahman launched the movement for autonomy with a six-point programme which he called 'a charter for survival' for East Bengal.[55] Though this move was characterized by the pro-Peking left (including the NAP) as an attempt by a vacillating leadership to forge independent links with the forces of international imperialism in an effort to create a new class of East Pakistani mono-polists and in no sense reflecting the aspirations of the East Pakistani peasants, workers and petit-bourgeois elements,[56] the EPAL received overwhelming support from the bulk of the population. It was in every sense of the term a mass movement. In fact, so successful was the movement that within three months of his election as President of the AL (1966), the central government arrested Mujibur Rahman and other leaders on a trumped-up charge of conspiracy to bring about East Pakistani secession with Indian help.[57] It also brutally put down a general strike in Dacca (June 1966), killing, according to official figures, thirteen.

The economic crisis that gripped Pakistan in the aftermath of the India-Pakistan war, the worst effects of which were simply passed on to East Pakistan, only served to keep the popularity of the imprisoned Sheikh at a high pitch as Bengali nationalism was stoked by the repression of the middle and lower-middle classes that had taken part in the AL's rebellion during the first half of 1966. At this stage, its grass-roots following had yet to move from its role as enthusiastic bystander into the more dynamic role of active parti-cipant in the Bengal national liberation movement. It had not yet shared the Sheikh's dream of *Sonar Bangla*. The vacuum in the leadership of the AL created by the imprisonment of the Sheikh was filled by student leaders[58] who led a movement against Ayub Khan based on an eleven-point programme of socialist policy, anti-imperialism, and pro-people reforms which received active mass support throughout East Pakistan. The slogans of *Swadhikar* (autonomy) and *Krishak Shramik Raj* (Peasants and Workers Raj) rent the air during the five months (November 1968 - March 1969) of mass upsurge throughout East Pakistan.[59] When, in February 1969, Mujibur Rahman was released in a gesture calculated to appease the people of East Pakistan, he became the national leader of East Pakistan *par excellence*, the popular hero of Bengali nationalism.

The resounding success of the AL in the elections in 1970 and the recrudescence of the fear of eastern domination of central politics to which it gave rise in West Pakistan[60] led to a new wave of repression under Yahya Khan with the collaboration of Bhutto. The AL responded to this new situation by launching a national resistance movement that developed into a national war of liberation involving a number of other political groups. With India's intervention, the national liberation war was brought to an end.[61] For our purposes, it is important to note that the seeds of East Pakistani separatism were sown in the language agitation of 1952. Yet, the language agitation by itself could not have led to secession without powerful economic factors coming into play - factors which emphasized the growing political imbalance between the West and the East even despite the fact that the class aspirations of the East Bengal leadership were substantially similar to those of the entrenched and economically far more powerful leadership at the centre.

5

The economic relationship between the Muslim masses in the different parts of undivided India which gave support to the formation of Pakistan and the economically powerful classes varied from region to region, even though the broad similarity manifested by the whole of India in this regard arose out of its exploitative (i.e., class) character. In Bengal, where the Muslims constituted a majority in the eastern part, an oppressed and impoverished peasantry which had no close links either with colonial government institutions or with the major political parties was swept into a nation-wide separatist movement led by a Muslim nationalist party, on the ground that Islam offered a special opportunity for national regeneration. In their acceptance of the idea of Pakistan, the Bengali Muslim masses were in fact reacting against the century and a half of economic oppression that they had suffered under a Hindu landlord and *rentier* class which was colonialism's contribution to the economic development of the Presidency of Bengal.

In effect, however, their adoption of the Pakistan solution was not dissimilar to the mass conversion

which the lower castes of eastern Bengal underwent to
Islam in order to escape from the repression of the
Brahman rulers of the early part of this millenium.
The cure, at least as far as the East Bengalis were
concerned, proved to be worse than the disease. The
potential bourgeois and petit-bourgeois elements in
East Pakistan were prevented from realizing their
economic ambitions by a powerful state at the centre
which sacrificed the interests of its eastern half in
order to augment the power of the western bourgeois
and petit-bourgeois elements. In addition to this
long-term obstacle placed in the way of indigenous
middle-class and lower middle-class elements in East
Pakistan, the vast mass of the Bengali peasantry was
squeezed even harder than during colonial times. The
economic colonialism of the east by the west was
thought to be buttressed by linguistic and cultural
domination.

The link between religion and politics which many
Western academic observers of Pakistan during the
first decade of its existence characterized as
permanently durable[62] soon became perilously tenuous
when the advantages of religious communality were
stacked against the disadvantages of linguistic (i.e.,
cultural) domination and economic oppression. Cultural
isolation from fellow Bengali-speaking Hindus with whom
they shared a common heritage might have been a price
worth paying if the offsetting advantages had been
considerable. But isolation from the mainsprings of
one's own culture, in addition to cultural (i.e.,
linguistic) domination by another part of the same
country against a background of progressive impoverish-
ment and internal colonization of the whole economy[63]
were, for East Pakistanis, burdens which religious
solidarity alone could not lighten.

Even so, we should be surprised not by the fact that
Bangladesh seceded from Pakistan, but by the fact that
it took so long to cut itself loose from the centre.
It is worth stressing that the East Pakistani opposition to Pakistan originally started and continued until
the last phase (i.e., December 1970 - March 1971) as a
movement not seeking to prejudice, in fact actively
seeking to avoid injuring, the integrity of Pakistan.
It was only when the agitation spread beyond the
confines of the middle class and lower-middle class to
include all classes of people that the movement in
favour of secession gathered momentum. Once the masses

were politically awakened, the major political party
(the AL) which had always been reluctant to sever
links with the centre[64] (for the very powerful reason
that unity between the ruling classes of East and West
Pakistan on the basis of some kind of Pancha Shila
would be infinitely preferable to starting on a clean
slate, as it were, in a newly independent state formed
as a result of a widespread political and economic
awakening involving the masses) had no option but to
follow; and their choice was further restricted by the
specific modalities of the developing conflict between
the centre and the AL. In other words, the case of
Bangladesh points to a clear *development*, over a
period of time, *from* limited opposition to the central
government spurred on by differences of geographical
location, the demographic balance, the relationship
between the classes within each region and between the
two regions, and cultural-linguistic-historical
peculiarities (despite religious unity) *into* an
implacable enmity which could be ended only by
secession.

Sathyamurthy, 'Language, Religion and Political
Economy: The Case of Bangladesh'

1. E.g., Selig S. Harrison, *India: The Most Dangerous Decades*, Princeton, N.J., 1960; Hugh Tinker,
'Events and Trends: India Today: A Nation in Making or
Breaking', *World Justice* 3 (December 1961), pp.199-224.
2. A classic example of this is the way in which
communal and linguistic politics were merged together
in the state of Madras during the mid-1960s to mount a
not inconsiderable opposition to the centre in which
the DMK was well placed to exploit the food shortage
and the near-famine and drought conditions prevailing
in parts of the state to discredit the corrupt Congress
government of Madras.
3. The attitude of C. Rajagopalachari who in the
1930s was the acknowledged leader of the Hindi Prachar
Sabha in the south and who, as the Prime Minister of
the Presidency of Madras, introduced Hindi in 1937 into
school education, was to undergo a radical change during
the 1950s. By 1957 he had become the most vocal
opponent of Hindi and protagonist of English in India.
4. In India the Congress party has always regarded
itself as the only champion of the Harijans and the
Muslims. Yet, during the 1977 election, it was dis-
owned by these two communities for very sound reasons
based on the harsh treatment to which the poor in
general (of whom the Harijans and the Muslims constitute a sizable segment) had been subjected under the
Emergency. The Janata Party, despite the past reputation of some of its components as communal parties,
was able to project itself as a party which evoked no
fear on the part of the Muslims and the Harijans and
to which they were prepared to give support. That
this reputation was to be short-lived does not invali-
date the fact that the Muslims and the Harijans did
detach themselves *en masse* from the Congress arty.
5. Berkeley 1970.
6. For an implicit recognition of this, see ibid.,
pp.229-30.
7. See I.H. Qureshi, *The Muslim Community of the
Indo-Pakistan Subcontinent*, Karachi 1962; *The Struggle
for Pakistan*, London 1965. In the south, too, the
existing non-Brahman administrative elite was replaced
by the Brahmans through a similar process of linguistic

anglicization of the latter as a prelude to giving
them the role of collaborators of the colonial power.
See V. Subramaniam, 'Emergence and Eclipse of Tamil
Brahmins', *Economic and Political Weekly* 4, 28-30
(July 1969), pp.1133-6.

8. Abdul Lateef founded the Mohammedan Literary
Society which took the place of the defunct Mohammedan Association in 1863. It was an association
committed to urging the acceptance of English education
by 'respectable Mohammendans'. See J. Das Gupta op.
cit., p.87. See also G.F.I. Graham, *The Life and Work
of Sir Syed Ahmed Khan*, Edinburgh 1885, passim.

9. Quoted in J. Das Gupta, op.cit., p.90.

10. (a) The work of the Nagari Pracharini Sabha
resulted in the recognition (in 1900) of Hindi in law
courts and the acceptance of Devanagari as one of the
three court scripts (in addition to Persian-Arabic and
Kaithi). (b) Sir Sayyid Ahmad Khan, during his tenure
as Member of the Viceroy's Executive Council (starting
1882), gave official support to Urdu leaders' efforts
to establish Urdu Associations for the protection of
Urdu. But these associations never spread their
linguistic and cultural influence to the Muslims
living outside north India.

11. The anti-colonial credentials of the Deoband
leadership go back to 1857 when they had taken part in
the sepoy insurrection. After the suppression of the
insurrection, they established a number of educational
institutions with a view to enabling the Muslims to
regain their cultural status. The Deoband movement did
not abandon its anti-colonial stance, and one of its
main differences with the Aligarh movement lay in the
latter's propagation of loyalty to the British rulers.

12. Its president was an Englishman. T.W. Arnold;
its secretary was the Deoband leader, Maulana Shibli.
By 1914, however, the Anjuman came to be dominated by
the Aligarh movement; its political complexion changed
accordingly. Eventually Maulana Shibli left it to
start his own academy devoted to literary and Islamic
research.

13. The supreme irony of the Khilafat movement lay
in the rejection of the traditional Caliphate by the
Turkish Muslim people themselves.

14. The cordiality between the Hindus and the Muslims during the Khilafat movement had already been
preceded by the 1916 pact of amity between the Muslim
League and the Indian National Congress.

15. This view was powerfully propagated through the Jami'yat-al-ulama-i-Hind started in 1922 by the Deoband-orientated ulema, with a view to safeguarding the religious and political interests of the Muslim community within the framework of united India. They detached the demands relating to Urdu from the demand for separatism. They gave institutional expression to their Urdu demand through the creation of the Jamia Milia Islamia at Aligarh (1920). The Jamia Milia Islamia represented, in the words of W.C. Smith, 'a secession movement from the official imperialist-entangled Muslim University of the Sir Sayyid tradition; students and some teachers "non-cooperated" by leaving the government-supported and controlled university; under a group of tents they set up a courageous but obviously improvised rival, thoroughly nationalist and free.' (Quoted in J. Das Gupta, op. cit., p.155.)

16. The leaders of the Anjuman Taraqqi-i-Urdu (especially Abd. al-Huq) which, as has already been noted, was the most important vehicle of the Urdu movement during the first two decades of this century, maintained close links with the Muslim League movement. They were particularly opposed to the syncretic possibilities for a fusion between Hindi and Urdu in which Gandhi reposed great faith. By 1930, however, it was clear that national integration, for which Gandhi worked, was the last thing that these Muslim leaders wanted.

17. No adequate discussion of this overall phenomenon is possible without examining the Indian National Congress in some detail and its relations with the Muslim League, for which this is clearly not the appropriate place.

18. A significantly larger proportion of people underwent conversion to Islam in East than in West Bengal. For a tentative explanation of why West Bengal was less affected by conversion, see Premen Addy and Ibne Azad, 'Politics and Culture in Bengal', *New Left Review* 79 (May-June 1973), pp.71-112 (see especially p.73).

19. See Ramkrishna Mukherjee, 'Social Background of Bangla Desh', *Economic and Political Weekly* 7, 5-7 (February 1972), pp.265-74; see also A. Karim, *Social History of Muslims in Bengal*, Dacca 1959.

20. The Muslim conquerors did not lose much time in taking upper-class Hindus over as functionaries; in due course, they drew in Hindu Baniyas from north India

(e.g., Jagath Seth) who eventually dominated commerce. Bengal was thus ruled by a Muslim elite which gave a dominant position in administration and commerce to high-caste Bengali Hindus and north Indian Baniyas.

21. P. Addy and I. Azad, op. cit., p.74.
22. Ibid., p.73 (see note 7).
23. K.M. Panikkar quoted in ibid., p.74.
24. Through the Permanent Settlement of Bengal.
25. The turbulent political and economic relationship between the newly emergent landlord-*rentier*, *bhadralok* class and the peasantry has been the subject of much recent scholarly writing, but the Hindu-Muslim aspect of this relationship has not been considered in great detail.
26. The Fara'izi (1810-30); the Indigo Riots (1859-60); and the Pabna Rent Riot of 1873.
27. P. Addy and I. Azad, op. cit., p.85.
28. Titu Mir and Dudu Miyan, a prominent Fara'izi leader, at various times organized Muslim and Hindu cultivators against European planters and Indian landlords. The success of the former's efforts in 1830 in establishing a partially liberated zone was met with government repression. The much wider indigo riots had their roots in this earlier mass movement. See P. Addy and I. Azad, op. cit., pp.84-6; Ranajit Guha, 'Neel Darpan: The Image of a Peasant Revolt in a Liberal Mirror', *Journal of Peasant Studies* 2, 1 (1974), pp.1-46.
29. During the same period, the *bhadralok*, under the leadership of such figures as Raja Ram Mohun Roy, was incorporated into the colonial system despite its ambivalent inclination towards some form of Bengali nationalism. See J. Das Gupta, op. cit., pp.44 ff.
30. A.Tripathi, *The Extremist Challenge*, Calcutta 1969.
31. The Hindu middle-class leadership was never really able to give up the religious overtone of the Swadeshi movement at this stage.
32. A careful study of Judith Brown's *Gandhi's Rise to Power*, London 1972, would show that, from the perspective of the political economy of the nationalist struggle, Gandhi's failure to characterize, in economic and political terms, the relationships involving 'the whole field of zamindars and their tenants' constituted the greatest single weakness of the nationalist struggle. See especially pp.75 ff.
33. P. Addy and I. Azad, op. cit., p.100.

34. Muslim mass organizations and their militant leaders were originally prepared to lend support to Gandhi. Being less integrated into the colonial structures than the Congress, they were prepared to be more uncompromising in their opposition to colonial rule. They were, therefore, frustrated by Gandhi's uncompromising stand on non-violence and what, to them, appeared to be his slow political evolution to the stage of demanding 'Purna Swaraj'. The misgivings of such Muslim leaders were compounded by the communal tinge which the non-cooperation movement acquired over time culminating in the virtual deification of Gandhi as 'Mahatma'.

35. Utsa Patnaik, 'The Development of Capitalism in Agriculture', *Social Scientist* 1, 2 (September 1972); see also the controversy generated by this article in subsequent issues in the same journal and in the *Economic and Political Weekly* (by, among others, N. Ram and Paresh Chattopadhyaya).

36. The Krishak Praja Party, a Muslim organization, attempted to win support from Muslim peasants by promising to put an end to the *zamindari* system. See P. Addy and I. Azad, op. cit., pp.105 ff.

37. Subhas Bose was, however, able to attract a few Muslim leaders (e.g. Shah Nawaz Khan and Habibur Rahman) to his side, but their influence among the Muslim masses was nothing like the Hindu following that Bose himself acquired throughout India and particularly in Bengal. See Jyoti Sen Gupta, *History of Freedom Movement in Bangladesh 1903-73*, Calcutta 1974, passim.

38. A detailed account of the dynamic social and economic factors underlying the emergence of communism as a political force cannot be undertaken here. Many of the original leaders of the communist movement in Bengal (e.g., Muzaffar Ahmed, Abdul Razzack Khan, and Abdul Halim) as well as those who joined it on the eve of independence were of Muslim stock. The development of the East Bengal fraction of the communist movement is well surveyed in Talukder Maniruzzaman, 'Radical Politics and the Emergence of Bangladesh', in Paul R. Brass and Marcus F. Franda, eds., *Radical Politics in South Asia*, Cambridge, Mass., 1972, pp. 223-80, though one need not accept his particular interpretation of the line followed by individual groups. See especially pp.234-52.

39. Hamza A. Alavi, 'Peasants and Revolution', *Socialist Register 1965*, (eds. R. Miliband and

J. Saville), pp.247-71.

40. See Keith Callard, *Pakistan:A Political Study*, London 1957, p.182. According to the Census figures of 1961 for Pakistan, the broad linguistic composition of the country was as follows: Bengali: 55.5%; Punjabi: 29.0%; Sindhi: 5.5%; Pashto: 3.7%; Urdu: 3.7%. Not even 1% of East Bengalis understood Urdu. See D.N. Wilber, *Pakistan: Its People, Its Society and Its Culture*, New Haven 1964, pp.71-84.

41. The first Chief Secretary of East Pakistan in independent Pakistan was a Punjabi who wielded 'extra-constitutional powers' to the extent of sending secret reports about the activities of East Pakistan ministers to the central government.

42. Begum Shaista Ikramullah.

43. Early in 1948 the Suhrawardy supporters among the students, led by Sheikh Mujibur Rahman (as Organizing Secretary), formed the East Bengal Students League. By February 1948, serious student agitation against Urdu had started in East Pakistan.

44. Khalid Bin Sayeed, *The Political System of Pakistan*, Boston 1967, pp.40-1.

45. The situation was further complicated by the fact that, as Chief Minister of East Pakistan, Nazimuddin had reached an agreement with the student leaders in 1948 over the question of parity between Urdu and Bengali as official languages of Pakistan. Fazlul Huq was the mover of the 1940 Lahore resolution referred to earlier in the text.

46. By May 1954, the AL-KSP agitators had won their main linguistic demand when the central government recognized the constitutional equality of Bengali with Urdu as a national language. See K. Callard, op. cit., pp.180 ff. None of the many subsequent changes in the constitutional and political arrangements in Pakistan ever brought into question the official parity of Urdu and Bengali. The Bengalis, for their part, unlike the non-Urdu-speaking West Pakistanis (with the possible exception of the Pashto-speakers, i.e. the Pathans), never really made a serious attempt to learn Urdu as a second language. It is significant, too, that after the 1954 elections, the EPCP was banned and remained underground throughout the rest of the period during which East Bengal continued to be part of Pakistan. In the 1954 elections, 22 communist candidates (of whom 4 had contested openly under the party label) sponsored by the United Front won; only 9 out

of 237 Muslim seats in the State Assembly were won by
the Muslim League. The Fazlul Huq ministry was
dismissed within a few weeks of taking office (29 May
1954).

47. Suhrawardy himself, once translated to the
centre, took a less active interest in the political
demands specific to East Pakistan and evinced a greater
interest in fashioning an all-Pakistan consensus. See
Talukder Maniruzzaman, *The Politics of Development:
The Case of Pakistan (1947-58)*, Dacca 1972, pp.53 ff.

48. The mullahs had always opposed both the
'Nationalist Muslims' who subscribed to the secularism
of the Indian National Congress and the 'Muslim
Nationalists' who opted for Pakistan on the rather
abstract ground that 'Islam enjoins faith in truth
only' and 'does not permit any kind of nation-worship-
ping at all'. In Pakistan politics, mullaism asserted
itself for the first time in the form of the anti-
Ahmadiya agitation provoking disturbances mainly in
the Punjab (1953). See Government of the Punjab,
*Report of the Court of Inquiry to inquire into the
Punjab Disturbance of 1953*, Lahore 1953 (also known
as the Munir Report). For a general discussion of
the relationship between Islam and politics, see Keith
Callard, op. cit., pp.194-221.

49. This period should really be broken into two
sub-periods: (1) 1958-62 when no attempt was made to
give any kind of constitutional justification for the
military rule, and (2) 1962-69 during which military
rule was continued in the garb of constitutionally
veiled dictatorship.

50. The economic policy of Ayub Khan, and its consequences for East Pakistan's development, is well
documented. See T. Maniruzzaman, op. cit., pp.256 ff;
'The Meaning of Bangla Desh', *The Radical Review* 2
(May 1971), pp.1 ff; T.V. Sathyamurthy, 'Indo-Bangla-
desh Relations: A Structural Perspective', Paper
presented to the 4th European Conference on Modern
South Asian Studies, Brighton, Sussex, 1974, pp.1-22;
Richard Nations, 'The Economic Structure of Pakistan:
Class and Colony', *New Left Review* 68 (July-August
1971), pp.3-26; Kamaluddin Siddiqui, *Indo-Bangladesh
Relations (1971-75)*, Unpublished M.A. dissertation,
School of Oriental and African Studies, University of
London, 1975; Ayub Khan, *Friends not Masters*, London
1967.

51. A brief historical note concerning the character

of this transformation is appropriate: With the
appointment of H.S. Suhrawardy (national convenor of
the AL) as Prime Minister of Pakistan, the AL
abandoned its anti-imperialist stand and toned down
its demand for 'full autonomy'. This provoked a
split as a result of which Maulana Bhashani along
with nine radical members of the Executive Committee of
the East Pakistan Awami League - joined by such radical
leaders of West Pakistan as Mian Iftikharuddin, the
Frontier Gandhi, a Sindhi nationalist leader, a
Baluchi nationalist leader, and the leaders of the
Ganatantri Dal, which had itself split off from the
EPCP in 1953 as a consequence of ideological differences formed the National Awami Party (NAP) (a
national 'anti-imperialist' front) on a platform of
anti-imperialism, anti-feudalism and the right of
self-determination for the various linguistic
nationalities of Pakistan. Bhashani became president
of the NAP; the NAP initially won the support of the
EPCP.

52. During the period 1958-62, all political
parties were banned by the military dictatorship of
Ayub Khan. But a large proportion of the NAP workers
were underground until 1964. A number of splits took
place within the EPCP which eventually resulted in the
formation of a number of Marxist-Leninist splinter
groups. The NAP, under the leadership of Bhashani,
however, moved steadily in a pro-Chinese direction and
this drift was utilized by the Ayub Khan-Bhutto
coalition to gather popular support for their new post-
1962 policy of friendship with China which they face-
tiously equated with anti-imperialism. Bhashani (who
was sent in September 1963 by Ayub Khan as leader of
a semi-official goodwill mission to China) and the
NAP lost some ground in East Pakistan as a consequence
of their endorsement of Ayub Khan's Policy.

53. The Students League (affiliated with the AL) and
the Students Union (affiliated with the NAP). Bengali
nationalist feelings were maintained at fever pitch by
these two organizations. 21 February continued to be
observed each year as Martyrs Day. Successful resistance was organized to defeat Ayub Khan's attempts to
destroy East Pakistan's cultural distinctiveness by
introducing the Roman script for the Bengali language.

54. The psychological effect of the India-Pakistan
War (1965) was, to say the least, traumatic, not least
because of the double sense of isolation that it brought

in its wake. The people of East Pakistan felt that
they had no contact either with neighbouring West
Bengal (i.e. India) or with the central power of their
own country. See also T.V. Sathyamurthy, op. cit.;
Kamaluddin Siddiqui, op. cit.

55. The now-familiar six points included demands for
political reform (parliamentary government based on
adult franchise), a confederal structure in which East
and West would be autonomous in all respects except
defence and foreign affairs, separate currencies and
state banks, separate taxation systems, autonomy in
international trade, and autonomy in the matter of
raising a para-military force. See Sheikh Mujibur
Rahman, *Six Point Formula: Our Right to Live*, Dacca
1966.

56. The EPCP, however, consistent with its anti-
Peking interpretation of the forces shaping the
political economy of East Pakistan, extended support to
the Six Point Programme of the AL.

57. The Agartala Conspiracy Case.

58. Student leaders from both the main student
organizations (see note 53 above) formed the East
Bengal Students Action Committee with Toafel Ahmed as
leader.

59. 76 persons were killed by the army and the
police during this period. Of these, 34 were workers,
20 were students, 7 were white-collar workers, 5 were
small shopkeepers, 1 was a school teacher and 1 was a
university teacher. See Talukder Maniruzzaman,
'Radical Politics and the Emergence of Bangladesh', op.
cit., p.260; see also Jyoti Sen Gupta, op. cit.

60. For a good account of the events which trans-
pired between the election victory of the AL and the
Sheikh's arrest, see Talukder Maniruzzaman, op. cit.,
pp.260 ff.

61. For a detailed analysis of Indian motives for
intervening in the struggle for the liberation of
Bangladesh, see Kamaluddin Siddiqui, op. cit.; T.V.
Sathyamurthy, op. cit.; see also Jambala, 'A Bizarre
Hotchpotch', *Economic and Political Weekly* 11, 17
(24 April 1976), pp.629-30.

62. See for example Keith Callard, op. cit., passim.
In sharp contrast, several Western academic observers
of India projected all but apocalyptic visions of her
imminent break-up into a Babel of nationalities. See
note 1 above.

63. The relationship in Pakistan between the

Punjabi Muslims (especially those belonging to bureaucratic officialdom and to the armed forces) and the Bengali Muslims was somewhat similar to that which prevailed between the Turco-Afghan *Ashraf* and the ignoble *Ajlaf*!

64. Even as late as September/October 1971, a section of the AL was reported to have entered into futile negotiation with Yahya Khan, using the good offices of the U.S.A., to secure the release of Mujibur Rahman and the grant of autonomy for East Pakistan within the framework of an undivided Pakistan. These efforts were discredited by a timely campaign launched by two influential pro-Moscow Bengali weeklies, *Nutun Bangla* and *Mukti Judho* which condemned 'CIA moves to foil the liberation struggle of Bangladesh'. See Talukder Maniruzzaman, 'Radical Politics and the Emergence of Bangladesh', op. cit., p.273.

THE CHANGING POSITION OF TRIBAL POPULATIONS IN INDIA

Christoph von Fürer-Haimendorf

The role of the aboriginal tribes as distinct elements
within the population of India has been recognized by
successive governments from the days of British rule to
the present day. Extensive legislation relating to the
'Scheduled Tribes', the establishment of tribal
research institutes in many of the Indian states, the
work of tribal welfare departments and a growing
literature on tribal societies ranging from articles
in popular magazines to the scholarly works of Indian
anthropologists all indicate the importance attached
to the problems of tribal populations. Though anthropologists have by no means a monopoly of the study of
tribal communities, they alone have both the expertise
and the motivation to undertake a prolonged investigation of the special circumstances which set the tribesmen aside from other populations.

According to the latest available census figures the
populations described as 'Scheduled Tribes' number 38
millions out of a total population of 548 millions.
Thus 6.94% of all Indians belong to one or other tribal
community and no less than 427 such communities have
been recorded in the census reports.

Considering that the members of scheduled tribes
exceed in numbers the combined populations of
Scandinavia, the Netherlands, Belgium and Switzerland,
one can well understand that the Indian government has
had to abandon its earlier policy of *laissez-faire* and
that politicians and civil servants have become conscious of the need to provide specially designed
facilities for tribal populations which stand outside
the main stream of Indian social and cultural life,
and are only inadequately covered by the normal administrative and welfare agencies. One may well ask why
populations which for millenia have persisted in a
state of almost complete self-sufficiency, developing
their own way of life and cultural individuality
without any need for outside assistance, have now to be
protected and aided by government? The simple answer
is that, through no fault of their own, many tribal
groups have had their traditional style of life
disrupted by alien populations which invaded their

habitat and introduced the paraphernalia of a tech-
nologically advanced civilization incompatible in
many of its aspects with the basic orientation of the
indigenous culture.

The single most important cause of this development
is the rapid growth of the population of India which,
between 1931 and 1971, has more than doubled and is
still increasing by close on 25% every decade. This
unrelenting expansion has led to a steady increase of
the pressure on all regions still capable of accommo-
dating the overflow from the more densely populated
parts of the country. Most tribal areas were
formerly regions of sparse population, because ever
since advanced populations spread throughout the
fertile valleys and open plains, the more backward
tribal groups have retreated into highlands covered in
dense forests and somewhat inauspicious for settled
cultivation. Even fifty years ago such regions were
still extensive, and it is only in recent decades that
many of them have been swamped by waves of immigrants
from some of the overpopulated parts of India, a
process which has often resulted in deforestation and
a transformation of the entire character of the
environment. It is obvious that in a situation of
mounting pressure on land the least advanced elements
of the population are the first to be dispossessed and
their weakest sections are almost exclusively tribal
groups.

Yet conditions differ from state to state and any
generalization about the fortunes of the Indian tribes
in recent years would inevitably be misleading. I
propose therefore to consider two contrasting areas of
which I have personal knowledge extending over close on
four decades. The one is Nagaland and the other Andhra
Pradesh, more specifically the highlands of Adilabad
district inhabited by Raj Gonds.

The situation in Nagaland and the neighbouring
districts of Arunachal Pradesh such as Tirap district
is characterized by the fact that by and large the
tribal populations have remained in full possession of
their land, and there are hardly any non-tribal
settlers competing for the natural resources of the
region. This situation has been achieved by a deliberate policy of excluding outsiders, other than government servants and members of the armed forces, from
the whole of Nagaland and Arunachal Pradesh, a policy
which goes back to the days of the British Raj, and has

244

been continued virtually unaltered by successive
governments of independent India.

The positive results of this policy are unmistakable.
Nagas as well as the various tribes of Arunachal
Pradesh have been protected against the danger of land
alienation, which is endemic in the tribal areas of
middle India. This does not mean, however, that in
Nagaland there is no pressure on the land. While any
substantial infiltration of outsiders has been
effectively warded off, the natural growth of the
population has accelerated, largely because of the
availability of medical facilities and the removal of
such checks on the growth of population as feuding and
head-hunting. Among the Konyak Nagas, whom I first
studied in 1936 and revisited in 1970, such growth is
beginning seriously to upset the ecological balance.
Villages have grown, the forest has shrunk, and the
cycle of fallow cultivation and regeneration, basic
to the control of shifting cultivation - the only
agricultural technique known to Konyak Nagas - has
been shortened from approximately fifteen years to not
more than seven to eight years. Anyone familiar with
the problems of slash-and-burn cultivation knows that
this is too short a cycle to allow for the natural
regeneration of secondary forest. Hence the likeli-
hood of progressive deforestation and the subsequent
erosion of hill slopes is a very real danger, and one
which the Nagas realize without being able to break
out of the vicious circle of over-cultivation and the
resultant diminution of the basis of agricultural
production.

Though, unlike other tribal populations, the Nagas
have not suffered from an encroachment of outsiders on
their land, they have yet been subjected to many alien
influences aiming at a transformation of their life-
style. The dilemma with which they are faced lies not
in the *failure* of the efforts of government to raise
their standard of living and change their outlook, but
in the very *success* of opening Naga society to the
modern world. By injecting large funds into Nagaland
the central government has created a situation in which
Nagas have become used to innumerable commodities of
outside origin, such as sugar, kerosene, cigarettes,
electric torches, matches, soap, various textiles,
metal vessels, bicycles and other articles not produced
in Nagaland. At present all these goods are bought with
money disbursed by government agencies in the form of

salaries and of wages for road-work and other public
projects. But the pattern of production of the Nagas
themselves has hardly changed, and their agriculture,
which is practised in the traditional manner of shifting cultivation, does not yield a surplus which could
be used for the purchase of the many manufactured
goods now available. Should the flow of funds provided
by the central government ever be turned off, the Nagas
would urgently need to produce goods marketable outside Nagaland in order to pay for all the imports
essential for the maintenance of their raised standard
of living, and so far it is difficult to see how such
a transformation in their economy could be achieved.

Closely linked with the prospects for economic
development is the problem of education. With a
literacy rate of over 27% Nagaland has nearly reached
the all-India average of 29%. In addition to hundreds
of primary schools covering virtually all Naga villages
there are numerous middle and high schools as well as
several colleges, and all of these English-medium
institutions turn out young men and girls educated in
subjects which have little relevance to the traditional
Naga life-style. Not unnaturally, educated young Nagas
expect to find work other than the agricultural
activities of their illiterate parents. The economy of
Nagaland has not yet become sufficiently diversified to
provide employment suitable for hundreds of men and
women with a modern education. At first newly
established government agencies, including the democratic machinery with elected members of regional
councils and the state assembly, provided an outlet
for many of the educated Nagas. But in view of the
youthfulness of most of the Nagas employed by government - older men with suitable qualifications being
unavailable - vacancies created by the natural process
of retirement are few, and one can foresee a situation
when educated young men and women will experience
great difficulties in finding any employment commensurate with their expectations. Hence there is the
danger that educational progress and with it the
unbridled growth of ambitions will outstrip economic
advance, and that in the long run the local economy
will be unable to carry the administrative and educational superstructure which is now being built up
with outside funds provided by the central government.
Members of the Nagaland government are not unaware of
this situation, but as elected representatives

they cannot easily resist the clamour of their constituents for ever-increasing educational facilities.
It is, of course, easier to establish schools and
hospitals, and even to provide electricity for
selected villages, than to transform the economy of
Nagaland to such an extent that in the years to come
the local population can create enough wealth to
sustain the new developments initiated by a government
able to draw on financial resources originating outside
Nagaland.

Notwithstanding these problems, which in any case
relate to the future rather than to the immediate
present, the tribal populations of Nagaland and
Arunachal Pradesh are in a much stronger position than
those of the middle-Indian states of Bihar, Orissa,
Madhya Pradesh, Maharashtra and Andhra Pradesh. For
both in Nagaland and Arunachal Pradesh tribes constitute the majority of the population and although
ultimate political control may still be in the hands
of officials appointed by the Government of India
the territories in question are administered for the
benefit of the local tribal population, whose
interests are given priority over any other considerations with the possible exception of those of national
security in strategically exposed frontier areas.

Compared to the tribals of middle India the tribesmen of the north-east frontier regions are consequently
self-confident, upstanding and uninhibited in their
dealings with non-tribal populations. Thanks to the
success of the government's educational policy many of
the tribes are well-represented in the state and
central services, and it is not unusual to find Nagas
or Khasis serving in other states as members of the
prestigious Indian Administrative Service.

In middle India tribal populations are in a very
different and far less favourable position. Indeed it
is no exaggeration to say that among the more backward
populations tribals are the least progressive and this
despite the government's long-standing efforts to help
them to overcome their disabilities.

Rather than enlarge on generalities, I propose to
sketch the fortunes of a specific tribal group whose
development I have been able to observe from 1941 up to
1977. The group in question are the Gonds of the
Adilabad district which used to be part of Hyderabad
state and is now included within Andhra Pradesh. Their
present position can best be understood by briefly

reviewing developments during the past fifty years.

In the 1940s when I first began to study the Gonds the time was still well remembered when a relatively small tribal population had lived in a large hill region much of which was covered by extensive forests broken only by enclaves containing villages surrounded by stretches of cultivated land. Although Gonds have for long been plough cultivators, both their settlement pattern and their type of cultivation were characterized by a high degree of mobility. Gonds moved freely from one village to another, sure to find sufficient arable land in the vicinity, and to be able to clear such land of existing forest growth. It was only when the government introduced a system of forest conservancy and notified large tracts of land as reserved state forest, that the Gonds began to feel the lack of permanent rights to cultivate land. For now they could no longer shift their villages at will and clear the forest wherever the land was suitable for cultivation. With large parts of the district included in the reserved forest, competition for the more desirable land became keener, and even among those Gonds who had secured rights to land, many lost their holdings to outsiders whose wealth and influence enabled them to contest the validity of the Gonds' title-deeds and to bring about changes in the land-records.

In the early 1940s, the process of land-alienation was already far advanced and many villages in the lowlands and particularly those close to some newly constructed motor-roads had fallen entirely into the hands of non-tribals. Some of the Gonds who had lost their lands resigned themselves to continue cultivating them as the tenants of absentee landlords, but others migrated to the interior of the highlands where they found fellow-tribesmen and possibly relatives willing to accommodate them in their villages. With the Gonds' system of optional residence in the wife's village, the fluctuations between plains and hills had always been fairly frequent, and the obvious refuge for those ousted from their villages in the plains and broad valleys was therefore the still relatively inaccessible hill region, where at that time they considered themselves safe from the encroachments of outsiders. Yet their position was insecure even there and had the process of land-alienation been allowed to continue the Gonds and other tribals would soon have been reduced to a floating population of landless agricultural labourers and tenants devoid of any occupancy rights.

In 1943 I was asked by the Hyderabad state government to report on the tribal problem in Adilabad district, and from 1945 till 1950 I held the position of Advisor to the Nizam's government for Tribes and Backward Classes and in this capacity exercised administrative control over the tribal policy of the state. It was then clear that only a coordinated programme of tribal rehabilitation could avert the material and social decline of the Gonds and other aboriginal tribes of the state. The cornerstone of this programme was a far-reaching land reform. For there could be no doubt that the Gonds' future would depend on their ability to retain the lands they were then holding, and to obtain new land to compensate them for the large areas from which they had been displaced during the previous thirty or forty years. In pursuance of the policy agreed in 1944 by the Nizam's government arrangements were made to allot land on permanent terms to Gonds and other aboriginals free of charge. Each householder was given an average of fifteen acres, an economic holding adequate to support a family. In order to satisfy the Gonds' need for land considerable areas were excised from the reserved state forest. Gonds from lowland areas, where no more vacant land was available were encouraged to move to the highlands and there whole communities were newly settled. The process of land allotment took several years to complete, for the population involved numbered close on 100,000, and many of those entitled to land were too ignorant or too much under the sway of landlords and moneylenders to grasp the implication of the new policy, and to apply for land in the manner prescribed by the rules. Yet, by the time I left Hyderabad in 1949 the majority of Gond householders of Adilabad had been granted permanent title deeds to cultivable land.

The allotment of land, moreover, was only one of the features of the policy of tribal rehabilitation. Various other welfare measures, and particularly the establishment of schools with Gondi as the medium of instruction created an atmosphere in which it could reasonably be expected that the Gonds would be able to resist any further encroachment on their land, and would thus develop as a community of self-reliant peasant proprietors capable of standing up to increasing contacts with other sections of the population.

249

In the course of a recent restudy of the Gonds and
other tribal societies of Andhra Pradesh I realized
that this forecast was too optimistic. The break-up of
the state of Hyderabad and the division of its territory between the states of Andhra Pradesh, Maharashtra
and Karnataka in 1956 had inevitably affected the
working of the tribal policies devised by the Hyderabad
government. With the incorporation of the greater part
of Adilabad district into Andhra Pradesh, the Tribal
Areas Regulation of Hyderabad, which had effectively
protected the Gonds against the inroads of more
advanced outsiders, was superseded by the legislative
arrangements of the new state.

When I visited Adilabad district in September 1970
I found many changes, and the position of the Gonds
seemed no longer as secure as it had ten years earlier.
The main cause of the transformation of the atmosphere
was an improvement in communications and the resulting
influx of newcomers even into those parts of the highlands which had until recently been the preserve of
the tribal populations. Newly constructed motor-roads
now cut right across the region previously notified as
a tribal area, and where traffic used to be only on
foot and by bullock-cart government buses and the
trucks of merchants and contractors now plied regularly.
As a result of this development shopkeepers and
traders established themselves even in the places
which only a few years ago were inhabited solely by
Gonds. To prevent them from acquiring land first for
house-sites and later also for cultivation strong
official action would have been required, but at a time
when the merging of part of Hyderabad state with
Andhra Pradesh created many administrative problems and
the powers of the district officials were curtailed by
the establishment of a form of basic democracy, such
strong action did not materialize.

In 1976-7 I found that affluent outsiders were once
again able to occupy land inside the tribal area and
some Gonds had been induced or forced to dispose of
the land which had been allotted to them under the
tribal rehabilitation programme of 1945-9. The growth
of population and consequent pressure on land in other
parts of Andhra Pradesh had caused land prices to
rocket and settlers belonging to advanced communities
used every device to obtain land in the highlands of
Adilabad. Many Gonds were led into debt and then
prevailed upon to sign away their land, while in some

cases force was used to dispossess tribals too weak
or ignorant to resist the pressure of men more
experienced in dealing with subordinate government
officials. In many respects these events are a
repetition of the wave of land-alienation of the
1930s and early 1940s. But there is one difference.
At that same time there was still a reserve of unoccupied
land which could be allotted to the Gonds. Now very
little cultivable land is left and the reserved
forests have already been seriously depleted, largely
by unauthorized fellings by non-tribal newcomers.

The Gonds' old tradition of mobility has now proved
a handicap, for in the face of the invasion of land-
hungry and aggressive immigrants from Maharashtra the
gentle and rather timid Gonds seldom put up a fight
for their land, but tend to avoid open conflicts and
retreat whenever the pressure intensifies and relations
with unscrupulous newcomers turn too acrimonious.

The magnitude of the problem becomes apparent if we
consider that between 1961 and 1971 the population of
Utnur Taluk, previously a predominantly tribal area,
increased from 55,099 to 93,823, while in conformity
with the average population growth in Andhra Pradesh,
the increase should have been 16% and not 60.13%.
The obvious conclusion is that most of the increase of
38,724 was caused by the influx of non-tribal settlers.

The laws designed to protect tribal land seem to
have proved largely ineffective, mainly because the
intentions of the legislators run counter to the
interests of politically powerful sections of the local
population. In the vicinity of the newly built motor-
roads there is hardly a single village where Gonds have
not been totally or partially ousted by newcomers, or
have been reduced to the state of landless labourers
tilling land acquired by affluent immigrants.

Commercial centres, consisting of shops and the
houses of traders, have grown up along many of the new
roads, but most of these 'growth-centres', as one may
call them, benefit the newcomers far more than the
tribals. Indeed, such growth-centres may turn into a
mechanism by which tribal assets are converted to the
use of members of advanced communities. A phenomenon
fraught with danger to the Gonds is the tendency of
shopkeepers and small entrepreneurs not to be content
with commercial activities complementary to the agricultural activities of the tribesmen. Thus, within a
span of ten years or so, an outsider who established

251

himself in a tribal village by opening a small shop,
is likely to succeed in acquiring land, first renting
it from Gonds, then strengthening his hold on it by a
mortgage agreement and ultimately obtaining permanent
possession.

In the short run the improvement of communications
and growth of commercial activity have undoubtedly
also brought some benefit to those Gonds who have been
able to retain their land. They are now within easier
reach of markets for their produce, and many have
switched to cash crops. Nowadays a great deal of
cotton is cultivated and sold at high prices, while
previously Gonds mainly raised food crops for their
own consumption. The influx of cash into the tribal
community is considerable and Gonds have become used
to such commodities as tea and sugar, which not long
ago were considered luxuries. Yet the reliance on
cash crops has also some disadvantages. To use a cash-
income economically needs skill and foresight, and
these are qualities which most Gonds have not yet
acquired. While grain used to be stored for home
consumption cash is easily squandered, and this
suggests that for the naive and improvident food-crops
may be preferable to cash-crops.

We may now consider the psychological effect of
social and economic changes on the indigenous tribal
population of the Adilabad highlands. The most
striking impression one gains of the Gonds after thirty
years' absence is an incipient disintegration of the
traditional structure of Gond society. Village
communities led by headmen, most of whom were men of
strong personality and authority, used to be characterized by a pronounced sense of solidarity and corporate-
ness. Today there is much less cohesion and mutual
helpfulness among Gonds, and many of the prominent men
have learnt to seek short-term advantages by cooperating
with wealthy newcomers, unmindful of the damage done to
other Gonds, and indeed too shortsighted to see the
danger to their own position.

The great majority of the Gonds feel insecure and
baffled by developments depriving them of a security
which even fifteen years ago they could still take for
granted. They are painfully aware of their inability
to compete with newcomers, be they Hindus or Muslims,
Marathas or Telugus, who are better educated and
organized than they themselves, and above all far more
skilful in dealing with government officials.

One of the causes of this situation is the disappointing progress in the field of education. Though primary schools specifically designed for Gonds have been in existence for more than thirty years few Gonds have succeeded in making the transition from these schools to the normal middle and high schools of Andhra Pradesh. The number of matriculates remains small and by the beginning of 1977 there were only two Gond graduates, one of whom was a member of the Legislative Assembly.

Like all other citizens of India Gonds have the vote, but as a minority community they do not greatly profit from their democratic rights. The two Gond members of the Legislative Assembly, both of whom stood for the ruling Congress party, have neither the skill nor the tenacity to represent the interests of their constituents with much effect. In the unfamiliar atmosphere of parliamentary life in a big city, they can barely hold their own, and have little chance of commanding attention to their views.

Notwithstanding a noticeable deterioration in the position of the Gonds of Adilabad in so far as the ownership of land and hence their general economic security is concerned, the prospects for their ability to retain many of their cultural characteristics compares favourably with that of many other tribal communities of peninsular India. A main factor in their resistance to any erosion of their identity as a distinctive ethnic group is the persistence of the Gondi language - an unwritten Dravidian tongue - as a powerful bond between all members of the tribe. As long as Gonds speak a language incomprehensible to most members of other communities, they remain conscious of their cultural separateness. Though economic interaction with the Hindu populations sharing their habitat is on the increase, Gonds still stand outside the caste system as a community which cannot be ranked in terms of the Hindu caste hierarchy.

I have described the situation among the Gonds of Andhra Pradesh in some detail because I had the opportunity of observing developments in Adilabad district as recently as the winter of 1976-7. Judging from reports on the fate of tribal populations in other regions of middle India, I believe that their position is fairly typical and that a somewhat gloomy view of the tribesmen's prospects in the foreseeable future is well justified. Nor am I alone in this assessment of

the situation. In a recent symposium on Tribal Economy
held in Calcutta, the Director of the Anthropological
Survey of India, Dr K.S. Singh, pointed out that the
census data of 1971 suggested 'an alarming deterioration in the economic condition' of tribal populations,
and that during the decade 1961-71 the percentage of
independent cultivators fell from 68% to 57.56% while
the number of agricultural labourers went up from 20%
to 33%, owing largely to mounting land alienation and
the eviction of tribals from their land.

Similarly, as highly placed a representative of the
Indian government as the Home Secretary stated
recently that 'numerous forms of tribal exploitation
... have resulted in large-scale land alienation.
Tribals have been deprived of their land by deception
and sometimes even under the cover of law.'
(*Illustrated Weekly of India*, 20 February 1977, p.19.)

The irony of the situation lies in the fact that
the central planners in the Indian government are well
aware of the tribals' precarious position and sympathetic to their cause, but that the legislation
designed to protect tribal interests has rarely been
fully implemented. Funds sanctioned for tribal
development have frequently failed to reach the
intended beneficiaries, and projects, such as extensive
irrigation schemes located in tribal areas, have often
benefited non-tribal landowners far more than the
indigenous population.

Yet, the Indian government is continuing to make
available large sums for tribal development. Thus
Rs 1,400 crores (approximately one billion pounds
sterling) have been set apart for this purpose in the
fifth Five Year Plan. What is required no less than
finance is trained and dedicated personnel to implement
the projects for tribal welfare, and it would seem that
such personnel is either not available, or is not being
employed in an effective manner. It is to be hoped
that sooner or later Indian anthropologists familiar
with tribal problems will be associated with administrative arrangements and projects designed to benefit
India's under-privileged tribal populations.

POLITICAL IDENTITY IN SOUTH ASIA

David Taylor

Identity is, first of all, a quality of the
individual; its development is part of the general
process of personal maturity and it must be studied
as much from the psychological as from the
sociological perspective. Erik Erikson posits an
identity crisis as an essential part of adolescence,
a period when different patterns of life are tried
out.[1]   How far such a crisis is characteristic only
of western, urbanized societies is a matter for debate,
but is beyond the scope of this paper. We can however
note that the individual only develops his sense of
personal autonomy through the testing of social links
with others, both within the family or other primordial
unit and outside.   Language and religion are each
important in this process. Language skills develop
within the primordial group and define the wider range
of those with whom easy and spontaneous contact is
possible. Religion, although the term embraces
philosophical tenets, rituals and symbols, and social
forms, can be seen as expressing the underlying
structural principles of the group and its relationships to the outside world.

Nevertheless, it is not possible to treat identities
in purely primordial terms. Cultural traits are
constantly changing, and the direction of such change
can be consciously manipulated, although the room for
manoeuvre may be severely limited by broader social
and economic developments which may occur simultaneously.   The individual, particularly in times of
technological or demographic upheaval, can choose how
far to adopt new cultural practices, or can try to
adopt another pattern of culture altogether from the
one in which he was brought up. *A fortiori*, political
identity, the parameters within which a man's political
actions take place, must be treated as malleable and
manipulable. The element of individual choice is in
some ways less, but the collective identities that
political leaders and dominant elites promote do not
flow naturally and uninterruptedly from Platonic forms
of nationhood. They spring rather from the dialectic
between struggles for power by individuals, factions
and classes, and the demographic, economic and

cultural situation.

Before turning to the South Asian experience, there are two conceptual points which must be considered. First, where a political identity, for example that of Italian, has ceased to be contentious and is broadly accepted by all the inhabitants of the relevant territorial unit, should one talk of it as political, or should one regard the fact of citizenship as having been absorbed into the pool of cultural symbols in which the individual sees his general identity reflected? The primordialist might well regard the absence of conflict as evidence of the appropriateness of the Italian identity, while the instrumentalist would point to the balance of forces in the country which had transferred attention away from the national to other areas of conflict. Even uncontentious identities are of course important in the international sphere. Conflicts which involve the mobilization of the whole population reveal not just how widely accepted an identity is, but how deeply it is felt. Ultimately, a man's political identity has to be seen as part of his total cultural identity, but it is important to note that the former is not a simple derivative from an amalgam of linguistic and religious practices. Indeed, we should look on a cultural identity as including successive layers of political and historical experience alongside more narrowly cultural symbols. Political identities must therefore be treated as separate phenomena.

The second point concerns the levels and the units within which political identities are studied. Purely parochial loyalties may perhaps be regarded as unimportant, but while the nation state may be a major focus for territorial loyalty it is by no means the only one. Nor need regional movements be seen merely as aspirant or as failed nationalist movements. The individual's political identity can combine elements from both levels. The more interesting question, however, is whether one can talk of a political identity expressed in terms of membership of a social class. As with religiously based identities, there are instances where class loyalties are seen as so important that all intermediate loyalties have to be eliminated. This can usually only be done through revolutionary action, and even then the older loyalties often creep back. Nevertheless, class-consciousness is of great importance not only in the way in which it affects the quality of political identity, but also insofar as it is a factor in the chain reactions brought about by economic change.

In South Asia, the various stratifications of language, religion, and history provide the raw material for a huge number of possible identities. Moreover, the segmented character of its social organization and the frequent absence of state power at the local level has meant that historical memories were not always expressed in political terms. Francis Robinson notes the close association between identity and power in his paper on South Asian Muslims,[2] but this is the exception that proves the rule in more than one sense, for it was the prolonged dominance of Muslim rulers from outside which deprived many parts of the subcontinent of recent memories of indigenous political power. Dagmar Bernstorff's account of the Telengana movement shows how the absence of an appropriate political memory forced the Telengana elite to refer to something as vague and elusive as 'cosmopolitanism' and refinement to justify their separatist ambitions.[3]

Even to write of South Asia (or the Indian sub-continent) is to prejudge important issues concerning identity, but in practice few would deny that the term has more significance than simply serving the convenience of conference organizers or of elites in New Delhi anxious to extend their sphere of influence. The question is whether the common factors that exist provide sufficient basis either for cultural communication or for political unity. In a famous passage, Strachey wrote in 1888,

> the first and most essential thing to learn about India - [is] that there is not, and never was an Indian, or even any country of India possessing, according to European ideas, any sort of unity, physical, political, social, or religious; no Indian nation, no 'people of India', of which we hear so much.[4]

But while any particular assertion about the unity of India can easily be challenged, it would be equally hard to deny them all simultaneously.

Strachey, for all his nineteenth-century
confidence about the unchanging East, does at least
provide us with headings for our discussion.
Physically, the Indian subcontinent is a self-
contained area, accessible of course by sea but with
only one major access route by land - a lobster-pot
of a country. Within it, since ancient times, there
has been no political unity but there have been a
remarkable number of links between regions. Pilgrimage routes, the use of Sanskrit, the recognition of
varna categories, all provide ways in which we can
trace the limits of the Indian *kulturkreis*; interregional trade, its finance through *hundis*, the
migration patterns of groups of traders and priestly
castes, provide more concrete indicators, although
the broad geographical divisions of the subcontinent
were at times only loosely articulated.

Despite all these common factors, however, it would
be anachronistic to talk of a South Asian or Indian
identity in the pre-colonial period. Although one can
distinguish a great tradition at the all-India level,
this provided only a pool of symbols which could be
drawn on selectively by regional elites as much to
bolster their dominant position as to add to the
richness of the local cultural identity.[5] The
fluidity of political power would in any case have
hindered the emergence of any persistent political
identities, but it should be noted that the caste
system, while its complementary patterns of mutual
dependence and separation generated a high degree of
mechanical solidarity, was a major factor in limiting
the development of a specific conception of the
political. This was particularly the case where clan
structure and land control coincided.[6]

Britain's conquest of the Indian subcontinent was
not peaceful, but it was gradual and at first not
perceived as part of an overall European expansion.
Even where it encountered more than purely dynastic
opposition, those who resisted were organized, with the
partial exception of the 1857 rebels, along the
inherently fragmented lines of clan. Displaced ruling
elites were able to come to terms with the British, and
the lessons of 1857 were quickly learnt by both sides,
so that the political identity (as opposed to the real
political power) of such groups changed only gradually.

In various parts of the country, Muslim revivalist movements sprang up in the nineteenth century, but in general colonial rule produced only isolated incidents of open discontent after 1857, for example the 1875 Deccan riots and the 1907 canal colonies agitation. Political identity in the countryside was still largely a matter of village and local caste loyalties.

The first challenge to the legitimacy of British rule which articulated a viable alternative political identity came from an area which had taken little part in earlier resistance movements but had been the first region to experience both the creative and destructive aspects of colonialism. The old centres of Bengal had been bypassed by the British, and Calcutta developed as a classic colonial port city, with a hinterland extending well beyond the Bengali-speaking areas and with a heterogeneous population. But the political activity and ideas that developed around Calcutta in the latter half of the nineteenth and early twentieth centuries, were predicated upon a specific sense of Bengali identity. Although Rammohan Roy and the Brahmo Samajists have attracted most attention, at least in the West, the more representative figures of the Bengal renaissance were men such as Bhabanicharan Bannerji and Bankimchandra Chatterji.[7] Their political identity, based firmly on the Bengali language and the rituals and beliefs of the upper castes of the region was extended in the twentieth century, rather grudgingly, to include the possibility of federation with other regions of the subcontinent, but only token gestures were made towards the majority Muslim population.

Are we then to assume that the Bengali identity was primordial? Particularly in the absence of memories of independence, the strength and speed with which it developed is striking, and certain symbols have persisted throughout. At the same time, its uses for a section of the population that had been disavowed by its colonial patrons are obvious. Any attempt to move from an elite to a mass posture (which would in any case have been foredoomed because of the strong grip of a Muslim identity among the majority of the rural population) would have meant unacceptable costs in terms of dismantling the zamindari system. It would also have meant allowing the development of rival (i.e., Muslim) elites. And yet, although in the

259

agitation against the partition of 1905 Muslims had
been excluded, in 1946 leaders in both communities
could seriously consider an independent Bengal in
which religious identities would be subordinated to a
conception of Bengal that drew both on language and
on a vaguely defined feeling of community among the
inhabitants of the delta. Independent Bangladesh has
chosen to stress the geographical element by its use
of Tagore's *Amar Sonar Bangla* as its national anthem.

In western India, a somewhat different type of
political identity developed among the educationalists
and officials who formed the Poona Sarvajanik Sabha in
1870. Not only were there recent memories of the
political power of the Marathas, many of the elite of
Poona were from the Chitpavan Brahman caste which had
been closely associated with that power. It was not
until the gradual development of the non-Brahman movement that a different interpretation of this historical legacy was put forward, so that no one challenged
Tilak's attempt in the 1890s to mobilize mass support
in terms of Maratha symbols, even if his rather
limited success showed that the identity he wished to
promote was most closely related to his own experience
and situation. It was by no means only 'extremists'
who put forward this Maharashtrian identity. Ranade
for example was the leading Maratha historian of the
time, and several other 'moderates' were similarly
engaged. Religion and language both had a part to
play, particularly the latter, but both were meshed
with historical specificity.

Bombay city provided a third pattern of identity
in the nineteenth century in which a pragmatic
approach to British power and to political organization
was matched by a concentration on the affairs of the
local community. The Parsis, in particular, who
unlike any other group in India except the Jews of
Cochin and some of the Christian churches could claim
to form a single *religious* community, were able to
combine active participation in business and politics
at all levels with the preservation of their community
institutions.

Political activity in other parts of India during
the nineteenth century similarly led aspirant
political leaders to examine the pool of symbols
available to them, but these three instances will
serve to illustrate the rather different views of

their identity which the leaders of the early
nationalist movement could hold. Although the
Congress was founded to draw together the various
political organizations in the country, the main
focus of activity was the district and the province.

If one is to fix on a date, 1920 marks the transformation of Congress into a movement that operated
on the all-India as well as the provincial level.
The factors at work were many. British policy,
which from the very beginning had allowed concessions
only at the provincial and district level, had run
out of steam, and the Montagu declaration of 1917
indicated the new paths that had to be explored. The
move to an agitational style of politics meant more
interregional contacts among the leadership and a
sense of being involved in a struggle between massive
and monolithic forces. At the same time, however, the
1920s and 30s were marked by an increasing articulation of regional interests. In part, this was a
response to the feeling in some areas that they were
being neglected by the new axis of power that ran from
Ahmadabad to Lucknow rather than Bombay to Calcutta.
It was also the result of the extension of the
political arena. This had been conceded by the
government in the vain hope that a greatly extended
electorate would in fact reveal the basic loyalty of
the people to the British connection. A major concern
of the Congress leadership after the 1937 elections
was to maintain control over the provincial ministries.

Despite the importance of regional politics, the
period after 1920 was of great importance in the
development of nationalist ideology. Rival identities
emerged which took the political and cultural unity of
India for granted. Nehru, the leading proponent of a
secular identity, unable to base his position on
linguistic homogeneity, nonetheless believed in a
natural unity in a way reminiscent of nineteenth-
century European nationalists. Geographically, India
was one country and the time had come for its ability
to absorb different cultural traditions to be
expressed politically. Savarkar was the most
articulate advocate of the view which held that
India's unity derived from its religious characteristics. The corollary to his position was that only
those who professed one of the truly Indian religions
could be full citizens.

Congress attitudes to language and religion changed during this period, and we must therefore consider them in further detail at this point.

The foundations of independent India's language policy were laid down during the 1920s and 30s, and we can also see the origins of several major language-based regional movements at this time. Fifteen languages (including English and Sanskrit) are recognized in the Indian constitution, and each state is primarily identified with one language. Only Hindi is spoken over a number of states. Quite apart from the problems raised by the use of English and bilingualism in certain areas, however, there is the well-known difficulty of establishing how particular languages crystallized out of the myriad dialects and languages that the *Linguistic Survey of India* identified. Nowhere is the difficulty more acute than in the north Indian plains, the area with which Paul Brass has been primarily concerned. It is important to recognize that each language has followed a different path to its current position. By the beginning of the nineteenth century, some of them were clearly recognized as regional standards, although in all cases a literary renaissance would modernize them; others awaited the attentions of British administrators or indigenous religious reformers to create for them a distinctive form. Important factors that affected the strength a linguistic identity might achieve include the existence of a separate, distinctive script, the literary tradition of a language, its religious significance, and its relationship to Sanskrit.

When in 1920 the Congress, or more precisely Gandhi, decided to reorganize the party structure, it set up what have since been regarded as linguistic provinces. An important point to notice, however, is that only those languages which had already declared themselves to represent self-conscious communities of speakers were given separate status. Those which had not, for example Konkani or Maithili, were ignored. Secondly, the language of no less than six provinces was stated to be Hindustani, and the borders of five of them coincided with British-imposed administrative units. By its action, the Congress leadership first of all recognized the fear elsewhere of domination by a single northern province (as well as the admini-

262

strative difficulties of organizing such a huge area).
It also by implication denied the overriding
importance of language as a basis of identity. Gandhi,
Nehru and others in fact hoped to make the ambiguous
character of Hindustani a source of strength by
developing it as the national language.[8] Such a
policy was bound to run into difficulties, as it did
in the 1950s, because of its too close identification
with north India. But it was also doomed to failure
because it did not come to terms with the significance
which certain Hindus and Muslims had come to attach
during the later nineteenth century to their respective versions of Hindustani.

On the religious front, the Congress leadership
had to respond both to those who wanted to insert a
specifically Hindu element into its ideology and to
those who felt that its secular posture, in so far as
it was not a sham, did not provide them with scope to
preserve or develop their own identity as distinct
religious communities. As Nehru once wrote, 'many
a Congressman was a communalist under his national
cloak',[9] but what is striking is the extent to which
Congress as an organization refused to make a
political issue out of the religious affiliation of
its members. 'Hinduism in danger' was not a slogan
often raised within it. What happened instead was
that Gandhi and his followers used religious symbols
to validate particular techniques of political
action and thus to mobilize wider sections of the
population, who were then left to develop their own
political identities in which collective religious
feelings played a variable part.

It is clear that up to 1947 Congress did not
attempt to dictate too closely the terms on which men
became politically conscious. Ideological consistency
was not required, and for the minority who cared a
range of positions could be accommodated. Although
its attitude was only a subsidiary factor in the
success of the Pakistan movement, Congress was not
able to withstand the strength of Muslim separatism.
In other ways, however, it was successful in
providing the underpinning for Indian federalism when
the constitution was framed, and for the integration
of the princely states.

Since independence, India's national leaders have
had the opportunity to educate its citizenry in their

political identity, but they have also had to cope
with the maturation of regional movements which
originated during the later phases of the nationalist
movement. In addition, they have had to contend with
the political consequences of initiating the planned
development of the Indian economy which in their more
optimistic or naive moments they had hoped would
reinforce a sense of national identity and reduce
regional pressures. Thus to the regional movements
which were noted twenty years ago by Selig Harrison,
one would now have to add the Mizo and Naga rebels in
the north-east, the Kerala Muslims, the rival movements in Andhra Pradesh, and several others.

A degree of diversity was of course expected and
encouraged. It is true that in 1948 the JVP committee
reneged on the earlier Congress commitment to linguistic provinces, but the basic principle of according
recognition to regional units was preserved. Given
Nehru's strongly historical view of India, it may be
that he felt that the existing provinces were in fact
more 'natural' than linguistic units. His judgment
in this instance was faulty, but once the mistake had
been rectified in 1956 (1960 in western India) it
might have been hoped that the problem of sorting out
regional identities had been solved.

Instead, two new aspects of the problem emerged.
First of all, fresh claims for regional autonomy or
separate statehood within the Indian Union have been
made, based on a wider range of criteria. On the
whole, these movements have, unlike their 1950s
predecessors, demanded the further subdivision of the
country, usually within the framework of an existing
state. Movements such as that for 'Vishal Haryana'
which would have meant mobilizing populations in
several states on a non-linguistic basis have had
little success. Secondly, where a linguistic component has been involved, it has either been a
palpable front for other symbols of identity, as in
the Punjab, or the language in question has been so
weakly developed as to make the movement's success
improbable, as in the case of the Maithili movement
described by Brass. With the exception of the tribal
upheavals in the north-east, the central government
has been able to contain regional pressures through
essentially political means. It may be suggested in
fact that whereas the earlier linguistic movements

264

represented, if not natural political units then at
least units with a substance which transcended the
interests of any one group within the elite, subsequent regional movements have more often been the
product of shorter term tensions arising from the
uneven pace of economic development.

The second new aspect of the regional problem has
been the demand from the states for additional power.
In the case of Tamil Nadu, where this demand has been
most forcefully expressed, the ideology of the DMK
even before 1956 stressed not just language but such
symbols as the idea of 'non-Brahmanness' which
simultaneously provided a basis for fuller autonomy
and named the oppressors of the Tamil people.[10] But
the central government has been able to contain the
DMK and now the A-IADMK by a careful strategy of party
alliances and policy concessions. Although it cannot
be denied that a Tamil cultural identity exists which
differs sharply from that of other parts of India, it
must always be remembered that a federal system such
as India's, where the centre exercises considerable
control over the states' finances, will always
encourage regional demands.

Whether the attachment of its citizens to the
notion of an Indian state would survive the total
collapse of central authority is perhaps doubtful, for
except among a relatively small elite, the concept of
a specifically Indian political identity is still in
its infancy.[11] What is important, however, is that
central authority is not likely to collapse as a
result of regional pressures. Nor is basic Indian
policy on language and religion likely to undergo
major changes.

NOTES

Taylor, 'Political Identity in South Asia'

This essay was originally written as a background paper for the series of seminars which led up to the conference on which this book is based. It has, however, been substantially rewritten, so that in any exchange of ideas with the other contributors I am the debtor.

1. 'The Problem of Ego Identity', in Maurice R. Stein *et al.*, eds., *Identity and Anxiety*, Glencoe, Ill., 1960.
2. Above, p.86.
3. Above, pp.138-50.
4. John Strachey, *India*, London 1888, p.5.
5. *Varna* categories, for example, developed at the regional level: Richard G. Fox, '*Varna* Schemes and Ideological Integration in Indian Society', *Comparative Studies in Society and History* 11 (1969), pp.27-45.
6. See, for example, Eric Stokes, *The Peasant and the Raj*, Cambridge 1978.
7. For Bannerji, see Christine Baxter, 'The Genesis of the Babu: Bhabanicharan Bannerji and Kālikātā Kamalālāy', in P. Robb and D. Taylor, eds., *Rule, Protest, Identity*, London 1978.
8. See, for example, Nehru's 1937 article on the subject, reprinted in *Selected Works*, Vol.VIII, New Delhi 1976, pp.829-45.
9. Jawaharlal Nehru, *An Autobiography*, London new ed. 1942, p.136.
10. The most complete account is Marguerite Ross Barnett, *The Politics of Cultural Nationalism in South India*, Princeton, N.J., 1976. The concept of cultural nationalism does perhaps exaggerate the force of Tamil feeling.
11. The situation in Pakistan is in sharp contrast. Although a sense of Pakistani identity is widespread, it is in direct contradiction to other bases of identity. The result has been both the generation of strong regional pressures and a lack of a sense of purpose among many élites. It would however require a separate paper to discuss these issues adequately.